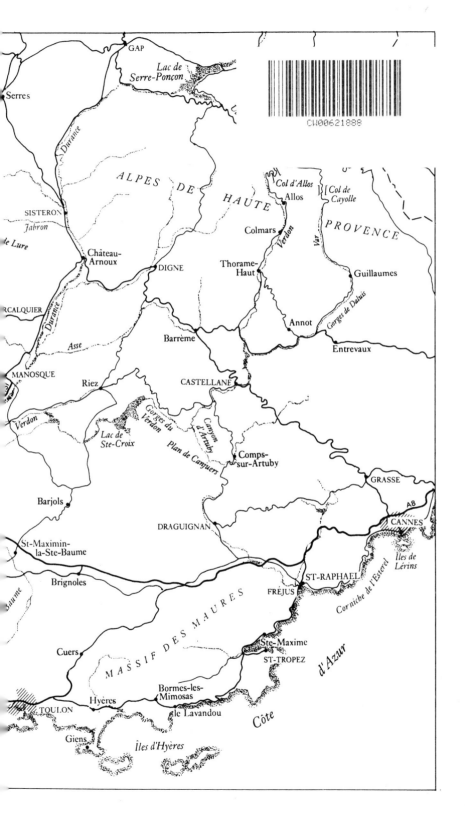

PROVENCE

PROVENCE

Francis Pagan

HARRAP
LONDON

First published in 1991 by Harrap Books Ltd.,
Chelsea House, 26 Market Square, Bromley, Kent BR1 1NA

Copyright © 1991 Francis Pagan

ISBN 0 245 60255 0

Book design by Vera Brice
Maps by Leslie Robinson

Typeset by Poole Typesetting (Wessex) Ltd., Bournemouth
Printed and bound by Mackays of Chatham plc, Chatham, Kent

Pour Une Femme d'Esprit

CONTENTS

ACKNOWLEDGEMENTS

My thanks are chiefly due to all those knowledgeable, patient and articulate guides who show visitors round the cathedrals, abbeys and châteaux of France, and more particularly to the owners of historic properties who have allowed me more intimate glimpses of their homes. Again in the general sense I have appreciated for years the friendliness and generosity of the people of the province, and admired the successful and continuing efforts of local communities to preserve and beautify their inheritance.

I am especially grateful to Mrs Duncan, of the *Centre d'Écologie* at Tour du Valat in the Camargue, for briefing me about the history and ecology of that endlessly intriguing area.

F.P.

COLOUR PLATES

All photographs by Audrey Pagan

PLATES

All photographs, unless otherwise indicated, are by the author

xii

Plates

Abbaye de Silvacane
Château d'If *(French Government Tourist Office)*
Provençal landscape
Draguignan: Tour de l'Horloge
Collobrières: Hôtel-de-Ville
Notre-Dame de Ben Va: pilgrimage chapel
Notre-Dame de Carami: pilgrimage chapel
Prieuré de Carluc: rock burial passage
Prieuré de Salagon: decorative detail
Sisteron: la Pierre Écrite
'Tardons' in the high pastures
St-Martin-de-Brômes: village church

MAPS

KEY

∴ Ancient monuments

✝ Churches, cathedrals or monastic sites

♜ Castles

xiv

INTRODUCTION

Provence has been called a state of mind rather than a geographical entity, which is not far from the truth. Even those who write about it tend to define it in different ways, perhaps so as to emphasise one or other of its individual qualities, but in a practical work such as this some geographical limits must be set. Its Roman origin is not much help, for the *provincia* of transalpine Gaul covered a good deal more of southern France than anyone would credit Provence with today. Under the early empire its capital was Narbo Martius, the modern Narbonne, and it extended from beyond Tolosa (Toulouse) in the west to Forum Julii (Fréjus) in the east and Lugdunum (Lyon) in the north.

Political events and tribal movements in the fifth century narrowed its frontiers, and Arelate (Arles) became the capital of a territory only roughly corresponding with the Roman province. In the north the distinction between Burgundy and Provence stayed fluid until 1032, the year when the kingdom of Arles was annexed by the emperor Conrad; thereafter Provence became identified with the feudal territory, or *comté*, of which the counts of Provence were overlords under the Empire. Nothing illustrates better the subsequent division between Provence and the rest of France than the practice of helmsmen on the Rhône who

xv

steered not to port or starboard but to the bank which they knew as 'France' or 'Empire'.

A neighbouring vassal of the emperor in the thirteenth century was the count of Toulouse, and between them the two *comtés* constituted an almost national identity which became known as 'Languedoc'. This name was first used to describe not a territory but a language – the tongue in which the word for 'yes' was *oc*, while in the north of France they said *oïl*, and eventually *oui*. It was the language of the mediaeval courts and their troubadours both west and east of the Rhône, the language which the nineteenth-century poet Frédéric Mistral and his circle succeeded in reviving for a while in literary form, and in which the Provençal dialect still has its roots. A cynical political and religious alliance between Louis VIII of France and Pope Innocent III led to a 'crusade' in which the people of western Languedoc were brutally crushed as heretics, and count Raymond of Toulouse submitted to the French crown. Provence remained an independent province of the Empire until 1481, when its last *comte* left it in his will to the French king.

In modern terms the most rational way of defining the elusive *régions* of France is by reference to the *départements*, but the trouble is that they hardly ever coincide – the departmental system having been imposed after the Revolution on the much looser regional one. In the case of Provence the discrepancy is not too great, and I have treated as the core of this book the departments of Vaucluse, Var, Bouches du Rhône and Alpes de Haute-Provence. This means that I have included the Camargue, most of which lies east of the Petit Rhône, while excluding places such as Nîmes, Aigues-Mortes and the Pont du Gard, all of which fall in the department of Gard and share few of the general characteristics of Provence. On the other hand the area known as the Tricastin, though strictly in Drôme, is inseparable on several counts from the northern parts of Vaucluse.

Where I admit to prejudice, though other authorities agree with me, is in excluding almost all of the department of Alpes-

Maritimes. This means going no further east than along the Côte d'Azur than Fréjus (which was the end of the Roman jurisdiction) on the ground that whatever regional qualities the rest of the Riviera coast once had have been sacrificed to make an international playground. There is still beautiful country and a good deal of interest in the hinterland of Cannes and Nice, but I have never felt at home there as I do in the rest of Provence.

Within the limits I have set, people will have different mental pictures of what Provence means to them. Some will immediately think of the Rhône-side cities of Orange, Avignon and Arles, with a possible extension to the more romantic parts of the Camargue. For others it will mean the still mainly authentic coastline from Marseille to St-Tropez, with the background which was painted so memorably by Van Gogh and Cézanne. A few will know and love the hills of the Lubéron, Vaucluse and Mont Ventoux, the gorges of the Nesque and the Verdon, but I wonder how many know anything of Haut-Var and Haute-Provence – to my mind among the most exhilarating scenes in France? I hope that all who know it would agree that if one city can embody the modern life and spirit of Provence, it is Aix.

So as to cover as varied a scene as possible, I have described a number of areas, and a sequence of journeys all of which I have myself undertaken at one time or another, and in which I assume that the independent traveller will be covering the ground mainly by car. None of these journeys are meant to be rigidly followed, but only as outlines for days of exploration which can be fitted in with common sense to the time available and the area selected. I hope the aspects of town and country which I describe will help people to appreciate a richly individual and sometimes eccentric part of Europe – for Provence as much as Corsica seems to enjoy a life apart from the rest of France. Its scenery, architecture, history and people should never be treated as separate subjects, but as facets in the proper sense used by jewellers.

To deal cards *à la Provençale* used to mean to throw them

down on the table anyhow, all mixed and muddled as they came. Likewise there is no standard Provençal scenery, only widespread varieties of it. The most familiar recipe combines the reddish earth, the grey-green olive tree, the dark cypress, the poppies in the cornfields (sometimes more like corn in the poppy fields), the wild flowers and flowering fruit trees, the evergreen *garrigue*, the white limestone outcrops and skylines. But what of the watery wastes of the Camargue and its reed beds, the stony acres of the Crau, the fertile river valleys, the endless vineyards of central Var, the lavender fields of the Lubéron, the plunging river gorges, the wild mountains of the far north-east?

The castles and churches of Provence are still part of its life, whenever they were built, and as much a part of its scenery as its mountains and rivers. Townscapes can be as arresting as landscapes, especially if we can find out who made them and when, and the village is still a distinctive unit in a sense which is vanishing in Britain. The sight of a Provençal hill town, with its red roofs at absurd angles, its church, clock tower and castle, all against a background like the Montagne de Lure, can be as uplifting as the Matterhorn or the Niagara falls. I often wonder, when I see some gaunt ruin of a castle on some unlikely summit, what the country was like when every hill-top had a *château-fort* full of real people, as most of them had until the Revolution levelled their world. The same is true of the empty abbeys and priories – take away the guides and tourists, people them with monks and lay brothers, and see how they come to life.

The Provençal weather? Much has been written about the *mistral*, that overpowering northerly wind which sours the temper and affects the judgement. It can be tiresome and disruptive, but you meet it mostly in midsummer and around the Rhône valley – which is its natural conduit as the air warms up and rises over the Mediterranean. The south coast is sheltered from it, and in central parts the main land masses and river valleys run east and west. The mountains of the north-east have alpine weather, and it can snow in April or September, while sudden storms can take you by surprise almost anywhere in this unpredictable land. For the most part the sun shines, and it can be scorchingly hot in July and August.

It was the Impressionist painters who first publicized the extraordinary quality of light in southern Provence, and you have only to cross over from Bagnols or Pont-St-Esprit into the valley of the Rhône to see what they meant. This almost unearthly clarity is really confined to Bouches du Rhône, Vaucluse and southern Var near the coast; the shimmering light off the estuary and sea has something to do with it.

The people of Provence are not unlike their weather – unpredictable, sometimes violent, but mostly warm, responsive and clear-sighted. If you listen to a midday gathering of men round a café table you may think a fight is about to break out until they erupt into shouts of laughter. Yet the native Provençal is also by nature a dreamer (the old word is *ravi*) and a great believer in fairy tales. In fact people of all sorts are not so different from those described by Daudet and Mistral a century ago; those two are a good combination, for Mistral was a romantic idealist (a *ravi*, perhaps) while Daudet was a sharp, humorous and tolerant observer. You will understand the region better after reading Mistral's *Mes Origines* and Daudet's *Lettres de Mon Moulin* – and best of all his two gloriously funny *Tartarin* books. Mistral's *Calendau* and *le Poème du Rhône* are heavier going, even when 'translated' into standard French. For a more recent account of the country poor, Jean Giono's novel *le Grand Troupeau* gives a marvellous account of the *transhumance*, the annual migration of sheep and shepherds from the plains to the hills, and the way of life it entailed.

Finally a few practical lessons, most of which will be familiar to habitual travellers in France. I have avoided giving lists of hotels and restaurants, as they can be found in any number of guide books and brochures. I have mentioned some in passing, but where I have spoken well of one my views are entirely personal. Others may not agree, and my recommendation may at any time become out of date and unhelpful. I do however stress the advantage the independent traveller has over the client of a travel agent, who feels bound to choose hotels which have extensive facilities including large bars, lifts, and television in the bedrooms. I have always been far happier with the welcome and ambiance of a small family-run place, even if it means stumbling with luggage up two flights of stairs and eating my breakfast in the corner of a tiny bar – which you can rely on to produce hot coffee. There are some splendid establishments in the more luxurious categories, but the choice depends on your taste almost as much as on your pocket.

There are few hotels even in the modest category today which cannot offer at least one room with a private bathroom *en suite*, and you are likely to enjoy the meal they give you in the evening as much as their local customers do. There are two warnings: make sure from your hotel guide which day or days they close, and book – or at least arrive – early enough to make sure you get the kind of room you want. The red *Guide Michelin* is still the most informative, but if you see the *Logis de France* sign over a hotel you can bank on it even if it has no mention in Michelin. The Michelin road maps in their regular 1cm:2km series are handy to use (for Provence you will need numbers 81, 83 and 84) but serious walkers interested in the Grandes Randonnées will find the whole system set out in *Topoguides*, which should be on sale at Stanfords in Long Acre, London.

Where possible I have given the usual opening times for visits, but they can vary from year to year. The green Michelin *Guide de Tourisme* (it takes three of them to cover Provence) does its best at the back of each guide, but the standard advice is to ask at the local Syndicat d'Initiatives. Museums and state establishments are almost always closed on Tuesdays, and they and most churches will close on the stroke of noon each day for at least two hours. Many small churches stay closed all week except on Sundays, simply to keep out thieves and vandals. A key is usually available if you can find it, either at the Mairie or with a good lady at a nearby house. If the *curé* has it, he may be more elusive, but if you ask locally you will usually get a helpful answer. On the serious matter of the food and the wines you can expect to find in Provence you will find a separate chapter at the end of the book.

1

Orange and Le Tricastin

When travelling south by car you have the choice of three roads which follow the valley of the Rhône from Lyon down to the frontiers of Provence. The most colourful is the N86, which sticks to the right bank of the river through Roquemaure and Viviers to Pont-St-Esprit, squeezing by between the river and the steep wooded hills of the Ardèche. The N7, at least during this part of its long journey from Paris to Monte Carlo, is duller and probably not worth the switch from the A7 autoroute – unless like me you hate all autoroutes.

Whichever way you go, once past Valence you will know you are in the Midi, as the narrow gap between the Rhône and the Grenoble Alps opens out into the wider broken country of Drôme. In spring and autumn the valley can be chilly and foggy, and sometimes the *mistral* will be howling round your ears, but in summer you will soon feel the heat rising from the earth, and at noon the sun seems to climb higher than anywhere else in France. Though never strictly defined, Provence is usually said to begin just north of Bollène, where you cross the border between the departments of Drôme and Vaucluse, but a little pocket of southern Drôme, known as le Tricastin, is as strongly Provençal in character and history as any of the country further south. Off the road appear vineyards, olive plantations and lavender fields; then you catch sight of ruined castles on rocky hill-tops, church towers in clusters of red roofs – wherever you look the colours seem stronger, the contrasts more striking.

First of the famous Rhône-side cities comes **Orange**, which could be a base for exploring not only the Tricastin but also the districts known as les Baronnies and le Comtat which adjoin it to the east and south. To reach Orange from the N86 you have to cross the river at Pont-St-Esprit, whereas both N7 and A7 deliver you to the gates – literally in the case of the N7. You will find it a busy and crowded town, as it always has been, hemmed in between a loop of the river Meyne and the hill of St-Eutrope which looks down on it from the south – a town to walk in rather than try to drive through.

Orange has a history of prosperity and independence. In 36 BC a colony of discharged veterans from Julius Caesar's Second Legion was established here, and they adopted the local tribal name for it, *Arausio*. The new town flourished and attracted more settlers, until by the end of the first century AD its population had grown to four times the size it is now. To serve such numbers of people the civic authority built temples, baths, a gymnasium, and a stadium over three hundred yards long; above all a **Theatre** which could seat about ten thousand spectators. This is the only one in Europe which has kept its gigantic Roman façade almost intact; even the topmost blocks of stone have survived, with holes for the wooden masts which carried the awnings to protect the stage and some of the seating. A hundred and twenty feet high, it dominates the southern part of the town with course upon course of its huge ochreous stone blocks. The vast semicircle of seats, cut into the hill above, is also mostly intact, with aisles, walkways and vaulted passages beneath. Only at Aspendos in southern Turkey has anything comparable survived – here it was saved by being incorporated into the defensive ramparts built by Prince Maurice of Orange-Nassau in the early seventeenth century.

With a population of over 100,000, a theatre even of this size

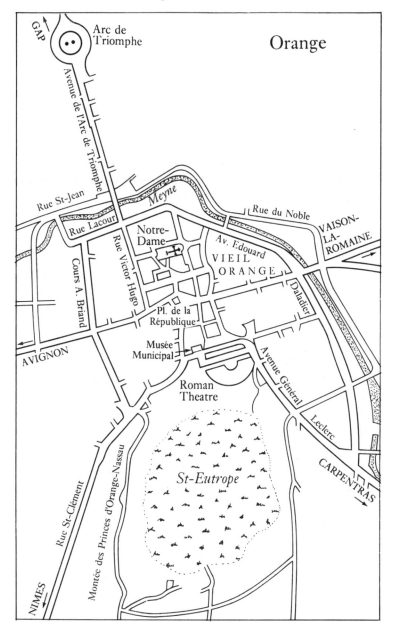

may not have been big enough for all occasions. It was meant not only for what we think of as theatrical productions, but for civic spectaculars and even wild beast shows and gladiatorial combats. You can imagine the roars of the crowd thronging the seats under the Provençal sun. Other sporting events were provided for in the stadium, though baths and gymnasium were reserved for the official classes. The centre of town life, the forum, was surrounded by shops and markets; in the side streets metal workers, carpenters and cobblers did their essential work. This kind of scene changed little during the Middle Ages, nor is it all that different today – except that (whatever may have gone on among the workers' tenements on the outskirts) the centre of Roman Arausio would have been a good deal more orderly than twentieth-century Orange.

These civic arenas disappeared from view in the seventeenth century, when all available stone was carried off for use in Prince Maurice's programme of fortification. They have only recently been excavated, and by no means all identified, in a long rectangular site extending northwards from beside the theatre. One other monument which also survived by being included in the fortifications is the three-arched gateway which bestrides the main road entering from the north, known a bit misleadingly as the **Arc de Triomphe**. Although elaborately decorated with carved reliefs of battle scenes by land and sea, it dates from only about 20 to 10 BC, after the foundation of Arausio and long after Julius Caesar's death and the pacification of Gaul. This suggests it was a monument to civic pride and the past achievements of the 'Second', rather than commemorating a recent victory by Caesar.

On the far side of the street which runs behind the vast back wall of the theatre you will find the entrance to the town's **Museum**, to which your 'theatre ticket' also admits you. Like so many of these excellent French provincial museums it has its surprises, and it is open all the year round at the usual hours except on 1 January, 1 May and Christmas Day. It is even at present open on Tuesdays, which is rare for French museums. The ground floor you might dismiss as the usual jumble of Roman fragments and later bric-à-brac, but for the unique reconstituted marble tablets which record government surveys of parts of the Roman *provincia* in the times of Vespasian and Trajan – times when the Roman civil service was at its most efficient. After this you will hardly expect to find on the first floor a large room devoted to the history and manufacturing techniques of what were called *toiles indiennes* in eighteenth-century Orange.

Cotton fabrics were first brought to France by the Compagnie des Indes (the equivalent of the East India Company of Clive and Hastings) in the seventeenth century, and became fashionable among the nobility – see for instance Molière's *Bourgeois Gentilhomme*. Their import was forbidden by an edict of 1686 because they competed with French silks and woollens, but they became so popular that clandestine factories took to manufacturing them, and in 1757 a Swiss entrepreneur called Wetter set up a business in Orange which copied all the Indian processes on a large scale. His highly efficient and practical organisation – among the fore-runners of the Industrial Revolution – employed hundreds of men, women and children, and prompted the government to rescind their decree in 1759. It was later in the eighteenth century that another Swiss called Oberkampf founded a factory at Jouy-en-Josas, and the products which he called 'tissus d'Orange-Jouy', with their distinctive classical designs in a light inky blue and a muted pink, are now universally known as 'toile de Jouy'.

In this room all M. Wetter's processes are illustrated by drawings and printed cards, while the walls on three sides are hung with an extraordinary series of eighteenth-century painted panels which came from his own house in Orange. It makes a brilliant pictorial account of the work done, the people involved and the social *moeurs* of the time – some of them very funny. We are told that while many colours were used for the blocks, the base for most of them was the *noix de galle*, or gall-nut, found on the plentiful local oak trees, which produced a tone rather like the must or lees of wine – hence that distinctive musty pink.

The rooms on the second floor, and the stairway leading up to them, are hung with a collection of pictures by two notable artists, Frank Brangwyn and Albert de Belleroche, whose paths seem to have crossed in this unlikely place. Sir Frank Brangwyn RA is well known as a draughtsman and engraver in England, but it is a surprise to find that he was born in Bruges in 1867 and died at Ditchling in Sussex nearly ninety years later. He is represented here by some powerful studies of men at work, done in pencil, crayon and colour-wash. On the other hand Belleroche, who met and befriended him in Orange, was born in Swansea in 1864 and died here in 1944. Though little known even in France he was a more remarkable artist than Brangwyn. His drawings on the stairway of his wife and family are delightful cameos in the manner of Augustus John, and his oil paintings in the main room on this floor look every bit as good as some of the post-Impressionist masters. A striking self-portrait and a bust by Van den Steen show a young man of sensibility with the eyes of a painter.

As we shall find elsewhere in Provence, Christianity spread quickly up the Rhône valley, and by the end of the fourth century Arausio was already a bishopric. However it was not till 1208 that the **Church of Notre-Dame**, off the rue Victor Hugo in the northern part of the town, was consecrated as its cathedral. It lost that distinction at the Revolution, and now it has a sad look. Only the apse and the transept crossing are genuinely Romanesque; the nave and side aisles were rebuilt in the seventeenth century, and there were other incongruous developments in the nineteenth.

The name of the town today has nothing to do with the fruit or its colour. The word for that comes from the Spanish *naranja* (or Arabic *narandj*), which lost its initial 'n' in the same way as a 'numpire' ('non-peer') became in English 'an umpire'. No,

Orange is a corruption over many centuries of the Roman Arausio, but it has a surprising link with the royal houses of Holland and England. An independent principality in the Middle Ages, it passed by an accident of heredity to William 'the Silent' of Nassau in the Netherlands, who thereby became the Prince of Orange-Nassau – a title which passed in turn to William III of England, popularly known as 'William of Orange'. It was even for a few years part of the kingdom of England, but it was awarded sensibly enough to France by the Treaty of Utrecht. It was William III's victory at the Battle of the Boyne which gave rise to the Orange orders of Northern Ireland, and the colours they assumed were spurious.

In between the narrow streets of the town are a few quieter squares. In one of them, the Place Langes, you will find the only quiet hotel in Orange, the Arène. It has no restaurant, but perhaps is the quieter for that. If in any case you find the bustle of Orange is too much for you, there are some delectable and secluded places to stay in if you make for the countryside away to the north-east – an area once occupied by a Gallic tribe called the Tricastini, and now known as **le Tricastin**.

You could reach the Tricastin earlier by striking off the autoroute at the Bollène intersection, but it would be just as appropriate to rejoin the N7 as it emerges from the Arc de Triomphe, and carry on in the direction of Bollène. You will soon see one advantage of this. Autoroute, *route nationale* and railway run side by side beneath a towering cliff face, bypassing at its foot two mediaeval villages, whose existence you would otherwise not have suspected. The first is **Mornas**, entered from the south through a fortified gateway, and the whole valley here is commanded by a vast ruined castle, built by the counts of Provence in the twelfth century; you can reach it quite easily by following a steep ravine behind the village.

The road is passable by car as far as the church of **Notre-Dame-du-Val-Romigier**, which lies athwart the ravine about half way up. *Romigier* is the old form of *roncier*, a 'bramble bush',

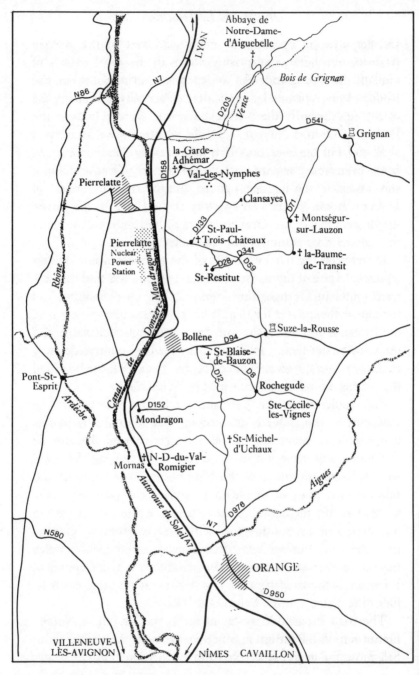

Orange and Le Tricastin

8

and helps you to imagine the scene where it was built. There was a church here as early as 818, but the present building is one of the first examples we shall see of pure Provençal Romanesque. With its tall square tower, its simple interior plan of a single barrel-vaulted nave, a central and two side apses leading off a short transept, it makes an ideal introduction to a style you will see a great deal of in northern Provence. It has been beautifully restored by 'les amis de Mornas', under supervision by the national commission of the Beaux Arts. To avoid disappointment by finding it locked, it is worth checking at the Secretariat of the Mairie in Mornas, where the key is kept.

A footpath leads up to the plateau where the castle was built. The scale of it is awesome, in its day encompassing the equivalent of a small town. There remains a massive keep, a chapel now fully restored, ramparts with corner bastions enclosing the whole site – and the width of the Rhône valley is spread out below. The view takes in the mountains of the Ardèche on the western horizon, and less romantically the atomic power station of Pierrelatte on the plain to the north. A mile or two up the road is **Mondragon**, the other bypassed village, but little is left of its barely accessible castle.

At this point the N7 dives under the autoroute to cross the Canal de Donzère-Mondragon, but a minor road goes on to Bollène, a decayed industrial town too close to the autoroute for its soul. If you follow the D158 north from here, a right-hand fork brings you to the market town of **St-Paul-Trois-Châteaux**, the most important in the neighbourhood. Its name was coined because of the supposed *tria castra*, or 'three forts' of the Tricastini, but not even one is to be found here. Instead there is the imposing cathedral of St-Paul, built in the light-coloured local limestone, and one of the most complete examples of Romanesque architecture in Provence.

There is a Provençal ring about its history too. The legendary first bishop of the Tricastin was none other than St Sidoine, or Sidonius, the man born blind whose sight was miraculously given him by Jesus. The legend has him arriving in an extraordinary boatload, without sails or oars, which made landfall on the coast of the Camargue, together with the 'three Marys' (St Mary Magdalene, St Mary Jacobé the sister of the Virgin, and St Mary Salomé the mother of the apostles James and John), their black attendant Sara, the Lazarus whom Jesus raised from the dead, and a martyred Roman called Maximius. All these figure in the folklore of various parts of Provence, but Sidonius made his way north up the Rhône valley and was welcomed as an evangelist in the Tricastin.

The man who later gave his name to the church of St-Paul was a slightly more historical character. A native of the Champagne in the fifth century, he fled to Provence during the barbarian invasions. Already respected for his simple piety, he was offered the bishopric, but with a dramatic gesture of humility he planted his shepherd's staff in the ground and refused the offer unless it should flower – as of course it did. Superstition has free range in Provençal folklore – indeed Christians everywhere tended to compete with Greek and Roman myth-makers in embroidering their early history. In Provence the stories are still told with gusto and conviction, just as they are in Greece today.

This majestic church, built early in the twelfth century, has a fortress-like nave and transepts which rise high above the surrounding roofs. The north transept (seen from the outside) is notable for a band of semicircular blind arcading which runs round it a little below roof level – said to be a Lombardic design introduced from northern Italy to break up otherwise blank wall areas, as it does here very successfully. The entry now is by the south porch, but if you go round to the west end you will find one of the best preserved Romanesque doorways in Provence. Its rich and varied semicircular mouldings are set in a plain façade, broken only by three beautifully placed round windows.

As you enter the nave the first impression is of height, dignity and simplicity. Only later do you take in the cunning with which the architects have introduced decoration at key points- sculptured corbels and friezes along the cornice of the nave, twisted fluting in some of the most exposed columns. The uninterrupted view eastward has probably not been altered since the church was built, except for the single later window at the centre of the apse, and the over-elaborate gleaming white stonework of the nineteenth-century high altar. These big Provençal churches have mostly escaped Gothic or Renaissance intrusions, as well as the heavy-handed restorers of the last century. To stand among the congregation at a Sunday Mass is an experience which has been repeated Sunday after Sunday, year after year, in much the same surroundings since the twelfth century. Only the form of service has lost some of its dignity since the changes ordained by the Second Vatican Council, popular though they seem to be with the congregations.

Nor are you likely to be bustled by crowds on weekdays, for few of these places are on tourist schedules. Instead there will nearly always be some knowledgeable resident, if not the sacristan himself, to show you round. I was grateful to one on my first visit to St-Paul, who pointed apologetically to the present high altar ('pâtisserie', he called it) and then showed us a gorgeous Renaissance altar front in gilded wood which used to stand there, but has been banished behind one of the bays on the north side of the nave. 'You can imagine', he said, 'how it glowed when struck by the evening sunlight coming in through the western windows.'

Its removal did reveal an even greater treasure, a twelfth-century mosaic floor with a vivid two-dimensional picture of the Holy City of Jerusalem, a fanciful vision of towers, windows and archways with no attempt at perspective. On either side of the nave there are a few remains of the mediaeval paintings which must have decorated the flat surfaces of its pillars and wall-spaces. On the south side is a Baptism, where the naked body of Jesus shows through the rippling waters of the Jordan, whereas the Baptist is substantially clad in ankle-length sheepskin; to the north, on the left of the bay facing the entrance, is a curious scene of martyrdom, where the victim kneels between two soldiers wearing a strange pointed cap such as one sees on the head of penitents in mediaeval paintings. On a pillar across the bay is an early carving in deep relief of the Last Judgement, and other decorative carving throughout the church shows how rich it was in this respect before it was so brutally mutilated in the wars of religion and the Revolution. There are masons' marks all over the southern face of the tower, some of them repeated many times on different stones.

Passing from St-Paul to the neighbouring village of **St-Restitut** you realize how quickly the scenery can change in Provence. From a market town in a bulge of the wide Rhône valley, the road to the south-east winds steeply up the face of a dry limestone ridge to reach a huddle of red roofs encircling another fine church of the twelfth century. The change of air in itself is exhilarating. In Latin the word *restitutus* means 'restored', and St Restitut is another name for St Sidoine, the man whose sight was 'restored' by Jesus. As the first bishop of the Tricastin, according to legend, he founded a community of Christians here is the first century. His church is a lovely surprise, and its walls of pale creamy porous limestone form one side of a leafy square where birds nest in spring and sing in summer.

Tradition says it was Charlemagne who built the first basilica here in the ninth century. That could be true, but few buildings of that period survived raids by Saracen and Norman invaders. On the other hand peace and security returned to Provence in the twelfth and thirteenth centuries. Abbeys and churches rose again everywhere, not only to foster religion and education but often specifically to house and display the saintly relics which the Crusaders were bringing back from the Holy Land. In this respect too they were a good investment, for they attracted pilgrims who brought wealth to the countryside.

The most striking part of the church is the big square tower at the west end – not the usual bell tower, but an extension upwards of a much older square chamber where pilgrims could look down into the crypt where the saint's body was buried. In 1249 the bishop of St-Paul had it exhumed, and the bones were put in a marble reliquary within the church. Sad to say they were burnt and scattered by intemperate Calvinists during the six-teenth-century wars of religion. Just below the coping which divides the older from the later part of the tower is a band of incised panels carved in relief round the three sides that are visible – it is in fact continued on the fourth side, visible only from inside the nave. The panels show an extraordinary medley of real and imaginary creatures of the animal world mixed with naively carved human figures. Masons' marks on the upper tower include some with the letters 'VGO', where the 'G' takes the form of a sickle. As this was among the marks we saw on the walls of St-Paul it suggests that the same team was employed on both buildings, perhaps with a 'Master Hugo' in charge. A pair of binoculars would be useful here.

With the tower blocking the west end, the entry porch is on the south side. Flanked by massive buttresses, its serene elevation is derived from classical traditions but speaks most eloquently for Provence. The doorway is crowned by a pediment supported by fluted Corinthian pilasters in the Greco-Roman style; it and the wide span of the semicircular arch above could have been copied from the amphitheatre at Nîmes, yet the composition is domestic and charming, with nothing of the stiffness of large-scale Roman architecture. On the western side of the square is the Auberge des Quatre Saisons. It has only ten rooms, but if you can find one free it would be a lovely place to spend a week – though it is not cheap.

At the same time if you are looking for a family base, or just a holiday for two, you can do no better than the Ferme St-Michel, an old family home cleverly converted to a small hotel without losing its original features. It stands in its own grounds just outside the village of Solérieux, on the left of the road from

St-Paul to la-Baume-de Transit. It has its own vineyard, a small swimming pool, a courtyard where you can eat or drink out of doors most of the time, and a kitchen which produces real Provençal food. The lady owner is *vraie Provençale* too, a small figure with piercing blue eyes, in constant motion and talking with a touch of her native dialect.

The village of **la-Baume-de-Transit** lies at the foot of a hill once occupied by the château de Baume, a fortress which belonged to the bishops of St-Paul. Of that only a gaunt fang remains, but on the slope of the hill on the far side of the village there is a fascinating little church which takes you back to an even earlier age and style than St-Restitut. In the late eleventh century a number of churches in Europe were built on the 'Greek Cross' plan, imitating the church of the Holy Sepulchre in Jerusalem, memories of which had been brought back by returning Crusaders. This was essentially a square central area surmounted by a cupola, with semicircular apses projecting at all cardinal points – a scheme which could be scaled down most attractively for small communities.

The church here, known as la Sainte-Croix, is puzzling to decipher on these lines, and you really need a compass to sort it out on the spot. The trouble is that only three apses survive, and though it was not unusual in the later centuries to demolish the western one and build an extended nave for the parish, this is not what happened here. As the ground falls away to the west, and the cemetery lay to the south and east, it had to be the northern apse which they got rid of in 1668, making the main entrance at the end of the nave and moving the high altar into the southern apse to face it. The earliest entry was through the 'porte des morts' leading to the cemetery on the south, but in the fourteenth century it was blocked up, a porch was added to the western apse, and a doorway cut through it to face what was then the orthodoxly placed high altar. Very recently the little southern door has been reopened, and the view through it to the inside of the church is a great gain.

In spite of all these complications that end of the church has much charm, and the eastern and southern apses still have their graceful decoration of blind arches below a plain half-dome, supported by four short columns; only in the western one have they disappeared to make way for the fourteenth-century entrance, but the nave of 1688 is a poor dull thing. The cupola collapsed in the 1500s, to be replaced by a Gothic vault, and the insouciant little bell tower was added later.

Just two kilometres north from here is **Montségur-sur-Lauzon**, the Lauzon being one of several streams which trickle down from the northern hills of the Tricastin to join the Rhône. The village church is modern, but on the rock above it a castle was built in the twelfth century, and beside it is a little church spliced into the rock. The castle is almost totally ruinous, though fascinating glimpses of its past can be seen all round amid the undergrowth and the rocks. One section of its curtain wall was built up again by a group of enthusiasts in honour of Frédéric Mistral, the Provençal national poet. Beneath a grandiose inscription which reads 'Grand Mur de l'Académie Gauloise' a seven-pointed stone star has been fixed to the face of the wall, with a tribute to Mistral at its heart, surrounded by tablets with the names of the academy's founders. Unfortunately this was as a far as their reconstruction of the site could go, but local enterprise has begun to restore the church, whose west end is embedded in the rock. From the terrace there is a superb view over the Rhône valley, carpeted with vineyards and fields of corn and lavender.

From here you can drive a few miles north to **Grignan**, a town which is still physically, if no longer socially, subject to the huge château at its heart; the high rock on which it stands occupies the whole of the upper town. What you see is Renaissance in origin, though the dead hand of the restorers has fallen on the main façade. The flanking tower to the left is original, and there is a more congenial fountain courtyard beyond it. The wide terraces are superbly planned and built, with views over miles and miles of sweeping Provençal country. This was the seat of the comtes de Grignan, one of whom married the daughter of Madame de Sévigné, that indefatigable letter-writer who seems to have had the run of all the best châteaux of her day, as well as the court of Louis XIV. Most of all she loved being here with her daugher and taking the air on these splendid terraces. She is buried in the seventeenth-century collegial church of St-Sauveur below the château.

North of Grignan the country becomes hilly and densely wooded, a secret world not suspected by drivers committed to the scorching autoroute which skirts it. In the heart of the Bois de Grignan is the Cistercian abbey of **Notre-Dame-d'Aiguebelle**, which may be your first sight of one of these establishments in full use today. It has recently celebrated the 850th anniversary of its foundation, and is occupied by a community of fifty monks who carry out the *activités fondamentales* of their order – Prayer, Work, Meditation. It was in 1137 that monks from Cîteaux in Burgundy first came to this green wooded valley, watered by many natural springs and threaded by the little river Vence. Its name is easy to understand – *aqua bella* in Latin, *aigo bello* in Provençale.

The abbey is much used today for *retraites* — visits by outsiders for periods of peaceful meditation. The comforts of a large hostel, the friendly atmosphere and the quite lovely surroundings should bring peace to any heart. The Cistercian rule keeps part of the monastic buildings (known as the *clôture*) closed to ordinary visitors, but that does not apply to the church of Notre-Dame, a pure and well proportioned example of Cistercian Romanesque which has been carefully preserved without any harsh attempts to restore it. The great barrel-vaulted refectory is just as impressive, and perhaps more human in its appeal. The projecting 'tribune' in the south wall is for readings during meals, which are otherwise taken in silence.

Monks work in the surrounding fields and vineyards, as well as in the neat vegetable plots within the walls. You will find in everyone who lives and works here a certainty of aim and clarity of view rare in other religious communities – even, one must say, in the Church of England; yet though intent on the articles of his faith the Cistercian monk enjoys contact with the outside world. Sunday visitors come from round about to hear Mass and greet relations who may be living here. The bookshop, which also sells honey, herbs and cheeses from the abbey estate, is served by a voluble young monk who is liable to break out into operatic airs if there is a gap in conversation. He prefers Mozart, but he is an expert on the Gregorian chants which are often sung in the church.

From the higher ground outside the entrance there is a lovely view down the valley of the Vence to the distant château of Roussas, while the slope is cut into by a big reservoir of spring water fed through two rushing stone chutes from the rocks above – *aqua bella* indeed.

Turning south down the valley you reach the main road from Montélimar to Grignan, from which a couple of left turns will put you on the long straight D158 which runs beside the canal and the autoroute back to Bollène. First, though, if you look up to your left you will see a ridge crowned by the village of **la-Garde-Adhémar**, stronghold of the once powerful seig-neurial family of Adhémar. You may hardly register the village at first, for out of it rises the high nave and octagonal tower of the church of St-Michel, a landmark for travellers heading north or south along the valley below.

Its plan, like that of St-Paul-Trois-Châteaux, is a noble basilica, though with broader aisles and without a transept; the side aisles run right through to end in separate apses. A very rare feature is a fourth apse which projects from the west end of the nave and forms the western entrance to the church. This is a ninth-century, or Carolingian, feature which survives in only one other instance in Provence, though there are examples of what architectural writers call 'westwork' in both Provence and Burgundy. The idea was to allow pilgrims an easier view of the church's holy relics, as in the upper narthex of St Philibert's cathedral at Tournus, which is also dedicated to St Michel.

The surrounding houses are dwarfed by the church and encircled by high walls, leaving narrow winding lanes between them. This kind of hill village is typical of Provence, but the country round about is specially beautiful – again a contrast with the plain below through which trains, cars and huge *camions* hurtle blindly along their allotted channels. Up above you can picnic in spring among fields of cowslips and grape hyacinths, with nightingales singing and butterflies dancing in their courting spirals.

In the twelfth century the church of St-Michel was dependent on the priory of **Val-des-Nymphes**, whose ruined chapel stands in a romantic glen below the country road leading east from la-Garde. This in turn was subject to the abbey of Tournus, and remained so until 1540, when the comte de Grignan persuaded Pope Paul III to detach it and St-Michel from Tournus and join them under the collegial church of St-Sauveur in Grignan. These were manoeuvres common among the land-owning aristocracy until the Revolution put an end to so many of them.

The result here in the sixteenth century was the decline and eventual ruin of the priory, but there is still enough left of the chapel in this delightful spot to attract local picnic parties. Especially charming is the delicate west façade, intact up to a small rose window in the gable. It seems natural to suppose that it was once a Roman or Gallic religious site, perhaps a *nymphaeum*. The ingredients are all there – springs, rocks, and a grove of oak trees.

So secret is the countryside away from its main roads that you could drive through it unaware of places like la-Baume-de-Transit and Montségur-sur-Lauzon. You would be even less likely to come across **Clansayes**, another hill village with strange embellishments. You will only find it if you take the next right-hand turn after Val-des-Nymphes which leads to St-Paul.

After crossing the little valley of the Echaravelles (what lovely names they have in the Tricastin!) you will see ahead of you a huge detached tower standing on a bare ridge to the left of the road. It proves to be an extraordinary polygonal *donjon*, or keep, of another long-ruined castle, with recessed arches on the angles and a walkway, or *chemin de ronde*, from which anything could be unloaded through the arched openings on unwelcome visitors. Above it stands an enormous and frankly incongruous statue of the Virgin, whose body looks as if it had been carved out of stratified rock to represent the folds of her robe. Alongside there is a tiny church, recently restored. The village is on the steep slope of the hill below, but parts of the ruined château have been bought up for private development into attractive dwellings with fantastic views.

That this is an ancient religious site (probably a priory or monastery) is proved if you poke around east of the tower. A now sunken enclosure has been revealed with three arched openings cut into the rock to form a row of three apses for a primitive church. Holes for cross-beams in the side walls show that it had a broad roofed nave. Another section of walling nearby has several courses laid in herring-bone pattern, usually a sign of Carolingian or even Merovingian building. All around is a pleasant confusion of rocks, scrub, gorse, wild flowers and butterflies.

You may be close now to your base at the Ferme St-Michel (at least as the crow flies) but if you are on your way back to Orange I would suggest taking what will now seem a very main road (the D59) from St-Paul to **Suze-la-Rousse**, where a dramatic fourteenth-century château rises from the trees above the town. The inside was mostly remodelled in the sixteenth century, though the twelfth-century kitchens survive from an earlier time and are much more interesting. There are guided visits, in the afternoon only, during most of the year, but you will find it – like so many French establishments – 'fermé le mardi'.

From here an even mainer road leads in the direction of

Bollène, but there is no need to get involved again in that industrial backwater. Instead turn sharp left on the D8 leading to Rochegude and Ste-Cecile-les-Vignes, and almost at once you will see the chapel and ruined castle of **St-Blaise-de-Bauzon** on a wooded hill to your right. This is all that remains of an eleventh-century feudal agglomeration which came into the hands of the church in the thirteenth century. The castle has long ago disintegrated, but the chapel ranks as one of the more eccentric little buildings of Provence. To reach it you must climb a rough footpath through the trees (there is safe parking beside the road) to find the lower part almost buried in the undergrowth.

What you will see is a short high nave ending in a semicircular apse, but the outer walls are strengthened by four unique rounded buttresses, and you enter through a sort of fortified annexe on the south side. There are hardly any windows, and they are small and a long way from the ground. Why this tiny place should need to display such strength is a mystery, but perhaps the builders of the castle were more used to military than church architecture. As things are, its status as a *monument historique* is doing nothing to preserve it.

For one more journey into remote Tricastin – we are only five or six kilometres from the autoroute, but might as well be a hundred – regain the main road to Bollène and take the next turning to the left. This is now the most direct way back to Orange and by far the most beautiful. After about ten kilometres, but only if you have time to spare, look for an entry road on the left which leads to a wooded area which is being developed for discreet housing. You may have to ask for help in finding the chapel of **St-Michel-d'Uchaux**, but sad though its state is today you will be rewarded by another intriguing miniature. An even more tragic victim of neglect than St-Blaise, this tiny building has all the attractions of small-scale early Romanesque architecture, but more importantly it contains three panels of thirteenth-century fresco painting in the apse –

delightful scenes of the Nativity and the Flight into Egypt on either side of a Virgin in Majesty. The entrance is now closed by a locked grille, and through it you can see that unless something is done there will be no point in letting people in to see them. They will have vanished, and the roof which still protects them will have been torn apart by the vegetation which grows unchecked through the tiles. This unusual situation in Provence is probably due to the uncaring and mercenary attitude of those who are developing the *commune d'Uchaux*.

These little buildings may seem of little importance in a busy world, but I write of them with concern in the hope that one day somebody will take notice. In the meantime go and look before St-Blaise and St-Michel disappear, then either take the tree-lined road south to Orange or make your way back to St-Restitut on its luminous hill, or to the vineyards and lavender fields round the Ferme St-Michel, which is still less than twenty kilometres away in the heart of the Tricastin.

2

Les Baronnies

I now suggest a wider sweep into country which will be even less
well known than the Tricastin. The name 'Baronnies' originally
described an area where the minor nobility held lands well away
from the centres of power on the Rhône; today it is mostly
applied to the first range of mountains you reach after leaving
the Rhône valley – though their rounded tree-clad summits,
none of them much more than 3,000 feet, in no way compete
with the magnificent limestone peaks of the Alpes de Haute-
Provence further away to the east.

The key to the Baronnies is the town of Nyons, which is easily
reached either from northern Triscastin or from Orange. The
latter is a slightly longer route, but if you go that way do not fail
to stop at **Sérignan-du-Comtat**, about eight kilometres out
from Orange. The town itself is a pleasant one, and popular with
commuters, but its great draw is an unobtrusive house screened
by trees beside the main road – on your right coming from
Orange. You might take it for a modest English country rectory,
the kind of place where Gilbert White would have been at home.
The house is called 'l'Harmas', which in Provençale means 'the
plot of land', and between 1879 and 1915 it was the home of
J. H. Fabre, the internationally famous naturalist.

His parents were poor and his education spasmodic, but with

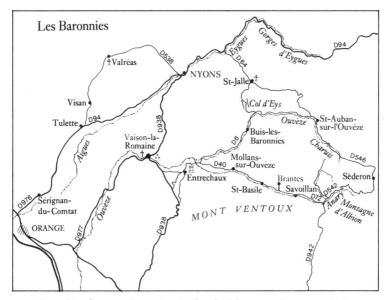

a university degree in science he held several congenial posts before being appointed by the Minister of Culture to lecture on the natural sciences in Avignon. Perhaps unwisely he chose as the subject of his first lecture the fertilisation of plants; his practical and evolutionary approach to it outraged both the parents of his pupils and the clergy of Avignon. He was forced to resign, and faced unemployment and poverty, but in 1868 John Stuart Mill (who was then living in Avignon) lent him three thousand francs to buy a house for his family in Orange and begin a career in writing. From the sale of his books he was able to buy his 'plot of land' in Serignan. Twice married, with ten children, he lived to be 92.

Inside the house, on the first floor, is one large room which was the study, library and workshop of a genius. On the walls you see a series of exquisite water-colour paintings of a hundred varieties of fungi. There are bookshelves full of his printed works and folders of scientific notes. Showcases of beetles and butterflies, birds' eggs, *trouvailles* of animal skeletons – one of a dolphin which he found while working at Ajaccio in Corsica.

23

A beehive, and a cell he used for studying the solitary bee. A glass-topped case with letters to and from other naturalists and famous men – Darwin among them. Little illustrated books catch the eye, which must have been written for his children. How about *le Crapaud Désobéissant* as a friend for Jeremy Fisher?

There is a small fee for admission, which applies to two hours in the morning and two in the afternoon, but if you have to wait there is an enchanted garden to sit or walk in. Just as Fabre left it, it has his favourite flowering shrubs, some of them rareties; herb plots, winding paths and wooden seats. Birds of many kinds sing and nest, and frogs croak in little pools. The garden is beautifully kept by a young gardener to whom Fabre, whom he could never have known, was clearly a genius.

Rather than follow the valley of the Eygues (or the Aigues as the maps call it in the department of Vaucluse) all the way to Nyons, you may find it more interesting to branch off the main road just after Tulette for Visan and Valréas. **Visan** as seen today is a seventeenth-century rather than a mediaeval town. It has a number of exceptional houses of that date, especially in the rue des Nobles, grouped round an earlier Gothic church of no great note; the wide clean streets are attractively paved in grey and pink stone.

This little area is marked on the map as a curious bubble-shaped extrusion of the department of Vaucluse into Drôme, an anomaly which arose when the Popes abandoned Rome for Avignon in the fourteenth century. John XXII, second of the Avignon Popes, bought Valréas from the French crown in 1317, and during the next few years he added the towns of Visan and Richerenches. A narrow corridor still divided this new papal territory from the Comtat Venaissin, the Provençal base of the Avignon Popes, and the later French king Charles VII refused to allow any further encroachment to unite them. This left the 'enclave des Papes' isolated, and you will find it still marked by notices telling you when you enter or leave it. Its low-lying and well watered terrain produces a surprisingly good Côtes du Rhône *rouge*.

The capital of the *enclave* was **Valréas**, another clean and well organised little market town, and its Hôtel-de-Ville is one of the finest in France. Originally the Château de Simiane, owned by the marquis of that name who married Pauline de Grignan, granddaughter of Madame de Sévigné, it now contains the Salon de l'Enclave on the first floor of what is a magnificent eighteenth-century mansion overlooking the Place Aristide Briand. More in the centre of the town is the church of **Notre-Dame-de-Nazareth**, whose outside is a curious mixture of styles and dates. Inside you will find it a typically plain and dignified example of Provençal Romanesque. The lack of ornament is almost Cistercian, and there are so few windows that to appreciate the tall sombre nave you will need to find the light switch on the wall to the right of the entrance and a one-franc piece to activate it. This solemnity is broken by a gorgeous baroque organ tribune at the west end, and under the single lancet window of the apse there is a lively fresco panel of the Assumption of the Virgin – probably part of a sequence which ran right round the nave.

Opposite the west end of the church is a gateway with an iron grille, beyond which is a path leading to some public gardens, with the little seventeenth-century chapel of the Penitents Blancs on the right. This was where at dawn on 13 June 1944 they brought the pitiful bodies of Resistance fighters and hostages who had been shot by the Germans on the evening before. Overlooking the chapel and gardens is the Tour de l'Horloge, once part of the Château Ripert. The gate is opened only for guided visits on Tuesdays, Thursdays and Saturdays, which leave the Maison de Tourisme at 1630. You should also register that there is a market in Valréas every Thursday, which leads to *circulation difficile*.

From Valréas the short drive to **Nyons** takes you into another world. The gateway to the Baronnies, it was built where the narrow valley of the Eygues broadens out into the plain of the Triscastin, but is so closely sheltered by mountains that it enjoys an almost exotic climate; you will find trees and plants here that grow nowhere else in Provence except on the Riviera coast. That it was a gateway not only to the Baronnies but to the alpine country of Haute-Provence is brought home when we find that the novelist Jean Giono was born here. He must have watched year after year the passage of the huge flocks of sheep and goats on their way between summer and winter pastures – the *transhumance* which he describes vividly in *Le Grand Troupeau*. Nyons itself he called a terrestrial paradise.

To get the best out of a visit, leave your car in the 'Parking de Tourisme' on the outskirts, look for the Place du Dr Bourdongle (a wartime resistance hero) and follow the road up to the church of St-Vincent. Leaving that on your right you come into a warren of narrow passages and stepped alleyways, of which the most surprising is the rue des Grands Forts, a covered passageway which runs for a good hundred yards under the walls of the mediaeval château. There are mediaeval smells of cooking too which greet you from unseen kitchens as you pass.

At the end of the passage there are very necessary signs which point the way up winding chains of steps to the **Tour Randonne**, a spectacular piece of mediaeval fortification which has been messed up by an elaborate neo-Gothic superstructure culminating in an absurd stone pineapple. Enshrined below it is the tiny chapel of Notre-Dame-de-Bon-Secours, which in spite of being tricked out in gaudy colours in 1863 has an odd kind of charm. From the terrace up here there is a marvellous view over the town below, which is well known for its truffle market and for its *moulins à l'huile*, and which still produce quantities of fruit and fine olive oil during the winter months. To get back to your car you can follow a straighter but steeper stepped alley which begins on the far side of the Tour Randonne; once in sight of the church of St-Vincent you should be able to get your bearings for Dr Bourdongle – though the topography of the old part of Nyons can baffle the most orderly mind.

Apart from Nyons there is only one town of any size in the Baronnies, and even Buis-les-Baronnies has little room to expand, hemmed in as it is on the upper reaches of the Ouvèze between 3,000-feet mountains. To reach it from Nyons you must set off up the gorge of the Eygues in the direction of Serre and distant Haute-Provence. After ten kilometres take a turn to the right which climbs to a narrow plateau where you will find the village and Romanesque church of **St-Jalle**. This wonderful little church stands on its own beside the road as you approach the village, and its short squarish tower perches like a great tawny owl, with two narrow windows for eyes, spreading its wings over a wide transept and a clutch of three semicircular apses. Inside, the twelfth-century architect has followed the common Provençal plan – one simple barrel–vaulted nave leading into a wide-spreading transept with two smaller apses projecting to the east, each with its little slit window.

Before you go in, take a good look at the decorations above the west doorway, for though it has features often seen in the Brionnais region of Burgundy you will find nothing like this in Provence. The capitals on either side, with their pierced acanthus-like foliage, support strange creatures below the abacus, and the decorated arches above frame a tympanum as charming in its treatment as it is mysterious in its message. It has two parts. On the extreme right a figure leans over a very early 'authentic' stringed instrument. Next to him an upright man with a large head seems to be picking fruit from a tree to put in a basket below, while an owl perches on his right shoulder. In the left-hand section a third figure holds a wallet and a pilgrim's staff, and is faced by a very large cock peering over a small bush. What on earth do we make of all this? The learned interpretation is that on the right hand we see earthly joys – music and fruitfulness – on the left religious duty in the person of the pilgrim. At the same time the owl could represent darkness, the

27

cock the coming of light, with the added thought that the Latin for cock is *gallus*, while *Galla* is a female Gaul, and the church's patron saint is now called Jalle! The lintel below adds a more graceful element, with its feathery interlaced rosettes, but we are a long way from the carefully planned spirituality of Gothic art.

After this the architecture of the little town of **Buis-les-Baronnies** may seem dull, but its arcaded shopping streets have character, and it can be a convenient starting point for one of many lovely drives through Provence. This one could be a cross-country way of reaching Sisteron from the west, but for our present purpose we can make it a round trip by turning back at the half-way mark for Vaison-la-Romaine. The outward journey begins with a steep and winding climb over open hillsides to the Col d'Eys, then drops you down just as steeply into the wooded valley of the Ouvèze. Your road (now the D546) follows a narrow course along the north bank, lined with cherry, olive, peach and apple trees – incredibly beautiful when the blossom is out in the spring – with mile after mile of lime trees marching beside you on either side.

After St-Auban-sur-Ouvèze you join the side valley of the Charuis, with the foothills of Mont Ventoux looming above you to the right. The valley gradually opens out, with more apple orchards and a few fields of maize and sunflowers. Eventually, just north of Séderon, the road turns south to its junction with the D542 on its way to the Gorges de la Méouge and the valley of the Buëch above Sisteron. For the present, though, follow it for two kilometres till it divides again, and take the right-hand fork. This begins the most exciting part of the drive, first along the valley of the Anary under the flank of the Montagne d'Albion, then turning right on the D72 close under the northern face of Mont Ventoux itself – that strange bald-headed mountain which seems from a distance to be permanently capped with snow. After Savoillan it will be more peaceful to take the minor D40 along the banks of the Toulourenc than to climb back over the cols into the Ouvèze valley.

This way also makes an easier approach to the romantic village of **Brantes,** an eyrie on a cliff face between the two roads. To call it 'romantic' may give the wrong impression, for this is no place for the tourist trade. The drive up is very steep, and you enter through a little archway next to the Mairie – beyond which your car will be of no use, so leave it outside. Rough lanes and flights of steps lead upwards in haphazard directions; at the head of one you come upon two little churches facing each other in friendly confrontation. As you wander around you will see how simple it all is; only here and there has an old house been done up for a pottery or an art exhibition. Further up the hill there is a modest *auberge* and an *épicerie* – the only shop in the village. Brantes is for the peace-lover, and the view over the valley to the tree-clad north face of Mont Ventoux is magical.

If you can tear yourself away to rejoin the road below you will have another lovely drive along the wide cultivated valley of the Toulourenc, especially in the autumn when the poplars stand up golden against the evergreen oaks and pines. To the left are the rich dark folds of Mont Ventoux, into whose shadow you will come by evening. Just before Mollans-sur-Ouvèze turn left for Entrechaux, where a ruined castle commands the skyline, and the main D938 road will bring you into **Vaison-la-Romaine**. This is one of the major historic sites of Provence, and it needs a whole day to explore. You can stay in comfort either at the Beffroi, a converted sixteenth-century house in the 'haute ville' south of the river, or in the Theatre Romain, a more modest hotel and convenient for the Roman excavation sites in the main part of the town to the north.

What you will see covers nearly two thousand years of the town's continuous life, from the first-century Roman bridge over the Ouvèze to the beautifully equipped modern museum which displays the evidence of its past. No other place has kept so much character alive from so many different periods, and the bustling, good-humoured *marché* which fills the Place du 11 novembre every Tuesday recreates the atmosphere of the third-century Roman 'Rue des Boutiques', whose ground plan is clearly marked among the excavations below. Without going into its nebulous Neolithic origins, we learn that 'Vaison' derives from 'Vasio', the name given by the Romans to the capital of the Gallic tribe Vocontii in the first century BC – and you will be familiar with the adjective *romaine* meaning 'Roman', as distinct from *romane* which means Romanesque and covers roughly the tenth to the thirteenth centuries of our era. Even by the first century AD its position in this fertile valley at a crossing of trade routes had made it a large and prosperous city, bigger than Arles and Fréjus, richer than Orange or Avignon.

The two main excavation sites go a long way to proving this, and everyone must be grateful to the abbé Sautel, who in 1907 'avec longue patience et la force de sa génie latine' brought so much to light that had been hidden for centuries, and to the civic authority which has made it such an attractive place to visit. As the ground rises from the north bank of the river you come first to the **Quartier de la Villasse**, which proves to have been a mainly residential area with many fine town houses, a busy shopping street, and the *thermes*, or public baths, which no Roman community could do without. Entrance is from the car park in the Place du 11 novembre, and you can wander at will round the houses of these wealthy Romans; the walls have been built up to three or four feet above the foundations, and some of the open spaces have been sown with green lawns and planted with dark-leaved maples.

Later buildings and roads have inevitably hidden much more than has been revealed. No public buildings other than the theatre and baths have been traced, but if you cross the Place and the Avenue General de Gaulle you come to the **Quartier du Puymin**, where the most luxurious of these town houses was built for a family called the Messii. It was on the scale of a small mediaeval château or an English country house, and must have been more comfortable than either. The different rooms and courtyards are clearly marked – the reception rooms and dining rooms, the kitchens, the private baths, the *atrium* with its little fountain, the *lararium* (a kind of private chapel where the busts of the household's ancestors were kept), the pillared peristyle for walking in sheltered shade, the under-floor central heating, even the multi-seated stone lavatory flushed by a channel of running water underneath.

To the north of these excavated areas a roadway lined with early Christian sarcophagi leads to the museum, but it would be sensible to leave that till after visiting the **Theatre**. The approach to this is on the right of the museum, and runs partly through a tunnel in the rock mass known as the Puymin which forms the back of the *cavea*, or semicircle of theatre seats. Though the whole theatre is nowhere near as big as the one at Orange, it still seats 4,500 during its summer international festival of dance and drama. There is a particular interest in the layout of the stage area, or *scena*, for though none of the backing for this has survived you can see the artists' dressing rooms and entrance, and the trenches cut into the rock which held the winding mechanism for raising and lowering the curtain in front of the stage. It seems almost incredible today that when the abbé Sautel surveyed the site in 1907 he could see only the heads of two arches protruding from the earth.

The **Musée Théo des Plans**, to give it the full title which commemorates its founder, is a clean, well lit modern building on a raised terrace, with plenty of space to avoid that crowded feeling you associate with many museums. It houses only objects found on the various sites, which include (from the façade of the theatre) marble statues of the emperors Hadrian, Domitian and Claudius. Notice Domitian's mean mouth and the sensitive features of the young Claudius. Also from the theatre came a dramatic tragic mask with gaping mouth and staring eyes, hair piled up in stylized ringlets. From one of the big houses in the Villasse quarter comes the famous 'Buste d'argent', which is a moulded portrait in silver of a typical low-brow *nouveau riche*

Roman with more money than taste. Collected from all over are toilet acessories, mirrors, brooches, pins – and the statue of Hadrian's wife Sabina shows how the more aristocratic ladies managed their hair. Displays of architectural features include one to illustrate roofing technique, and the whole museum brilliantly complements the gound work of the excavations.

If after all this you are feeling faint, dry or famished, the terrace of the Theatre Romain hotel in the Place Abbé Sautel is just right for an aperitif or a delicious lunch before going any further. Sooner or later, though, you must move down beyond the western end of the excavations to the cathedral church of **Notre-Dame-de-Nazareth**, where you will see how the artistic and religious life of Vaison continued almost uninterrupted through what have been misleadingly called the 'Dark Ages'. Christianity, as we saw in the Tricastin, came early to Provence, and by the beginning of the fourth century Vaison had its first bishop, while recent excavations have made it clear that there was a Gallo-Roman 'church' on the site of the present cathedral. Inside the south porch, by which you enter, are three conjectural drawings of what successive churches in the sixth, eleventh and thirteenth centuries would have looked like when first built – and that shows you how old and hallowed is the site.

The present church is still basically that of the thirteenth century, a late Romanesque basilica with three aisles, though the main apse is almost unchanged on the inside since the sixth century – notice the row of stone seating round its circumference for the clergy, with the bishop's throne raised in the centre. The drawings in the porch show that the first two churches had wooden roofs. The present barrel vault with its slightly pointed arches belongs to the thirteenth century, as does the beautiful octagonal cupola where figures of the four evangelists occupy niches at the heart of the fan-shaped corner squinches. The smaller apse at the head of the north aisle has a beautifully decorated marble altar which must have been carved in the early Christian, or at the latest in Carolingian times, and at the west end of the same aisle the ground has been excavated to show the base and first three drum sections of one of the colossal fluted columns of the sixth-century building. More signs of the earliest building can be seen from outside the east end, where the outer wall of the main apse has been squared off, leaving exposed the sixth-century foundations and the re-used drums of pillars which support it. The cloister, unusually placed to the north, was added to the eleventh century church, but it has been harshly restored in recent times.

About a quarter of a mile to the north, reached either by a winding lane through allotments or by way of the Avenue General de Gaulle and the ring road, is the curious **Chapel of St-Quenin**, named after a sixth-century bishop of Vaison. It was certainly another very early religious site – some say it was based on a temple of Diana, but the oldest remains are early Christian and Merovingian fragments built into the west façade, attractively carved with leaves and vine clusters. Inside, the nave (which was entirely rebuilt in the seventeenth century) leads to a unique triangular apse, which with all its detail dates from the twelfth century, and looks very odd indeed from the outside.

The course of life in Vaison was changed decisively in the Middle Ages, for in 1160 the then Count Raymond of Toulouse attacked and captured the defenceless town, and in the true mediaeval spirit built a great castle on the high rock south of the river. Most of the population took advantage of the protection and employment it offered, and the lower town was largely abandoned. Even the bishop eventually moved up to the 'haute ville', and a suitable church was built for his successors in 1464. For once the Revolution proved good news for Vaison, by abolishing the bishopric and dismantling the castle, so that in the nineteenth century the population gradually returned to the original site of Vasio Vocontorum. Yet time never stands still here. Though little remains up there to attract the tourist, apart from the Hotel Beffroi, and the climb to the castle ruins is unrewarding except for the view, local people have bought up and refurbished a number of the old houses, thereby escaping the crush of tourists and enjoying a lordly mediaeval view of town and countryside.

3

Le Comtat

The 'Comtat Venaissin' is the core of the confused mediaeval history of western Provence. When in 1032 the ancient kingdom of Arles was taken over by the 'Holy Roman' emperor Conrad II, the overlords of the various regions became feudal subjects of the Empire, with the title of *comte*, owing no allegiance to the Capetian kings of France. Avignon, in Latin *Avenio*, was then the chief town of the *Comitatus Avennicinus* and a fief of the counts of Toulouse. When the cynical alliance of the French king Louis VIII and Pope Innocent III had crushed the 'heretics' of Albi and Toulouse in the so-called Albigensian Crusade, Avignon fell to the French army, and in 1226 their defeated leader Raymond of Toulouse pledged his lands east of the city to the Pope as a surety for his future behaviour; in 1274 the Comtat Venaissin was formally annexed to the Holy See.

This had an unexpected result. In 1305 a Frenchman called Bernard de Got, archbishop of Bordeaux, was elected Pope. Once installed as Clement V he decided to move the whole fabric of the Papacy away from faction-ridden Rome to his native France, and he chose this little outpost of Papal territory as its new home. The only problem was that Avignon itself had been excluded from the deal with Count Raymond, and the capital of the Comtat was now Pernes-les-Fontaines, not nearly such a prestigious place. However, though he never lived there himself, Clement negotiated with its new overlord the count of Provence to allow him to establish his court in Avignon, where he made a solemn entry in 1309.

The Comtat of those days extended from Vaison on the Ouvèze to Cavaillon on the Durance, and included the cathedral towns of Carpentras (which became its capital in 1320), Pernes-les-Fontaines and Venasque. For its size it remains one of the richest concentrations of man-made and natural attractions in France. Central to it is the distinctive mountain ridge called the **Dentelles de Montmirail**, where the jagged teeth of its limestone crest are a technical challenge to rock climbers, and its green slopes a joy for walkers. There is no better centre from which to explore it than the long-established climbers' hotel Les Florets, close up under the Dentelles and a mile or so from the famous wine-growing centre of **Gigondas** – though you will need to book your room well in advance during the summer.

If you should be driving south in this direction from Vaison, try taking the little road which leads south into the hills off the D977 soon after leaving the town. It should be signposted to **Seguret**, which you might call the 'show village' of the Comtat, though its setting is so magnificent that you can understand and forgive it being so popular. Built on the side of a rock-crowned hill, its tiers of houses in cream-coloured stone are a setting for the gentler side of tourism – *ateliers* for pottery, exhibitions of *santons* (doll-like figures of typical Provençal types), *salons de thé*, and a communal bread-oven complete with faggots and fittings. Even the Mairie has a mediaeval signboard, and its walls are covered with Virginia creeper. There are ruins of a castle, a tiny central *place* with a fountain and wash-house, and a strange-looking church with its nave jammed up against the rock. You can stay here if you wish at the picturesque Domaine de Cabas on the road to Sablet, or dine (if you can afford it) at the rosetted Table du Comtat off 'petits choux fourrés au foie ¿ s et

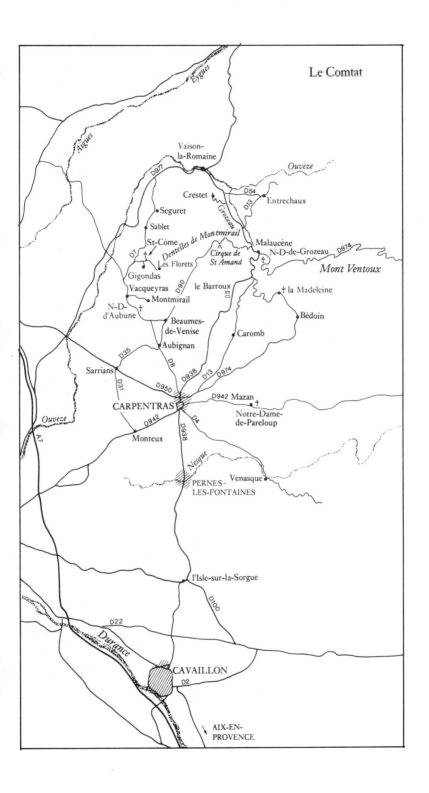

Le Comtat

langoustines' and 'filet mignon d'agneau à la barigoule' and watch the sun go down over the distant valley of the Ouvèze.

It is through Sablet that you can reach Gigondas and les Florets, and here one plunges into a sea of vineyards which not only line the roads but climb higher into the hills than is normal in France. Some rate the red wines of Gigondas and Vacqueyras as highly as the more famous bottles of Châteauneuf-du-Pape, and to my mind they go better with the strong and gutsy flavours of Provençal food. Beside and above the road from Gigondas to Les Florets look for the tiny chapel of **St-Côme**, or rather of Saints Côme-et-Damien – a saint too many, you may think, for so small a place, but the two are often paired together and are said to have been doctors who never took money from their patients; they were martyred under Diocletian. When the chapel was built in the twelfth century it was much bigger, but the nave was destroyed in the wars of religion and never rebuilt.

Instead they put a door in the south end of the transept and treated that as the nave, leaving the three endearing apses apparently misplaced to the side – though in fact they still properly face east. A minute's scramble up the bank beside the road is well worth it. Throughout Provence you will come upon these chapels, often in the remote countryside, and many of them built on the site of an early Christian hermitage with their own feast-days and mini-pilgrimages; few have the immediate charm of Sts-Côme-et-Damien. On the hill above Gigondas there is another little church, slightly later than St-Côme, but this was attached to the château of the local *seigneur*. Not as badly ruined as some castles, and of a comfortable size, it is now being done up by 'les amis de Gigondas', and the church of Notre-Dame, with its intriguing bell-tower and sundial, is included in the project.

If you drive on south of Gigondas you will soon join the D8 to Carpentras. The vineyards are forever till you pass Vacqueras, when the road begins to skirt the lower slopes of Montmirail. Long before you reach it you will see ahead a tall and elegant

Romanesque tower on the left of the road. This belongs to the church of **Notre-Dame-d'Aubune**, which began as barely more than another roadside chapel but was dignified by this marvellous bell-tower in the late twelfth century. When you come closer you can appreciate the touches which have turned a plain square structure into such a delight to the eye – the fluted pilasters at each corner and in the middle of each face, the perfectly placed windows, their arches carried in pillars variously marked with vertical or twisted fluting. At the base of the tower proper, just above roof level, the design is completed by a delicately carved corniche. Neither time nor weather has harmed it in seven hundred years.

The church below began as part of a small priory, built on an early Christian site, though there is a stirring legend that Charlemagne celebrated a victory here over the Saracens in the first light of day by dedicating a chapel to Our Lady of the Dawn (*aube*). More prosaically the name can be related to the Celtic word *alp*, meaning the foothill of a mountain. The east end has the familiar group of three apses, but it also has an *oculus* window over the middle one which lets in the light of the rising sun. Its solid walls date mostly from the early twelfth century, and there is a remarkable barrel-vaulted passage leading from a gate on the south side to the only entrance. The key is kept by a friendly family who live in the farmhouse set back from the road below, but you should be warned that the inside has not been improved by nineteenth-century decorations.

As we leave this green hillside we are soon back among the vineyards, and close by is the village of **Beaumes-de-Venise**, a place remarkable not for its ruined castle, or indeed for anything but the most fashionable sweet dessert wine east of Château Yquem. At **Aubignan** too, a little further along the road to Carpentras, the vineyards are more obvious than the remains of its fourteenth-century walls. A detour from here will take in **Sarrians** on its little hillock, where the choir and crossing of an eleventh-century priory have survived, while down on the plain at **Monteux** just one tower is left of the château where Clement V spent much of his time when avoiding Avignon. This low-lying area now grows huge quantities of fruit, vegetables and other market produce, including the earliest naturally grown strawberries in France.

Carpentras has never renounced its status as the capital of the Comtat. Avignon may draw the crowds of tourists and art-lovers, but Carpentras is the centre of local trade and a busy market for all that perishable produce, including truffles, and it has kept some notable monuments from its past. The commercial bustle makes it a difficult town to explore, and the points of interest are unfairly scattered. Among them one would pick out the high battlements of the Porte d'Orange, its old northern entrance and all that is left of its fourteenth-century walls; the cathedral of St-Siffrein, of which more later; the remains of a first-century Roman arch behind the Palais de Justice, next door to the cathedral; and a group of museums, the most important of which was founded as a library for the collection of Bishop d'Inguimbert, the most celebrated native of Carpentras.

Born here in 1683 and bishop of the diocese from 1735 to his death in 1757, he was a cultivated man of great energy and enthusiasm for the arts. This is the man responsible for the many fine rococo buildings you will be surprised to come upon in this frankly commercial setting, and especially for the world-famous **Bibliothèque Inguimbertine**, which contains about 200,000 volumes and thousands of manuscripts – ranging from rare editions of Petrarch (who lived in Avignon) to an auto-graphed score by J. S. Bach. The same building (which is in a side street off the Boulevard Albin-Durand to the west of the town) has on the ground floor the **Musée Comtadin**, where local curiosities include a fascinating collection of sheep and goat bells with a great variety of tone. Shepherds were supposed to be able to pick out their own animals by the sound of their bells from the hordes which took part in the spring and autumn *transhumance* – and maybe they still can.

To return to **St-Siffrein**, which is in the central Place General de Gaulle, you will find it a large and handsome Gothic cathedral in the Provençal tradition, interesting mainly for the few remains of the Romanesque building it supplanted, and for the flamboyant south portal which incorporates a mysterious carving of a sphere being gnawed by rats – a piece of symbolism which has defeated everybody. The doorway is known as the Porte Juivre, because Jews who had been converted to Christianity came through it to be baptised; there must have been a good deal of tension over this between the cathedral and the nearby **Synagogue**. Founded in the fourteenth century to serve a ghetto of more than a thousand Jews, it is the oldest synagogue in France, though it was given an elegant rococo décor in the eighteenth century which makes it look more like a Louis XVI *salon*; in the 1950s it was reconstituted as a modern venue for the still active Jewish community in Carpentras. Guided visits are allowed during the week, but it stays shut to visitors on Saturdays and Sundays, and on all Jewish festivals. The town museums are of course closed on Tuesdays.

Seven kilometres east of Carpentras is **Mazan**, another busy but a more agreeable market town. The interest here is the cemetery (just outside the town to the east), but not for those rows of marble headstones and vases of artificial flowers which can crowd rather too close round a simple Romanesque church. This one has a more uncanny feeling about it, for the earliest burials here were possibly pre-Christian; certainly many are of a very early Christian date, and its limits are marked on two sides by rows of Gallo-Roman sarcophagi set end to end. The name of the chapel is **Notre-Dame-de-Pareloup**, and on the analogy of *pare-brise* (the windscreen of a car) the word *pare-loup* has been interpreted as 'wolf-scarer'. This fits in with the superstition that signs of Christian occupation would at least keep at bay the demons and were-wolves who came to break open the tombs and prey on the dead. No skeletons have been found, though some of the sarcophagi have suspicious openings broken into their sides.

The chapel itself has an eerie feeling. Half sunk in the ground, dimly lit and obviously very ancient, it has been left entirely plain within – a simple nave, a single apse with the ritual openings of *armorium*, sacrarium and *piscina* round its walls. The walls themselves may not be older than the eleventh century, but the stone altar slab, with a hole in the middle and resting on stumpy columns, looks much older.

Your circuit of the Dentelles could take in **Caromb**, with a mildly interesting church and a typical detached Provençal bell-tower with an ironwork top. If you are going directly north from Carpentras you can pass under the walls of the gigantic castle of **le Barroux**, so big that it looks like a cuckoo nudging the surrounding houses out of their lofty nest. Privately owned, it must inspire its occupants with a certain *folie de grandeur* even today, but it is a magnificent piece of military architecture.

More rewarding than either of these places is to take the D974 north-east to **Bédoin**, an enterprising and lively little town which has a stylish and brand-new Mairie and a perpetual *marché* in its main street – on Mondays no traffic can move. There are roadside cafés where the gossip would have made Tartarin and his friends feel at home. Bédoin is not the only reason for coming this way, because if you carry on towards Malaucène you will soon embark on a lovely winding woodland road which passes the most delectable of all roadside chapels, called simply **la Madeleine**. Go slowly round those bends, not just for caution, but so as not to miss seeing its delicious little tower of pinkish stone among the trees to the left of the road. But for the tower you might miss the wooden gate which leads to it, though the proper approach is through the grounds of the pleasant large house on the bend below. The Madeleine is owned by M. Roland Ricard, whose father bought it and the surrounding property from a farmer in 1939, and to them we' owe the preservation of this enchanting place.

The misty origins of the site are again pre-Christian, for the stone altar inside is inscribed with a dedication to a local Celtic deity called Excanus. Early Christian sarcophagi appear in the foundations of the present eleventh-century building, and pieces of one with fourth-century decorations were found here after it had mysteriously disappeared early in the last century from a farmhouse near Carpentras. The chapel originally belonged to a small priory which was presented by the *Seigneur* of Bédoin to the abbey of Montmajour near Arles. It was first dedicated to St Peter, but later reconsecrated in honour of Provence's favourite saint, St Mary Magdalene.

The Ricard family lived quietly during the war in the manor house next door, but afterwards they set about the delicate business of restoring its precious fabric. They also converted the farm buildings between it and the road for use by a small party of Benedictine monks, but in 1980 the monks withdrew to join a large new community at le Barroux. The inside of the chapel is unique in that its structure of three parallel and almost equal naves, with their respective apses, has never been altered since it was built in the eleventh century. The masonry, despite its age, is finely tailored with clean-cut edges, and the perspective of semicircular arches is wholly satisfying and harmonious. Yet it is the view from outside the east end which you will never forget. The tower is in two stages, capped by a shallow dome, and here it would seem that the upper stage and the dome were added perhaps a century later; yet nothing can detract from the sheer simple beauty of the eastern elevation, set off as it is by tall dark cypresses and a background of green woods.

You can sneak a view of the outside from a few vantage points, but for a proper visit you should apply to the Mairie in Bédoin who will contact the occupants of the 'château' of la Madeleine to authorise it. This is really just an attractive house of nineteenth-century character, with wide sunny terraces, and it was the home of the novelist Henri de la Madeleine (1825–1887). Part of it is let for family holidays – it sleeps six.

From here the road wiggles on blissfully through the trees to join the D938 just south of **Malaucène**, a town with an old quarter which the Michelin guide describes as 'un dédale de ruelles, où l'on découvre au hazard d'une promenade des maisons anciennes, des fontaines, des lavoirs, des oratoires, et au centre un vieux beffroi'. This is all true, and the word 'dédale' (from the Cretan Daedalus who built the labyrinth) is an apt one. Before plunging into it, though, you will see immediately on entering the town the startling south front of the church of St-Michel.

It looks more like the outer wall of a castle, and it was in fact built as part of the town's fortifications in the fourteenth century, though not, as was once believed, by Clement V. There are just five round-headed windows high up on the south side, and the rectangular blocked-up openings above them were the casemates of a defensive *chemin-de-ronde*. The defences continued at the west end, which has the kind of machicolations over it which you associate with a castle entrance. More remarkable still are the doors themselves, coated entirely with iron plates on the outside, which are fixed to the wood with iron bolts. It seems strange to think of armed men patrolling these battlements, or waiting to unload unpleasantness on enemies battering at its iron doors; yet, though the fourteenth century was a fairly peaceful time for the Comtat under the Popes, the town and its church must have been glad of this kind of protection during the sixteenth-century wars of religion.

The inside is an interesting mixture of late Romanesque and eighteenth-century classical styles. The nave belongs to the earlier period, while the choir, the stately apse and the side chapels were completed between 1703 and 1714 by the Chevalier Mignard, son of the Avignon painter Nicolas Mignard. The ingenious *trompe l'oeil* painting in the chapels was copied on either side of the 1713 organ when it was restored in 1965.

At either end of the church there is an arched gateway which leads into the 'dédale' of the old town, where among other surprises you will find that the street signs are in Latin as well as French. The newer part of the town is pleasantly laid out with broad streets lined with plane trees, and as at Bédoin there is a lively spirit abroad.

You now have the choice between following the main road down the valley of the Grozeau to Vaison, or branching off along the D80 back to Beaumes-de-Venise and Gigondas. The latter is an uplifting drive through the bare hillsides east of the Dentelles, with wonderful views from the Cirque de St-Amand, but whichever way you go you ought first to drive just a mile up the road which runs close under the north face of Mont Ventoux, as far as the curious church of **Notre-Dame-de-Grozeau**. Architecturally there is not much to see – just the remains of a small priory church with a wide Renaissance porch added to the west end – but it was in this peaceful place at a turn in the winding river that Clement V spent some of the happiest hours of his ten years as Pope, preferring the simple community of monks to the formality of the château of Monteux and the city life of Avignon.

If you prefer to head back towards Vaison you will have the choice of visiting **Crestet** – and that is not a place to miss if you are anywhere in the neighbourhood. The village stands high on your left three kilometres short of the town, and like Brantes and Seguret it clings dizzily to its cliff face. You reach it by a steep winding ascent from the main road, but cars have to be abandoned before the final climb – which as at Brantes is by steep cobbled steps leading to a series of terraces. As at Seguret the church is built hard up against the rock, with no room for an apse, but it has an unusual tower with a four-sided stone spire. The village is less sophisticated than Seguret, but the château at the top has a distinguished history. First heard of in 850, and the favourite residence of the bishops of Vaison until the Revolution, it underwent various transformations from Romanesque to Gothic. Total neglect in this century left it a ruin by 1982, when it was bought and restored by a private owner.

Although its formidable defences are now turned against the unwanted visitor, who is faced by a high wall and a fortified entrance with iron-plated doors (just like the church at Malaucène) you will be happy to share its eagle's view from the terrace outside. To the east is spread out the valley of the Ouvèze, with the château of Entrechaux in the middle distance and Mont Ventoux closing the southern end of a line of lesser hills. From Seguret you can watch the sun set over the Rhône valley, but it must be a wonderful moment here when it rises over the Baronnies – and those are the boundaries of the Comtat.

Two of its towns remain to be visited, both lying south of Carpentras, and close enough to the western end of the plateau of Vaucluse to be a convenient starting-point for the journeyings of the next chapter. **Pernes-les-Fontaines** is an intriguing town, much of it dilapidated, but carrying a good deal of history within and beyond its walls. They date from the fourteenth century, the time of its greatest importance, though it had been the capital of the Comtat since 968. Of the castle at its heart only the keep remains – since 1486 it has been the town's clock-tower, and in 1763 it was given one of the most elaborate of iron belfries. Another tower, the Tour Ferrande, was part of a Hospice of the Knights of St John, and the inside was decorated with contemporary frescos. Only a few rather battered ones survive on the upper floor, but their mixture of warlike, religious and romantic themes is typical of Provence.

Below the walls runs the river Nesque, and in the most attractive part of Pernes a leafy terrace shaded by big plane trees has been built alongside one of its channels, with willows on the far side; this is now sensibly used, even if not so designed, as an arena for the national game of *boules*. The Porte Notre-Dame is the northern entrance to the town, a picturesque low-arched opening with corbelled balustrades, approached by a bridge over the channel. Beyond it stands one of the stone 'fontaines' you will expect to find here, the one called 'le Cormarin' in which the bird has a fish in its beak. There are about thirty others, but most of them are not as impressive as those in Aix or in some other provincial towns; the oddities include 'le Gigot', which is supposed to look like a leg of lamb, while the waters of 'la Lune' are said to make drinkers run mad – which could be a useful excuse for antisocial behaviour.

Well outside the walls and beyond the water is the ancient priory **Church of Notre-Dame**, never included within the defences. It was rebuilt at least twice after different disasters, and the only survivals from the eleventh century are the apse and a curious doorway east of the south porch, which is thought to have led to a cloister for the monks of an earlier church priory. It may remind you a little of St-Restitut in the Tricastin, though the triangular pediment has almost disappeared. The church is usually kept locked, but if (by applying to the Mairie) you manage to get in you will find the single lofty nave with side chapels common in Provence. No attempt has been made to decorate the capitals between the bays; instead an unusual frieze and cornice runs the whole length of the nave on both sides, broken where it crosses above the pillars by panels carved with a typical mixture of biblical and contemporary scenes – there is Adam and Eve, a *chevalier*, Daniel with his lions, and a man with an ox-cart. There is nowhere much to stay in Pernes these days, but just off the road from Carpentras is the Hermitage, a beautifully quiet and well ordered hotel.

Venasque is both more conventional and more surprising. For some years it has been a favourite town for people wanting to buy and restore mediaeval properties for modern living, and on the whole they have done it with feeling and discretion. To appreciate the importance of the place you must realise that between 500 and 900 the bishops of Carpentras used Venasque as their seat, feeling safer up here from the fire and slaughter threatened by barbarians and Saracens. Its mediaeval history can be imagined from the massive towers and gateway which still protect its southern entrance, but long before they were built the church of Notre-Dame stood at the northern end of this rocky spur – now high above the Nesque.

The church is a complex building, though it stands so casually beside the village street, with its irregular wall surfaces, stumpy tower and jaunty spire. Entering from the west you will find it dark and forbidding at first, and most unusual in its plan. Not properly cruciform, it has a very short nave and an elaborate ribbed cupola over the crossing, but the chapel to the north which pretends to be a polygonal apse was added in the eighteenth century. The arches of the crossing are solidly Romanesque, but so far we have seen nothing earlier than the beginning of the thirteenth century; it is only the apse – set slightly askew from the nave and disguised on the outside by a straight wall, which takes us back to the eleventh century.

To find something as old or older we have to follow a path round the east end of Notre-Dame and enter by a side door a separate little church which has puzzled antiquarians for centuries. It was built on the pure Greek Cross plan, and so primitive in its construction (four irregular colonnaded apses not properly aligned to the cardinal points) and with such an air of mystery about it that it was for a long time assumed (on the authority of Prosper Merimée himself) to be a sixth-century baptistery attached to the cathedral church by a vaulted passage. The experts now declare that the building itself, though it uses some early Christian and possibly Roman materials, is no earlier than the apse of Notre-Dame, though they admit that it may have been developed from a much earlier funerary chapel – even such as might have contained the body of St Siffrein, bishop of Carpentras in the sixth or seventh century. The crushing blow to the more romantic theory was to find that the sunken 'baptismal font' was put there by nineteenth-century restorers. In spite of all this the atmosphere in this little place is extraordinary, and it would not be the only hill site in France which began as a temple of Mercury and ended as a Christian chapel.

4

Le Plateau de Vaucluse

One of the joys of exploring Provence is never knowing what you will find round the next corner. Nothing is predictable, and whatever you may have read about a place beforehand the reality can be a surprise. In among the familiar red roofs, cypresses, ruined castles and bell-towers, something you had never dreamed of is sure to materialise. The *département* of Vaucluse has more surprises than most. It includes the whole area between Drôme in the north, Bouches-du-Rhône in the south, and Var to the south-east, though the name itself applies only to the immediate locality of its best known attraction, the 'Fountain of Vaucluse'. In the language of the south, *vau* means 'valley' and *clausa* in Latin means 'closed' or 'shut in' – which is a good description of that rather claustrophobic place. The Plateau de Vaucluse is something different, a wide hilly area stretching a long way eastward from Carpentras, and there are as many surprises among its dry uplands as in the valleys which eat into it from the south.

If you set out from the neighbourhood of Carpentras along the D942, past Mazan, you soon reach Villes-sur-Auzon, which is the starting point for one of the great drives of Provence, the traverse of the **Gorges de la Nesque**. The Nesque, which we last saw in more open country at Venasque and Pernes-les-

Fontaines, marks the northern limit of the plateau, and after a steady climb through the woods you suddenly see the floor of its deep-sunk valley more than a thousand feet below. A high corniche road winds its way round and up the folded hillsides, densely covered with dark green *garrigue*, till cliffs of rock appear on both sides of the gorge; sometimes the road has had to be blasted through the rock to give it room to pass under the crags. Spring is wonderful for most of Provence, but autumn is the time to come to these deep gorges, when the carpet of evergreen is lit up by fiery red flashes from the deciduous shrubs scattered all over the slopes.

There are caves in the cliffs on both sides, and just before you reach the *belvedere* on the col you will see on the right of the road the strange outcrop known as the Rocher du Cire. This has been so much hollowed out by the weather that the wild bees have filled its crannies with wax (*cire*) and turned it into an enormous hive. Mistral tells us in his *Calendau* how young men used to be let down on ropes from the top to collect the honey – which seems a risky practice on more than one count. The beautifully engineered road climbs on to the final col, then descends through a more varied and domestic landscape to **Sault**, which is a pleasant clean-looking market town assembled round the church of St-Sauveur.

One is inclined to dismiss this kind of church as run-of-the-mill Provençal Romanesque with the usual sixteenth-century additions, but there will always be a few details to catch the eye. Here look for the huge recessed *oculus* on the west front, with its chain of *rosaces* all round the inside of its outer rim, and the exceptionally fine Romanesque window in the south transept – which has been converted to a chapel with modern furnishings. Many will be content to linger in one of the peaceful *places* round about, and it is rare to find a town which even smells as fresh as this – understandably when its main industry is the gathering, crushing and marketing of lavender. Lavender for the perfume trade is a staple product in several parts of Provence,

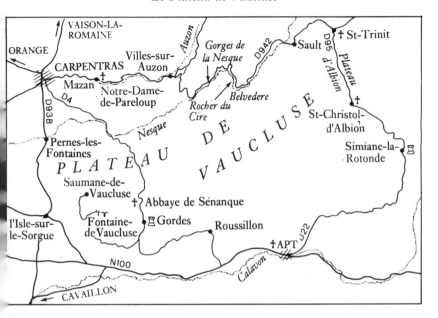

Le Plateau de Vaucluse

but unless you have seen lavender fields in full flower you can have no idea what that means. Hundreds of acres of a dry sunny plateau will be planted with tufts of deep rich blue – the sea come to the hills – in lines as straight as vines in a vineyard. June is the peak flowering time; when the flowers fade the tractors straddle the rows to crop the plants, and on the roads you will pass trucks crammed with the glorious aromatic stuff. The march of the seasons in Provence produces so many glories – the only problem is to be in the right place at the right time to enjoy them.

It goes without saying that there will be lavender fields on all sides as you move towards the boundary of Vaucluse and Alpes-de-Haute-Provence, but there is general farming too around the tiny hamlet of **St-Trinit**, seven kilometres east of Sault. It has no shops – a baker's van comes in from Sault for half an hour on Saturday mornings, and they say the bread is so good that it lasts the week – but its fifty inhabitants live happily in good stone houses, and their church is a small Romanesque gem. You will succumb at once if you see it first from the east; the choir is the earliest part of a church mentioned in 1118 as a priory belonging to the abbey of St-André in Villeneuve-lès-Avignon. Small indeed for a priory church, it seems that it was never served by more than one monk, and the lucky man was the prior.

A little square bell turret sits on the roof of the almost square choir, from which projects an apse which does everything right. Its rounded surface is varied by flat buttress-like pilasters, with a beautifully composed central window – the actual lancet is recessed between the pillars of a miniature Romanesque arch. The southern approach is nearly as delightful: the plain narrow round-headed door is offset to the left, and a delicately decorated window sits high in the wall to light the southern end of the crossing. A rare interior arrangement is the cupola, not based as usual on an octagon, but with four tapering segments which meet at the top. Notice how casually the bell ropes fall down from the centre to be gathered in a bunch by the entry door. The squared-off pilasters in the apse go all the way up from floor to vault and give it great dignity, but the last word must go to the carving of the Lamb of God *passant* above the eastern arch, balancing his eight-pointed cross neatly on the sole of his upturned right fore-foot.

If this is a rare discovery, one of a different order will hit you if you drive south from St-Trinit in the direction of **St-Christol-d'Albion**. Why has such a minor road been made so wide and surfaced so well? The answer is that the French air force has used the bare scrubby tableland of the Pays d'Albion to build a nuclear missile station which makes Greenham Common look like a football field. Traffic is discreetly diverted, with suitable warnings, but nothing prevents you from joining the main road south from Sault.

At St-Christol you are back among the lavender fields, though you will see that many of them have been neglected and allowed to become waste land. This is partly because the economic value of the crop is not what it was, but also because the local labour force has been mopped up by the nuclear missile site; the environs of the plateau d'Albion are more prosperous than they have been for generations. The church here is more sophisticated than St-Trinit, and in one respect unique. The pentagonal apse is furnished inside with six short pillars of astonishingly varied ornament, even the shafts of which are carved in intricate designs by a virtuoso sculptor.

They all show a fertile invention and a great sense of style, but the two outer ones are the most remarkable. The one furthest to the right has two *griffons* – mythological monsters with the head and wings of an eagle and the hindquarters of a lion – with their heads back to back and caught in a halter of rope. The pillar furthest left is encircled by *entrelacs* enclosing little panels of grapes, birds and flowers. The capitals have conventional acanthus-leaf decoration, but they are all quite different, and there is nothing conventional about the carved bases of the four inner columns. All portray disturbing monstrosities, trodden as it were symbolically under foot. From right to left we have first the not uncommon symbol of Lust – a bare-breasted *sirène-poisson*, or mermaid, with her twin tails held seductively apart; next we have a two-bodied lion crushing in its teeth a snake which turns its head to bite its enemy behind the mane; in the third the head of a bearded man is attached like a sphinx to the bodies of two lions; in the fourth a winged female head with long hair and staring eyes is blowing into a double horn – *a sirène-oiseau*, they call her.

The symbolism of these hybrid monsters is baffling, and much argued about, but their symmetry has been cleverly worked into the overall design, which is more than just a riot of mediaeval fantasy. The altar fits in too, though it was only in 1975 that this was recognised by putting it back where it belongs. Since the eighteenth century it had been banished to an obscure part of the church, but you can now see what they missed. A triple arcade on the frontal slab is supported by short columns with branching capitals, and it encloses concentric circles from which a petrified spout of water falls to a base identical to those of the columns. The side panels, not so original, are carved with flowing foliage.

The church as a whole is curiously arranged and represents two periods – a north aisle having been added to the twelfth-century nave in the seventeenth, while at the same time the oddly placed tower was attached to the south-east corner. The important thing is to spend as much time as you can looking at those carvings, frustrating though it is that we know nothing of the man who did them. The entrance is at the east end of the north aisle, but if the door is locked call at the first house on the right of the street which faces you as you stand on the steps. You may have to be patient, but the lady occupant does have the key.

If St-Trinit is the most delightful, St-Christol the most intriguing, the village and 'castle' of **Simiane-la-Rotonde** is the most unexpected of the three. The Pays d'Albion is the eastern extension of the Vaucluse plateau, but why the name 'Albion' was attached to it is far from certain. The whiteness of the stone quarried here is a more likely explanation than any connection with the British Isles, perfidious or not. The name of the village sounds odd enough, but is more easily explained, for it was the family of d'Agoult-Simiane whose magnificent town house was turned into the Hôtel-de-Ville at Valréas, and virtually all that remains of their country castle here is an extraordinary circular keep, or 'rotunda'.

The village, which climbs the southern face of the steep hill, is itself unlike any other hill village in Provence. Its secret and silent stone-paved streets run between high-fronted houses – some of them four storeys high – with fine seventeenth-century doorways. There is no wheeled traffic, and little gardens and flowering trees point up the surfaces of biscuit-coloured stone. The *halles*, or covered market place, is a wooden-roofed space with a view to the south through a loggia of four columns. A bell-tower stands beside one of the few level streets, with a panel near the top dated 1582 and an inscription which reads DIEU SOIT LOUÉ ('God be praised').

The climb is steep, but rewarding at every turn, and you come out on top to find this round tapering *donjon*, looking like the base of a gigantic windmill. In fact, only the outer defensive skin is round, made up of an unbroken surface of rough stonework tapering towards the top and crowned by a little square look-out turret. On the inner side, which used to face an elliptical courtyard with a defensive wall to the north and domestic quarters to the south, the plan is polygonal, and most of the surfaces have been restored with clean white stone. This shows off a fine Romanesque window, which was originally a doorway at the top of a stairway leading into the large upper chamber which would have been the *chambre d'honneur* of the castle – big and splendid enough for assemblies and other formal occasions. Now it is used for a chamber music festival in July and August – a strange but happily contrived venue for Bach and Vivaldi. Restoration was still going on in 1988, but there were indications that later on visitors would be allowed inside during the afternoon (except on Tuesdays), and you can always climb up through the village and walk round outside. If you wander on up past a few cottages into the country beyond and look back, the *rotonde* may remind you of the kind of sand castle you make by inverting a bucket of sand on the beach – though it would have been a giant at play.

Simiane marks the end of the plateau, where the land falls to the valley of the Calavon, and the road south leads through orchards of pear, plum, apricot, peach and cherry to the much larger town of **Apt**. However important this was as a celtic tribal capital or as the Roman *Colonia Apta Julia*, it wins fame today by producing those delicious boxes of *fruits confits* which are so popular at Christmas. Likewise the **Cathedral of Ste-Anne** no longer has a bishop, and its overall architecture is a sad muddle of the taste of many centuries. Little remains above ground of its twelfth-century state except the transept crossing and the east end of the south aisle – which was handsomely restored not long ago and has had its Romanesque altar put back where it belongs It does however have a remarkable system of crypts.

As in the great Burgundy cathedrals of St-Philibert at Tournus and St-Etienne at Auxerre, the principal crypt lies immediately beneath the sanctuary of the church above, and follows closely its original shape; indeed, it probably dictated it. The purpose of these crypts was to expose in convenient and impressive surroundings the sacred relics of their particular saints, which were such a regular source of income for the community. In this case they were the bones of St Auspice, first bishop of Apt in the third century, and of St Castor, a fifth-century bishop who built the first church on this site. His body had earlier been buried in a little oratory nearby, but in 1179 it was transferred to this crypt beneath the new Romanesque church. It was well planned for the purpose, with a gathering space for pilgrims and a wide ambulatory round the inner sanctuary. From there they had a clear view of the altar through the gaps between the pillars.

Far more ancient is the lower crypt, which begins as a narrow tunnel about seven metres long, but only one metre wide and just over two metres high; its roof is formed partly by carved stone plaques which came from the Carolingian church replaced in the twelfth century. The tunnel leads into a short *cella*, twice as wide but no higher, with a rough barrel vault. It was probably an early martyr's burial chamber, though the two openings in the south face of the tunnel are believed to have contained relics of Ste Anne, mother of the Virgin Mary and the patron saint of the cathedral. It was this primitive structure which dictated the exact placement of the sanctuary in the crypt above, and in the Carolingian and Romanesque churches on top of that.

Crystallised fruits are not the only industry in Apt, which is one reason why it seems less attractive than Sault. It is in fact the centre of the biggest ochre industry in France, which produces about 3,000 tonnes a year from a rich seam of deposits in the neighbourhood. Ochre is basically a mixture of sand and iron oxide, and the iron content is what stains everything it touches with a coating of rusty reddish brown. The end products, after an elaborate process of washing down and drying out, are the valuable pigments used in paints, colour washes and dyes. The livid faces of the ochre quarries scar the landscape, and even in natural form the misshapen outcrops of red, orange and tangerine rock are an astonishing sight – especially round the small town of **Roussillon**, built on a narrow ridge a few miles west of Apt. All the houses here have been colour-washed or rendered with the local product – no wonder its name is Roussillon. The highest point of the ridge is occupied by a handsome high-walled citadel known as the *castrum*, and so probably with Roman antecedents. The climb up there is worth it, if only for a view which avoids the ochre outcrops and takes in the green slopes of the Vaucluse plateau away to the north.

Difficult as it is to time your visits anywhere to suit conditions, it would be a pity not to approach **Gordes** at least once in the evening from the west. The stone here is not ochreous but honey-coloured, and when the setting sun catches it the whole hill-top glows with golden light. From Roussillon you are more likely to be coming in the opposite direction, but in either view the powerful turretted château and the high-naved church stand out above all the roofs. Much of this handsome and sophisti-cated town was destroyed by the Germans in 1944 as a nest of the Resistance, and has been rebuilt on commercial lines, but a few original corners and alleys survive. Unfortunately the barn-like seventeenth-century church has been hideously decorated in gaudy colours.

There is parking right under the walls of the château, which was another possession of the Simiane family; it was Bertrand de Simiane who changed it in the sixteenth century from a mediaeval fortress to a Renaissance palace. Open for visits morning and afternoon throughout the year, it has a *salle d'honneur* on the first floor with a magnificent chimney-piece dated 1541, but five other rooms have been made over for an exhibition of modern art by the Hungarian 'mathematical' designer Vasarély. A peaceful spot at the heart of a busy town is the Place du Château, where the bar-restaurant 'La Renaissance' will supply anything from a beer to a full meal in the shade of plane trees – shade more than welcome here in midsummer.

Much has been made of what is known as a 'village noir' in open country a mile or so west of Gordes. It consists of a large group of dry-stone dwellings known locally as *bories*, in shape rather like an old-fashioned beehive, which were once thought to have survived from prehistoric times. Dry-stone walls are quite common in the neighbourhood, and this group was probably built not earlier than the seventeenth century. Some were used for storage or tool sheds in the last century, and have now been turned into a kind of museum for bygones. Some have even been done up for letting as holiday cottages, but you will often see a single example of a *borie* standing on its own in a field, where it could have sheltered a shepherd or quite a number of sheep, and that seems a more natural use.

With two of the most visited sites in Provence not far away, there is no lack of hotel accommodation in these parts, much of it very expensive. Places like the Mas de Garrigon, just outside Roussillon, the Domaine de l'Enclos between Gordes and Senanque, or the Mas de Herbes Blanches at Joucas (which has a *cuisine renommée*) are not for the ordinary traveller who needs only a comfortable bed for a night or two and some good local cooking and wine. At that level the Hostellerie des Commandeurs at Joucas is a possibility, with the temptation of going out for just one meal at the Herbes Blanches up the road towards Murs.

No one, I think, would wish to stay too close to the **Fontaine de Vaucluse,** though it still remains just possible to conjure up

romance at the spot of which Sir Theodore Cook was able to
write in 1905:

> 'The syllables of Petrarch and the sighs of Laura are on
> every breeze. Theirs are the images reflected in the crystal
> surface of that mysterious pool which wells from the deep
> heart of the mountain and pours forth its everlasting
> streams through the cascades of the young river towards
> the village of Vaucluse.'

Francesco Petrarca was born at Arezzo in 1304. When he was
nine his family moved to Avignon for much the same reason
which persuaded Clement V to move the seat of the Papacy
there from Rome – the violent faction-ridden life of northern
Italy. As he grew up under the later Popes he observed both the
luxury and the squalor of papal Avignon, and preferred to spend
time among the beauties of the *vallis clausa* of the river Sorgue.
It seems that among its natural beauties was a young girl called
Laura, but though Petrarch in his sonnets has described her
beauty in passionate detail, we know nothing about her for
certain except her Christian name. He later indignantly denied
that she was only a romantic fiction, such as other poets have
used to decorate their sonnets, but we have to choose between
such extreme theories that she was a chaste maid, the daughter
of a poor farmer, who died unmarried at the age of thirty-seven;
or that she was the daughter of Audebert de Noves and bore
eleven children to her husband, the comte Hugues de Sade,
before dying of the plague in 1348.

Petrarch says they first met – he doesn't say where – at six in
the morning on Good Friday in 1327, when he was twenty-three
and she was sixteen; this is what he tells us:

> 'Erano i capei d'oro a l'aura sparsi,
> Che 'n mille dolci nodi gli avvolgea;
> E 'l vago lume oltra misura ardea
> Di quei begli occhi, ch'or ne son si scarsi:
> E 'l viso di pietosi color farsi,

Non so se vero o falso, mi parea:
I' che l'esca amorosa al petto avea,
Qual meraviglia se di subit' arsi?
Non era l'andar suo cosa mortale,
Ma d'angelica forma; e le parole
Sonovan altro che pur voce umana.
Uno spirto celeste, un vivo sole
Fu quel ch' i' vidi; e se non fosse or tale,
Piaga per allentar d'arco non sana.' *

After what seems to have been a vain pursuit of an idealised
love, Petrarch (according to one account) retired here in 1337
with a dog and two servants to brood over it all for the next
sixteen years. This conflicts with the fact that he was crowned
poet laureate in Rome in 1341, but he must have come here
often to visit his close friend Philippe de Cabassole, a young
man of almost exactly the same age who lived in the château
whose ruins overlook the path to the fountain. They met here in
1338, by which time this precocious young churchman had been
appointed bishop of Cavaillon by Pope John XXII, and was
destined to be made a cardinal thirty years later. Petrarch
himself became an influential politician and diplomat, and he
played an important part in persuading Pope Gregory XI to
return to Rome in 1376.

I have dwelt on the romantic past, because there is little
romance in the present-day scene. The dark pool itself, at the
foot of a high cliff under which the river Sorgue bursts out from
its underground source and wells to the surface, does catch the
imagination; by the time of the spring floods the river has been
swollen by winter rains falling on the plateau, and the water
pours over the lip of the pool in an emerald green cascade.
Though what emerges from the pool is thereafter known as the
Sorgue, the source is not just one underground channel but a
vast reservoir which extends far under the plateau of Vaucluse.

*translation at the end of the chapter

Divers have tried to explore its depths since the end of the last century, even Pierre Cousteau has been down there, and in 1935 a radio-controlled mini-submarine with a video camera reached a depth (or a distance) of 315 metres, but we are no nearer knowing where all the water comes from. To reach the place at all you must run the gauntlet of one of the most depressing displays of *tourisme* in France – including several buildings which claim to be the 'maison de Petrarch'.

Only a short distance away to the north, in the foothills of the plateau, the little village of **Saumane-de-Vaucluse** could not be a more peaceful contrast. Near here they dig some of the most succulent truffles of all, and the dwellers in the big château of Saumane must have had the pick of them for centuries. Nothing is left of the twelfth-century fortress, but it was reconstituted in the fifteenth and sixteenth centuries by the de Sade family, which is a big name in this part of Provence. It was tarnished somewhat by the reputation of the eighteenth-century marquis de Sade, who after his controversial literary career died in a madhouse at Charenton, but for the most part they were respected owners of several properties in Vaucluse and the Luberon. It was an abbé de Sade, a contemporary of the marquis, who claimed as an antiquarian to have identified Petrarch's Laura as the Laure de Noves who married Hugues de Sade, so he may not have been disinterested. On the whole the poet's account of his love is more worthy of belief – and far more romantic.

I have left to the end of the chapter what is rightly its climax, a visit to the **Abbaye de Sénanque**. Only four kilometres from Gordes, it belongs to a different world in both the physical and the spiritual sense. The lush plain between Gordes and Roussillon gives way to the dry, stony, steep-sided valley of the Sénancole, and there is always a moment of disbelief before you realise that the long grey bulk wedged across the valley is what you are looking for – one of the four great monuments built by the Cistercian order in twelfth-century Provence. Its moods

61

change with the season and the light. In winter a bitter wind funnels down the valley from the north; even in summer a dull day may find it grey and forbidding, yet at noon in midsummer it can be a sultry place – the heat trapped between the stony hillsides. The best time is when the morning light in June catches the east end of the abbey church across a rich blue field of lavender – which was planted by the monks and is still cultivated by their successors.

The east end, did I say? Alone among Cistercian abbeys its church is aligned north and south, as the stream running through the floor of the valley left too little room to build it on the traditional east-west axis, so ritual east became compass north. Sénanque was the latest of the Provençal abbeys to be founded in St Bernard's lifetime, and the founding monks came from the abbey of Mazan (not the place near Carpentras, but a vanished community in the Ardèche) in 1148, five years before his death.

It may be a help now and in future chapters to recall some key dates in the history of the Cistercian order. It was in 1098 that Robert, abbot of Molesme in northern Burgundy, and Stephen Harding of Sherborne Abbey in Dorset broke away from what had become the lax Benedictine regime of Cluny to found a monastery on strictly ascetic lines at Cîteaux, a few miles south of Dijon. In 1114 they were joined by a young man of good family and tremendous energy called Bernard le Roux, with a party of thirty friends all like him in their twenties. I think it makes a difference to our view of this kind of community when we realise that it was set up not by soured elderly churchmen but by young idealists who wished to shape a new world for their faith.

In fact the very next year Bernard went off with some of his friends to found a new abbey at Clairvaux in the Champagne. Within three more years the original 'four daughters of Cîteaux' had been established, and within the next hundred years more than a thousand monasteries had appeared, covering the

western world from Ireland to Palestine, all following the rule of
St Bernard. The earliest foundation in Provence was at le
Thoronet (1136), followed by Aiguebelle in the Tricastin
(1137), Silvacane in the valley of the Durance north of Aix
(1147) and Sénanque in 1148.

The Cistercian rule required all monasteries to be laid out on
the same plan, so that a new monk could fit in immediately on
arrival with the regime of prayer, work and meditation – which
was as tightly organised as in a beehive. The *dortoir*, or
dormitory where they slept, was always to be at right angles to
the nave of the church, and on an upper floor; it had a stairway
connecting it with the transept, so that monks could reach the
choir easily for their nightly offices. Underneath was the
chapitre, or chapter house, where the official and communal
business of the monastery was conducted, and the *salle des
moines* where work such as the copying of manuscripts could be
done if there was no library. Next to this was the *chauffoir*, the
only room other than the kitchen which could be heated by a
fireplace, which helped to thaw the frozen fingers of the copyists
in winter. Off the far side of the cloister, which could be either
to north or south of the church, depending on the lie of the land,
was the *refectoire*. All meals were taken in silence, though
passages from scripture or theology were read aloud from a
raised tribune in the side wall. Next to the refectory was the
kitchen, and all this area was known as the *clôture*, into which no
outsiders were allowed. The third side of the cloister (for which
the different word *cloître* is used) gave access to the quarters of
the lay brothers – refectory and cellar, with their own *dorter*
above – and it had a separate entrance to the west end of the
abbatiale, or abbey church.

The rules for building an *abbatiale* were just as strictly laid
down. The body of the church had to be in the form of a
basilica, with a central nave and two side aisles, and a *narthex*, or
covered porch, at the west end. The monks' choir was at the east
end of the nave, with an entrance from the cloister as well as

from the transept. As in all churches, the sanctuary with the high altar projected to the east of the transept, forming the head of a Latin cross, but the Cistercian plan had two or sometimes three chapels with their own altars ranged along the east wall of both arms of the transept. All interior decoration was forbidden. There were to be no statues. Pillars and capitals had to be plain, there was no triforium, and the few windows allowed were to have plain glass only. The outer walls and the western façade had no decoration, and no tower was to be built except for a short belfry.

In spite of, or possibly because of, these limitations the Cistercian abbey churches include some of the most beautiful buildings in the world. We find too that however strictly the rules were observed they all have a different character. One reason is the difference in the colour and texture of the stone, another is the setting of the buildings in the landscape; a third is the variety of ways in which the architects have handled the window openings, and so influenced how the light falls on the inner surfaces.

Sénanque was built here because the site had been given to the Cistercians by the family of Agoult-Simiane (of Gordes, Valréas and Simiane-la-Rotonde). Their motto illustrates the civilised approach to life by the nobility of Provence and Languedoc in the twelfth century: *sustentant lilia turres* means roughly 'the arts are our strongest defence', and some governments we know could take that to heart. The hard grey stone was quarried only half a mile away to the north, most of it simply lowered or slid down the hillside into the valley. It has never mellowed, nor does it warm in the sunlight; even within the church, noble and dignified though it is, there is a coldness which emphasises its austerity.

The cloister, which here lies on the 'north' or compass east side of the church, has a lighter and more congenial feel about it. This is mainly because the architect allowed himself more freedom of design and decoration. The arcading on all four sides is made up of four wide arches supported by three rectangular pillars (square ones at the four corners) each enclosing three smaller arches divided by pairs of columns standing on a raised base. This, we are told, is part of the mathematical symbolism at the heart of Cistercian architecture, where 'four' represents the world perfected by God and 'three' is the number of the Trinity. The proportions are indeed satisfying to the eye, but the effects of light and shadow are magical.

The carving of the capitals, on both the main pillars and the intervening columns, is stylised but varied and elegant; in this context it comes as a shock to find a devilishly malignant head carved under the corbel of one of the transverse arches of the vaulting. The stylised capitals are repeated on the pillars which support the vaulting of the chapter house – a fine room, with the original stone seating round the walls. The dorter is a magnificent barrel-vaulted chamber which runs the length of the first storey above the chapter house and *chauffoir*. The refectory, which to avoid that tiresome stream had to be built parallel instead of at right angles to the cloister, is used for exhibitions. This leaves the cloister itself as the happiest and most accessible part of the monastery.

It will be interesting to see what happens next to Sénanque. Having survived fairly peacefully until the sixteenth century, it was drawn into the religious controversy surrounding the Vaudois, a reformist sect who followed the teachings of one Pierre Valdo and were particularly numerous in the Luberon district. They were denounced as heretics and ferociously persecuted by the Catholic hierarchy, so in revenge they attacked the abbey in 1544 and burned down a good deal of it. It was rebuilt by the end of the seventeenth century, but never attracted more than a handful of monks after that. By 1770 there were none left, and it was sold as public property in the Revolution.

Fortunately the fabric was preserved, and in 1854 it was

bought back for the church by the abbé Barnoin, resumed its Cistercian way of life, and in the 1870s had a community of seventy-two monks. Anti-clerical legislation in 1880 forced them to disband, and though a small party returned in 1926 they finally withdrew in 1969 to join the ancient mother-foundation of St-Honorat on the Îles de Lérins off the Riviera coast. Sénanque is now administered and preserved by an association of 'les amis de Sénanque', which also promotes general mediaeval research and a surprising study of the history and culture of the Sahara. According to the terms of the thirty-year lease the Cistercians may return if they wish, but it is hard to see how they could now cut off the profitable flood of tourism and live in tranquillity again. Whatever happens, the lavender has to stay.

Translation of Sonnet XC by Petrarch

'Flung to the breezes was her golden hair,
Into a thousand knots its tresses wound,
Beyond all telling glowed the sunshine fair
From those soft eyes where now no light is found.
I cannot tell if it be true or no,
Methought her face to pitying colours turned;
My breast love's touchstone was; at love's first glow
What wonder that with sudden fire I burned?
Nor did she walk like any mortal thing,
But every motion was celestial grace,
Her words were like the angels' when they sing;
A living sun, a heavenly spirit's face
Was what I saw. If such it is not now
No wound is healed by slackening the bow.'

William Dudley Foulke, 1915

5

Le Lubéron

On the map it would be difficult to draw a clear line between places associated with the plateau of Vaucluse and those on the margins of the Montagne de Lubéron, but you will soon see the difference on the ground. If there is a physical boundary it could be the river Calavon, which runs a serene course from a mile or two north of Apt until (under the *alias* of the Coulon) it joins the Durance north of Cavaillon. The mountain itself is split in two by the valley of the Aiguebrun and the Combe de Lourmarin; its highest point is in the eastern half, where the Grand Lubéron rises to about 3,500 feet, only a few hundred feet lower than the Colline de Berre on the plateau. This is wonderful walking country, criss-crossed by the Grandes Randonnées, and in its more accessible parts a wide, rich and gentle countryside; the people too seem gentler, perhaps because they see fewer visitors than Vaucluse does today.

It would be possible to reach much of the Lubéron from Avignon, if that suits your plan, but for a leisurely exploration there is no better centre than **Bonnieux**. This is a quiet, unsophisticated, hospitable community which enjoys a superb site overlooking the valley of the Calavon, and there is a choice of two hotels which may appeal to different tastes and pockets. The Hostellerie du Prieuré declares its origin, having been

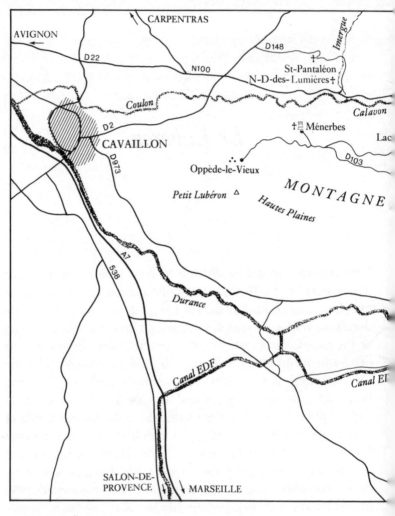

Le Lubéron

attractively converted from a fifteenth-century priory, and occupies a quiet spot in the lower part of the town. The César is simpler and more unexpected, with a friendly management and rooms (with restaurant) overlooking the rest of the town and the wide plain to the north and west.

The old town was built in tiers connected by steep slopes and flights of steps. Right at the top, above a few remains of ramparts

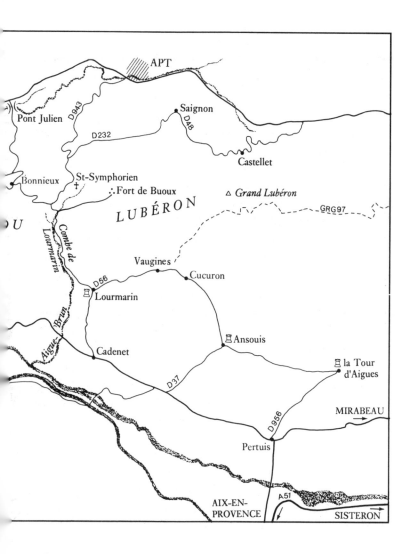

and surrounded by tall cedars, is the Romanesque parish church. Only the three western bays remain of the twelfth-century nave, the rest of the church having been altered or added to in the fifteenth, but it looks solid and dignified compared with the larger but characterless modern church in the lower town. Interesting in a different way is the **Musée de la Boulangerie** in the rue de la Republique, the beginning of the main road out of the town to the south-east. In the original bakehouse you can see the stone-built oven with its round-arched opening and all the paraphernalia of the trade – you might almost call it an art – set out in adjoining rooms. This is the kind of local exhibition which the French do with pride and modern skill; it was inaugurated in 1985.

From here there are three distinct areas which invite visits, to the east, south-east and north-west of Bonnieux. The smallest group lies to the east, and though the distances are short it includes one place which will need at least a morning to itself – and preferably an early start to avoid the heat of a summer day. If you leave Bonnieux by the D36 to Cadenet, but turn left when you reach the deep valley of the Aiguebrun, then right at the first fork on to a minor road, look out for a tall slender tower rising among the trees below you to the right. This detached campanile is all that is left of the twelfth-century priory of **St-Symphorien**, and it seems remarkable that it has survived after centuries of neglect – at one time it did duty as a *pigeonnier*. You can appreciate its beauty even from a distance, and though access is restricted during restoration there may be a chance later on to get closer. The sad thing is that we can only guess at what has been lost elsewhere on the site.

The morning's main objective is the **Fort de Buoux**, only a mile or so further east but along a road which otherwise leads nowhere. Avoid the left turn to the village of Buoux, and carry straight on following the signs which point to the Fort. For the driver the road ends in a clearing with parking for cars and a little shelter which sells drinks and snacks for the hungry and thirsty walker. The path beyond is steep but mostly shady, in one place passing under the overhang of a vast Cyclopean cliff, and it leads to the point of entry where you need to buy a ticket from the *gardienne*. From there it is still a walk of some fifteen minutes up the mountain side till you reach the outlying bastion of this huge fortress area. The final climb is by steps cut in the rock which lead to the gateway of its first ramparts – which in their present form date from the sixteenth century.

At this point the reader as well as the walker may be ready to pause and consider why a place like this needed to be built in a natural fastness of the Lubéron. If you ignore all the modern roads in this area, you will see from the map that the valley of the Aiguebrun is part of a continuous route northward from Marseille, which passes close to Aix-en-Provence, crosses the Durance just south of Cadenet, and here penetrates the Montagne on its way to Apt – where it joins the east–west highway between Avignon and Forcalquier. This was the route taken by primitive peoples moving to north or south, and in the Middle Ages by carriers of salt from the Étang de Berre. It was protected by many now vanished castles, but by none so extensive and formidable as the Fort de Buoux, whose primary object was the defence of Apt. To follow its ramifications you can hardly do without the illustrated booklet by René Bruni which is on sale where you buy your ticket.

The first fortified area is striking enough, but hardly prepares you for what is to come. The path crosses an open space, then skirts a ravine at the head of which is a vaulted stone reservoir full to the brim at most seasons with spring water. Past the head of the ravine the path turns south, and it will be another ten minutes before you reach the next stage of the fortifications. At about 1,500 feet you pass the remains of a mediaeval village and a Romanesque church, and then embark on a gradually narrow-ing ridge with precipitous drops on either side. To your right as you climb there is a rocky ledge with about a dozen round holes drilled into the rock, about six feet deep and anything from five to seven in diameter. They were used for food storage – silos, in fact – and to contain essentials like the salt brought up from the coast. Several heavy stone lids are still in place or to be seen round about. One realises now that this was not just the fortress home of some potent mediaeval *seigneur*, but the site of a sizeable village where his retainers and their families lived.

We know nothing of those who held it until the sixteenth century, when the family of Pontevès-Buoux emerge as overlords in the neighbourhood. This was the time when the Luberon became involved in some of the most furious episodes of the wars of religion. The 'heresy' of the Vaudois, a reformist movement inspired by the teaching of one Pierre Valdo in the thirteenth century, had taken a firm hold on the Lubéron; in 1573 their military arm captured Buoux, and soon afterwards Ménerbes, hoping thereby to defend themselves against the crusading Catholic wrath to come. It came, and Ménerbes fell after a fifteen-month siege, but it was only by a trick played on the governor of Buoux that Pompée de Pontevès-Buoux recovered his castle. Once up here you can appreciate that sixteenth-century cannon could never be brought to bear in this kind of terrain.

To continue the tour, our path enters the line of fortifications which defended the thirteenth-century fortress – two lines of ramparts, each preceded by a dry moat. The large square building in the centre of the open space behind, of which one substantial wall and its doorway survives, was probably where the *seigneurs* lived when not under threat of siege; a flight of steps behind it leads to another water cistern, now dry. Finally we climb to a point where the ridge is less than fifty feet wide, and look down on ravens – perhaps even an eagle – circling hundreds of feet below on either side. This is where the third and last ditch and rampart were built, and the keep itself stands on the edge of a sheer drop to the east – surely the most fantastic position for any last stand, and one which could never have been taken by force. Almost as a postscript, and inaccessible from where you are, there is a flight of rock-hewn steps leading down and away from the cliff face to the west – a secret escape stairway which could be reached only by a path from a postern beside the second line of fortifications.

You will understand by now that this is not a visit to hurry, either mentally or physically, and if you can carry the ingredients of a picnic lunch up there you will never forget the meal. Except where rock and scrub take over at the very top, there is plenty of shade and greenery. Otherwise the nice family who run both the ticket office and the snack bar below will provide refreshment when you come down.

From here there is nowhere to go but back to the D943 which leads to Apt. Passing another turn to Bonnieux you quickly reach a right-hand fork signposted to **Saignon**. You will be startled to find this village spread across a slope below what looks like the most enormous castle ever built. In fact there are two vast outcrops of rock on the skyline with a fissure between them, below which is Saignon, a peaceable place which has a pretty central *place* with a plashy fountain and a simple *auberge* restaurant. Its church is of mixed dates, as so often in these parts, but it has a strong western façade with a long band of blind arcading over the doorway – there seems to be a touch of arab or Saracen influence here. The doors themselves are eighteenth-century and very fine.

If not already sated with scenery, take the D48 south over the hills to **Castellet**, another delightfully simple village with old houses, before returning by the main N100 to Apt and thence back to Bonnieux.

Next in the programme could be a group of places on the lower ground to the south-east, a country threaded by small streams on their way down from the Montagne to join the Durance. To reach it you take the spectacular route down the Combe de Lourmarin, at the bottom of which you come to **Lourmarin** itself. An outcrop of rocky ground here was first used to build a castle which protected the southern entry to the Combe, but it was on nothing like the scale of the Fort de Buoux. There was no room for it to expand, and by the fifteenth century there was no longer any need for its defences. At this point the fief of Lourmarin came into the hands of Foulques d'Agoult, baron of Sault and the head of a notable Provençal family – cousins, incidentally, of the Simiane. Foulques was

Grand Chamberlain at the court of King René in Aix, and a very rich man who shared his master's cultured tastes and had a large library. He was also a good business man, and he reorganized the industry and agriculture of the neighbourhood by bringing in skilled workmen recruited from among the Valdensian population of the Lubéron.

In 1470 the old castle was abandoned and Foulques planned to build a family home on a site about half a mile north of the village, where he already had a country house where he stayed when on the move between Aix and Sault. This ended up as one of the most famous Renaissance châteaux in Provence, which is still a centre of all kinds of cultural activity. Foulques's building was a haphazard affair, still in the Gothic style, never finished, and known today as the *Château-Vieux*. He died in 1492 and his successors set about building a *Château-Neuf* in the Renaissance manner. It was begun in 1526, but it too was never properly finished after constant interruptions caused by the wars between François I and the emperor Charles V, as well as by the interminable conflicts of the religious wars. In particular there was a furious onslaught in 1545 by Jean de Meynier, baron of Oppède, intended to exterminate the Valdensians (or Vaudois) who had settled all over Lubéron, in which the village of Lourmarin was virtually wiped out.

The château survived, but it was never extended beyond the beautifully proportioned rectangular block we now see. The death of King René in 1480 had meant the end of Provence as an independent state, for his successor Charles III made a present of it to the French crown. The early d'Agoult, including Foulques, had resisted the union with France, but François Artaud de Montauban d'Agoult – a man whose importance matched his string of names – received François I here on his return from Italy in 1537. Over the following centuries country estates were neglected for court life, and in 1790 the château was only saved from destruction by the revolutionaries when the mayor of Lourmarin persuaded them to turn it into a hospital.

During the nineteenth century it gradually decayed, until 'roofs and floors collapsed, walls cracked, the lower rooms became stables or lumber rooms, the upper parts of the towers were used as pigeon-lofts, and ground floors were taken over by squatters'.

At what must have been its last gasp, Lourmarin was saved by a miracle. In July 1920 four friends set out by car from Lyon to see the Roman temple near Vernégues. They drove first to Apt and then down the Combe de Lourmarin, to find at the bottom of the defile 'the proud silhouette of an ancient château whose towers stood out against the sky'. They stopped for lunch in the village and discovered that the owner of the property was on the point of selling it to a builder for demolition. They swallowed their lunch and rushed off to have a closer look at this romantic-looking place, only to find the ruinous reality. One of the four, Robert Laurent Vibert, saw through the universal decay to the still beautiful bones of the château, called up the local *notaire*, and within a few days had bought it at auction for 8,000 francs.

Vibert was a Renaissance man of his own times, which may be why Lourmarin had such an immediate appeal. He was born Robert Laurent in 1884, orphaned at the age of ten and adopted by his godfather, François Vibert. After military service he went to the *École normale superieure*, where he studied the history of the French Renaissance, creative art, and political economy – a combination of subjects such as our universities have not yet achieved. When his adoptive father died in 1912 he took over all his business interests. Twice wounded in the Great War, he was among the first to win the *Croix de Guerre avec palmes*. In 1916 he was stationed in the Middle East, and when peace came he set up his own petroleum agency, which gave him both the money and the opportunity to travel and collect works of art in that part of the world.

This was the man who rescued Lourmarin, and within four years not only had the essential rescue work been done, but true to his character Vibert had installed a library of 10,000 volumes.

He was to die in a road accident in 1925, but not before he had bequeathed the château in his will to the Academy of Aix, with a clause calling upon it to establish the *Fondation de Lourmarin Laurent Vibert*. Revenues of his estate were to be set aside to complete the restoration and to maintain the fabric, with any surplus going to provide free lodging for three or four months in the year for an unspecified number of young artists, musicians, writers or researchers. In 1927 the Academy granted the foundation a 99-year lease of the whole property. Between them these two men of vision – Foulques d'Agoult in 1526 and Laurent Vibert four hundred years later – created an *ensemble* where the arts and values of the Renaissance still flourish in a materialistic age.

I have dwelt on the history of Lourmarin both because of its human interest and because it aptly illustrates the history of Provence over several centuries. Visits to the château are at fixed intervals during the day and accompanied by lucid and intelligent guides, so it seems unnecessary to detail here what you are going to see. Perhaps the most striking architectural feature is the great newel staircase which rises through the quadrangular tower to serve all floors of the *Château-neuf*. Its rope-like twists of stone follow the newel post itself all the way to the top. The formal rooms are on the lower floors, with a curious selection of furniture and *objets d'art*, but on the higher levels you will find rooms set apart for music (with several pianos of various dates) and one devoted to paintings by young artists who have worked here. There are two libraries, one of which contains a unique collection of local manuscript archives, bound in vellum, covering the years 1495 to 1822.

The anteroom to the *Château-Vieux* contains portraits and photographs of notable visitors to Lourmarin. One expects to find traces of our Queen Mother in such a place, and even (considered as an artist) Churchill, but Montgomery is a surprise. We should not forget, by the way, that Albert Camus (1913–1960) lived in the village and is buried in the parish church. In case your guide leaves you on your own to visit this part, make sure you go down to the courtyard behind the polygonal tower, from where you look up at the wooden galleries reconstructed in the mediaeval manner, and poke your nose into two rooms now used for art exhibitions. One was the bakery, and still contains the huge bread oven which seems to go back for miles; the other was the cellar, and over the door you can see the date 1513 and read the exhortation: 'Bois et t'en vas'. There is indeed a great deal at Lourmarin to drink in before you go.

In **Vaugines**, five kilometres east of Lourmarin, there is a thirteenth-century Romanesque cemetery chapel with a curiously off-centre apse which belonged to an earlier building. Two kilometres further on is the small town of **Cucuron**, a huddle of grey and ochre roofs below the remains of a château and a Provençal bell-tower. Its centre is Notre-Dame de Beaulieu, a big church for a little town, and in the mix of styles we are used to hereabouts. It has a good western façade, with simply moulded arches and a tympanum with geometric patterns of intersecting circles – all made to look rather odd by the extremely tall bare trunk of a plane tree beside the doorway, which sprouts only at the very top. The inside (not in the best of repair) has an intriguing combination of a barrel-vaulted nave, Gothic side aisles and a vast baroque altar which entirely fills the apse.

From Cucuron the road goes on south to **Ansouis**, where the château is every bit as interesting as Lourmarin, and is still lived in by the family who have owned it since the thirteenth century. It was in 1285 that a son was born here to the comte de Sabran, and christened Elzéar. In an age when piety and faith counted a good deal, he and his wife Delphine devoted themselves to good works and were both canonised in 1369. That there is still a room in the old part of the château called the 'room of the saints' shows how old it is.

As at Lourmarin there are two distinct parts, but here the older one dates from as early as the twelfth century, and it provides some telling evidence of life in the Middle Ages. The *salle de justice*, where the *seigneur* sat in judgement over his feudal subjects, has a convenient man-hole in the floor through which the condemned could be lowered into the prison below – which is now more humanely used as the family chapel. In the chapel is a deep well shaft by which – quite credibly – an underground passage could be reached as an escape route in time of trouble, and your guide will give you a graphic description of its use.

The seventeenth-century part is not such a perfect piece of architecture as the Renaissance wing at Lourmarin, but it makes up for that with a good deal of charm – not least because it remains above all a family home. The ramifications of the Provençal nobility being what they are, it is no surprise to find that the de Sabran were related not only to their near neighbours the d'Agoult and the de Simiane, but to the Pontevès of Buoux and even to the sovereign counts of Forcalquier. The thirteenth-century *comté* is now a twentieth-century dukedom, and the daughter of the present duc de Sabran (she was a professional concert pianist) married the comte de Paris, royalist 'pretender' to the throne of France.

The principal staircase is a fine example from the time of Henri IV, and all the adjoining rooms are beautifully furnished; the dining room has a set of Flemish tapestries telling the story of Dido and Aeneas. After all that formality there are comfortable family rooms on the ground floor, and the kitchen (still in use) is an informal delight, set out with all the ingenious implements and equipment of the 1900s. From the outside the château looks more mediaeval than Renaissance, but not the terrace gardens, which would be a lovely setting for any home. They look out to the north over a rich plain, planted with vines, fruit trees and lavender – a temptation for a family to put down its roots here for ever. Visits are guided, sometimes a little hurried, and limited to the afternoon. There are none on Tuesdays.

A branch of another Provençal family put down its roots only ten kilometres further on, at the eastern end of the plain. There had been a mediaeval castle on the banks of the Lèze at **la Tour d'Aigues**, but in 1511 this property was inherited by a sister of Raimond d'Agoult of Lourmarin. In 1545 the Italian architect Ercole Nigra was brought in to transform the old building to suit contemporary taste, and the result was a Renaissance château on a much larger scale than any of its neighbours – big enough to receive a state visit from Catherine de' Medici with all her retinue in 1579. We have to imagine its superb appointments and furnishings, because it was destroyed by two disastrous fires in 1782 and 1792. Luckily the entrance façade survives mainly intact to give some idea of its magnificence. Built more on the lines of a Roman *arc de triomphe*, adorned with Corinthian columns and pilasters, warlike friezes and a classical pediment, it makes a startling and incongruous backdrop to the *place* at the centre of this unassuming little town – which has a weekly market and is sometimes taken over by a travelling fair complete with dodgems. Performances of *son et lumière* are given in front of it during the summer, and the Vaucluse authorities have undertaken to restore what they can of the body of the château behind – a long and speculative task. The quickest way back to Bonnieux is by Pertuis and Cadenet, and up once more through the Combe de Lourmarin.

The western end of the mountain is called the Petit Lubéron, and though not as high as it is to the east it has some exciting scenery. Before setting out in that direction you may like to have a look at the only authentic relic of Rome in the neighbourhood, the bridge over the Calavon north of Bonnieux known as the **Pont Julien**. Built in the time of Augustus, it carried the section of the *via Domitia* which here coincides more or less with the N100 running west from Apt. This was the great trunk road, called after Cnaius Domitius Ahenobarbus (Mark Antony's bluff general Enobarbus), which linked the Mont Genèvre pass from Italy with Narbonne and the Spanish border, so the bridge must have carried important traffic. It looks a typical Roman structure, self-confident, balanced and practical, with an air of effortless strength. Its three wide arches would have spanned a wider river bed than the present one, and just in case of extra pressure from flood water both the intermediate piers have arched openings at a higher level – a practical idea which also improves the design.

A little further along the N100 you come to the pilgrimage village centred on the church of **Notre-Dame-de-Lumières**. There was an early Romanesque chapel here beside the river Imergue, just before it joins the Calavon, but it only became a famous spot when mysterious lights were seen in the river valley and an old farmer was miraculously cured of some ailment. This seemed a good opportunity to attract pilgrims, and in 1663 a new church was built over the old chapel (now the crypt) with a statue of Our Lady and other relics. It has little architectural interest, apart from the crypt, but the gardens laid out for the pilgrims are pleasant to walk in. They still come in large numbers.

There is a much more interesting church at **St-Pantaléon**, lost among country roads to the west of the Imergue. Its layout is eccentric, with a high Romanesque nave and two side aisles, consisting of only one bay, beyond which is a large central apse and two little ones flung wide to north and south – in other words the church is wider than it is long. This may be something to do with the site, which is an outcrop of natural rock. The base of the main apse has simply been cut out from it to form a semicircle, and the bare rock shows up all round – a natural formation which has been put to a strange use.

Outside the west door a large tomb has been hollowed out of the rock, looking like the base of a sarcophagus, with a few smaller ones round about. Then if you walk round to the east end you will find a whole nest of irregular little oblong cavities similarly hacked out round the base of the northern apse. Rock tombs are not uncommon in Provence, and though there is a temptation to link them with early Christian burials they are not as a rule very ancient. In this case it seems to have been the custom in the early Middle Ages to bring to Mass at St-Pantaléon the bodies of infants who had been still-born or had died before they could be christened. There was a comforting belief that during Mass the child would revive enough to receive the sacrament of baptism, after which the little body was committed to its rocky tomb. St-Pantaléon therefore seems to have been one of the *sanctuaires de répit*, of which there are a few other examples in Provence – though what you see here leaves a lot of questions unanswered. Even the date of the church is uncertain, and though most of it is probably no older than the twelfth century there are three much earlier-looking columns inside, to the right of the main apse.

Time now for a last run to the west from Bonnieux into the heart of the Petit Lubéron. First stop will be at **Lacoste**, after a short but scenic drive. You can see the hill on which it stands clearly from the terraces of Bonnieux, but the top of it has no room for anything but the château de Sade, for thirty years the chief residence of the eighteenth-century marquis of ill repute. He evaded the law here for a time, but in the end he was committed to the Bastille on information laid by his mother-in-law. The château would have been the biggest for miles around, but the Revolution left only the shell. You enter through the Portail des Chèvres – this is goat country – from where a cobbled street leads up to an idiosyncratic bell-tower. This one has a very odd topknot, with the usual ironwork held up by four short stone pillars with decorated capitals. There was room for a whole village inside the castle walls; a house or two has been restored and re-occupied, but most of it remains deserted. You can see now that the west-facing walls of the keep are built directly on the rock, a formidable piece of fortification.

The Petit Lubéron is not unlike Tuscany, with *villages perchés* rising out of a fertile rolling countryside, each one as it were within signalling distance of the next. So from Bonnieux to Lacoste, and now to **Ménerbes**. There is more to see than at

Lacoste, because the spine of the hill has room for a château at one end, a church at the other, and the Place de la Mairie in between. The château was deeply involved in the fight put up by the Valdensian Calvinists against the brutal Catholic assaults. In 1573 they managed to secure it as one of their three bases in the Luberon, and they held on to it in a siege which lasted six years before they were dislodged.

Today Ménerbes is a favourite with the French house-hunter, and you can see why. There is great peace and silence up here in its traffic-free streets, and there are enough good solid houses which can be done up at a reasonable cost. The views to both south and north are wonderful, and some unexpected little corners have been cleverly converted. The château is a conventional four-square affair with corner turrets, well restored after its sixteenth-century troubles and nine-teenth-century neglect. The interior is mostly in either civic or private hands and not visitable, but do look carefully at the light stone block set in the wall over the entrance. The subject carved there is the weighing of souls in the Last Judgement, with a snooty-looking angel handling the scales and a posse of horned devils waiting for the rejects. One of the turrets has a corbelled-out extension like a romantic gazebo, and this has been snapped up by a discriminating private buyer.

The church at the other end is one of the usual mixtures, none of it older than the fourteenth century, and with a tower set rather strangely over the east end at an oblique angle to the nave. The view to the north across the valley of the Calavon takes in both Gordes and Roussillon (you can even make out the ochre quarries) against the green southern slopes of the Vaucluse plateau. The belfry-cum-clock-tower at the end of the *place* has a disarmingly simple iron crown, and its stonework tones well with the old houses and cobbled streets around it. There are no false notes in Ménerbes.

So to **Oppède-le-Vieux**, next in the line of *villages perchés*, and a place so extraordinary that it must be seen to be believed.

To call it a village is misleading, because the inhabitants deserted it for a more convenient site in the plain nearly a hundred years ago. What you have now is a steep-sided cone of rock, overgrown with every kind of vegetation, its slopes punctuated by ever more bizarre ruins appearing out of the undergrowth and poised dizzily on the edges of cliffs. The climb from the car park begins sedately with a paved and stepped *sentier*, but once you are through what would have been the gatehouse of a castle you will have to scramble through thorny scrub to reach stage after stage of its now unravellable fortifications and domestic quarters. The *donjon* on the final spur is one of the best preserved fragments, and the view from it invites every kind of cliché. The only place where the ground is level enough to form a terrace is occupied by the still handsome shape of a Romanesque church – a big one, too, with nave and side aisle and a partly fortified tower.

The site must have been occupied in Roman times, for Oppède is clearly the Latin *oppidum*, the word used in the provinces to indicate a native settlement, and distinguished from the Roman-occupied *colonia*. The castle was first built by Raymond VI, count of Toulouse, round about 1200, though he was forced to cede it to the Pope after the catastrophe of the Albigensian crusade. It would have been added to later, when it came into the hands of the masters of les Baux, and again in the sixteenth century when it was held by Jean Meynier, whose family had been created barons of Oppède by the Pope. This was the man who crushed the life out of the Valdensian 'heretics' of the Luberon in 1545, and this was the base for his savage campaign.

The past few years have seen contradictory developments at Oppède-le-Vieux. On the one hand what was left of the old village centre below the castle has been re-animated, a few houses have been expensively restored, and a pleasant small *auberge* has been opened to refresh the visitor. Yet up among the ruins the undergrowth has grown unchecked for several years now, and the roots of fast-growing trees are undermining the ancient walls. You need to watch your step on the steep slippery paths, and at some points you can easily miss your way down again. Such is the magic of the place, though, that on a fine morning I know of no more exhilarating experience in this part of Provence. It will leave you with a last and lasting memory of the Lubéron.

6

Avignon

Avignon is such a famous city that many people will want to make it their first stop in Provence. Others may come to it only after long meanderings through the countryside, but if you have never seen it before the best approach is from the west or north. As you cross the highest point on the road from Pont-du-Gard, or drop into the Rhône valley at Pont-St-Esprit, you can instantly appreciate the brilliant light and luminous air which painters and writers have always associated with Provence; the contrast with the atmosphere among the soft green hills of the Ardèche is striking.

Only from the west bank of the river do you have the view of the city which every camera knows (and which was painted by Corot): the cliff-like battlements of the Palais des Papes rising from a screen of trees and red roofs across the two wide channels of the Rhône, and the appealing remains of the bridge of St-Bénézet – the Pont d'Avignon of the song we all know. You may get there quicker by belting down the autoroute to the eastern suburbs, but the approach from there is featureless and depressing.

In planning a visit to Avignon the most important decision is where to stay, assuming you will not be content with a day trip by coach from some other centre. Inside or outside the walls? The

VILLENEUVE-
LÈS-AVIGNON
←

Rhône

Pont St-Bénézet

Île Piot

Pont Edouard Daladier

Boulevard du Rhône

Boule

Musé
Petit

Place du Palais

Rue des Grottes

Porte de l'Oulle

Hôtel des
Monnaies

Allées des Oulles

Boulevard de l'Oulle

RAMPARTS

Rue Joseph Vernet

Theatre

Hôtel-de-Ville

Pl. de l'Horloge

Rue St-Agricol

Rue Victor Hugo

Musée
Calvet

St-

Boulevard St-Dominique

Rue Joseph Vernet

Rue de la République

Pont de l'Europe

Boulevard Raspail

Cours Jean Jaurès

Porte de
la République ←

Boulevard

Avignon

guides give you a big choice of hotels in either category, but Avignon always seems easier to come at from outside. Ville-neuve-lès-Avignon on the west bank is not so much a suburb as a riverside town in its own right, and it has accommodation ranging from the superb Prieuré, where if you have the money you can spend a luxurious week in blissful peace and relaxation, to the simpler but comfortable Residence des Cèdres in the western part of the town. Another idea would be to go even further out, perhaps north along the D980 to the Hostellerie de Varennes in Sauveterre or the old-world Château de Cubières in Roquemaure. At any of these places you will be far from the noise and confusion of a city which lives by tourism, and a short drive will bring you across the Pont Daladier into the huge parking area outside the ramparts. Unless you have a hotel inside with a garage, it would be a mistake to bring your car any further.

To penetrate the outer ramparts (which were heavily but accurately restored in the nineteenth century by Viollet-le-Duc) you have to walk along under them to the Porte de l'Oulle, from where you pick your way through a mostly residential quarter to the southern end of the Place du Palais. At the height of the tourist season, and especially during the festival period in July and August, things are uncomfortable even for the pedestrian, but in spring and autumn – best of all in May – the scene is pleasant and relaxed. Avignon is altogether more attractive than it was ten years ago. Most of the Palais des Papes has at last been restored, the warren of mediaeval streets behind it has been cleaned up, some of them reserved for pedestrians, the long throroughfare which begins with the Place de l'Horloge and continues down the rue de la Republique and the Cours Jean-Jaurés has been cleared of clutter, and the Petit Palais has been adapted to make a museum of art in the best modern French tradition.

From the first sight of Avignon fiom across the river you can see why the Rocher des Doms was so important in its early days

– in fact it was the only reason for its existence. An outcrop of rock some two hundred feet high, it commanded a natural crossing point. It was inhabited even in palaeolithic times, and attracted a large population in the Bronze and Iron Ages. The Massiliots built a trading post in the fifth century BC, and the Romans fortified it. The Rocher was the strong point of the early walled city, which from the ninth to the eleventh century was part of the Kingdom of Arles, or Lower Burgundy. The kingdom's western boundary was the Rhône, so that when in 1032 it was annexed by the Emperor Conrad II the left, or eastern bank of the river was regarded as belonging to the Empire, while after the crushing of Languedoc in the Albigensian crusade the right bank belonged to the kings of France. This explains why Villeneuve on the right bank was first fortified by Philip the Fair of France in the thirteenth century, and why the castles of Tarascon and Beaucaire threaten each other from opposite banks further down stream.

There seems to have been a Roman bridge over the Rhône here, perhaps the only one between Vienne and Arles, but it disappeared during the barbarian invasions. From then till the end of the twelfth century only a ferry service joined the Empire to the Kingdom at Avignon. It was when Beaucaire, a little further down the river on the French side, turned into an important commercial centre that its merchants began to agitate for an easier way to bring their goods into the city. As to how the bridge of St-Bénézet came to be built, you can choose between the romantic and the prosaic accounts. According to the chronicler Robert of Auxerre, who died in 1212, a young shepherd boy in the Ardèche was looking after his mother's flock when he was told by an angelic voice that God wished him to build a bridge over the Rhône. As he was only twelve, with just three farthings in his pocket, this seemed a tall order, but he gave the ferryman his three farthings, crossed the river and boldly confronted the bishop of Avignon in the cathedral with his message.

Challenged to show his qualifications, he prayed for help and confounded everybody by carrying an enormous block of stone down to the river bank as a first step. The miracle was accepted, and work began. The chronicle ends with the words 'but before it was all accomplished Bénézet died, in the 1184th year after the birth of Christ; and he was buried in the chapel on the bridge itself, and four years later the bridge was finished *by his companions*'.

Now it is known that there was at the time a guild or fraternity of bridge-builders, in the tradition of the *collegium pontificum* of Rome. It had a semi-religious status – had not the Pope inherited from the Roman priesthood the title of *Pontifex Maximus*, the Supreme Bridge-builder? Furthermore, a legal document has come to light, dated 1185, by which a toll was fixed by the consuls of Avignon for crossing it, and which mentions 'Frère Bénézet' as the builder. At the same time it appears that following the custom of the brotherhood Bénézet also bought land in Avignon to build a hospital and a hostelry for pilgrims. This paid off after his death, when large numbers came to see his relics (by then advertised as those of a poor shepherd boy) and their contributions enabled the 'companions' to buy out the rights of the ferry owners who were contesting their monopoly. By 1202 Bénézet is officially described as 'Beatus Benedictus', and the legend was born. Now it seems a pity to demolish it.

What also emerges from the archives is that the roadway of this first bridge was made of planks of wood, not of stone, and that it was wrecked by the crusading army of Louis VIII when he captured the town in 1226. Ten years later it was replaced by a bridge built entirely of stone, with the roadway on a higher level. This was the reason why the original Romanesque chapel of St Bénézet was given an upper storey with an entrance on the new level, the upper chapel being dedicated to St Nicholas, patron saint of mariners. The curious building which resulted is a mixture of Romanesque and Gothic styles, and it can be visited every day from June to August (at other times not on Tuesdays). The approach to the bridge is by a stairway from the Boulevard de la Ligne on the up-river side.

What is left of the thirteenth-century bridge is such a graceful structure that the loss of the rest was a tragedy. There were twenty-three arches in all, spanning not only the two main river channels but the intervening shallows and sandbanks too. Although the design (as at Pont Julien on the Calavon) incorporated openings in the piers to let flood waters through, it began to disintegrate in the fourteenth century and needed repair after every winter by the guild of bridge-builders. The worst damage came with the winter floods of 1669, and after that the river was allowed to have its way. As for the dancing, current wisdom says we should read '*sous*' for '*sur*' in the old song, and that '*L'on y dansait tout en ronde*' on the Île de Piot between the two channels, and so 'underneath the arches', as it were. It spoils another picturesque vision, but maybe they are right.

At the beginning of the chapter on the Comtat, I have explained how Avignon was besieged and captured by Louis VIII, and how in 1309 Pope Clement V came to be installed in the Dominican monastery of Avignon, though it was still not Papal territory and not even the capital of the Comtat Venaissin. The city itself had been left out of the deal which gave the Comtat to the Pope, so for the time being he had to be content as a vassal of the Emperor. There was no official Papal residence, but Clement's successor John XXII was already bishop of Avignon and decided to use his existing palace for the purpose. Though he laid his plans and put aside money to build a new and stronger one on the empty ground to the south, it was the next Pope, Benedict XII, who transformed Avignon when he was elected in 1334.

A former Cistercian monk called Jacques Fournier, the new Pope lived long enough to build a new base for the Holy See, and to make it a fortress as well as a palace. As John XXII had planned, the new building went up on the lower ground to the south of the Rocher, away from the river bank. All available materials and resources were concentrated on the project, which meant demolishing the earlier buildings on the Rocher and elsewhere, so there are virtually no remains from Roman or early mediaeval times in the vicinity. Its architecture reflected the Pope's Cistercian upbringing, and Benedict's part of the **Palais des Papes** is as austere as it is magnificent. It forms the left section of the long battlemented frontage which faces you across the Place du Palais, ending in the tall square Tour de la Campane on the extreme left, close up against the tower of the cathedral of Notre-Dame-des-Doms.

Benedict died in 1342, to be succeeded by a very different character. Cardinal Pierre Roger de Beaufort was nobly born, and his tastes matched his birth. As Pope Clement VI he saw no reason to break off his affair with the beautiful Cécile de Comminges, and he enobled his 'nephew' Guillaume de Beaufort as Vicomte de Turenne. He extended the palace further to the south on a grandiose scale, and in the flamboyant Gothic style he had come to admire in northern France. His *rapport* with beautiful women had another useful outcome when Queen Jeanne of Naples (who was also Countess of Provence by her descent from Raymond Bérenger IV) came for an audience and to ask for help in a little family difficulty. She had been accused of murdering the first of her four husbands, Prince Andrew of Hungary, and though probably not directly involved she hoped for absolution from the sin of complicity, and was anxious for her second marriage to be declared valid. As she was only twenty and very lovely she had her way; in return she agreed to sell the city of Avignon – which still belonged to the Counts of Provence as vassals of the Emperor – for 80,000 florins, which was only five times what Clement VI had spent on his inaugural banquet. At last the Pope owned the ground on which he lived.

Although visits are unaccompanied (except for groups with their own guides) there is enough literature available to help you to find your way round the two palaces that it seems unnecessary to describe it all in great detail. The official booklet on sale has a curiously garbled English translation but the information it gives is mostly to the point, and the green *Guide Michelin* for Provence shows the preferred route very clearly. After buying your ticket (and it may be worth remembering that at State establishments *les agés* get in at half price) you cross the *Grand Cour* to enter the ground floor of the **Palais Vieux** of Benedict XII. From the *Salle du Consistoire* you reach the *Cour du Cloître*, a simple two-storeyed cloister, from where a stairway leads to the plain but magnificent *Grand Tinel*, or banqueting room, which is hung with Gobelin tapestries. The kitchen tower beyond is fascinating, with a wonderful fireplace and a tapering smoke-hole in the centre of the ceiling. There are two small chapels on this side of the building, that of St Jean on the ground floor and of St Martial above it, leading off the *Grand Tinel*. St Martial has some bright Italian frescos painted by Matteo Giovanetti in 1345.

The long room to the right is the *Chambre du Parement*, a sort of anteroom for papal audiences, and beyond it the Pope's private quarters – study and bedroom. Though the bedroom is architecturally simple it has the most bewitching wall decoration with swirling patterns of branches and leaves, with birds and squirrels cavorting against a sky-blue background. You are now on the upper floor of the *Tour des Anges*, and from here you can pass directly into the corresponding private quarters of the **Palais Nouveau**. Clement VI's study, known as the *Chambre du Cerf*, is decorated with entirely worldly scenes of hunting, fishing and falconry. As these wall paintings were also by Giovanetti, it seems likely that those in the Palais Vieux were added to please Clement VI rather than his austere predecessor, and that they used the same bedroom.

We now enter the principal rooms of the Palais Nouveau, and the biggest on this floor is the *Chapelle Clementine*, or 'private' chapel of Clement VI. This is a noble high-vaulted Gothic chamber, whose proportions exactly fit the *Salle de la Grande Audience* immediately below it, which you can visit on your way out into the *Grand Cour*. The tour as organised at present leaves out a good deal of both palaces, in particular the upper floor of the wing associated with the Conclave. This was where all the cardinals were lodged during the election of a new Pope, and the rooms could be reached only from a narrow gallery overlooking the great courtyard. During the election the whole area was shut off *con clave*, or 'with a key', from the outside, except for a passage for the supply of food and drink – and even that was supposed to be scaled down if the cardinals took too long to make up their minds.

Avignon in the fourteenth century must have been an extraordinary place. Most of France beyond the Rhône was heavily involved in the Hundred Years' War with the English kings, but in Avignon the peaceful arts found wealthy patrons. The old gracious life of Languedoc, the troubadours and the 'courts of love' had never been quite extinguished even when the southern nobility had been all but wiped out in the Albigensian crusade. Now the spirit of the Italian Renaissance came to join it in the new Papal capital; architects and painters could be sure of employment. Yet the Popes (apart from Benedict XII) were practical administrators as well as spiritual leaders and patrons of the arts: John XXII had been Chancellor to the Count of Provence, Clement VI to Philip VI of France, and a university was founded which taught civil law. The wealth of the city was protected by the walls of its palace fortress, which the French chronicler Froissart thought was 'the finest and the strongest house in Europe'.

Under Clement VI in particular the spiritual functions of the Papacy were kept in the background, and the life of the flesh came to be accepted by clerics and officials as well as by the aristocracy. The walled city had become a sanctuary for vagabonds and criminals, so that a disillusioned Petrarch could describe it as 'an abode of sorrows, the shame of mankind, the most abominable of towns. . . . God is there despised, money is adored, laws human and divine are trampled underfoot.'

It was not until 1376 that Petrarch found an ally in St Catherine of Siena, who was on an embassy to Avignon from the city of Florence, and they persuaded Gregory XI that it was his duty to return to Italy and try to restore order among its warring states. He left Avignon in September that year, accompanied by thirteen of the twenty-three cardinals, though the horse he first mounted refused to carry him away from the palace. There was little chance of a clean break, and before long a group of dissident cardinals had elected their own Pope, who returned to Avignon as Clement VII. 'Antipopes' were elected there until 1403, when Rome reasserted its authority and a succession of Papal legates were sent to govern the city. The last of the antipopes, Benedict XIII, had to be smuggled out of the palace by a secret passage after a five-year siege by French troops.

Revolutionary France annexed the Comtat Venaissin and with it Avignon. The new regime cared nothing for ancient buildings, and both the Dominican and the Franciscan convents were destroyed, together with the cathedral cloister. The Palais des Papes was ransacked and became first a prison, then a barracks. A barracks it remained until the early years of this century, so no wonder the *École des Beaux Arts* (interrupted by two wars) has taken so long to restore it all, and they deserve great credit for its present condition.

The Place du Palais is a magnificent open space, running all the way from the Grand Palais entrance, past the tower at the west end of Notre-Dame-des-Doms, to the façade of the Petit Palais which faces you across the far end. It must have been quite a scene when Queen Jeanne disembarked from her galley at the jetty near the bridge, and processed up to the palace gateway under a canopy of cloth of gold; she was escorted by the papal guards and followed by eight cardinals in their glory. The building which faces the palace across the Place would not have been there, for the **Hôtel des Monnaies** was built in 1619 to house the city mint. Its façade looks thoroughly Italian, with its swags of fruit, its strutting cockerels and Borghese coat of arms. Its present role as Avignon's School of Music seems to suit it better.

The cathedral of **Notre-Dame-des-Doms** is difficult to assess as a building, so many different styles having been imposed on it over the centuries. It began as a single-aisled Romanesque church in the twelfth century, not long before Bénézet arrived to build his bridge, and was probably built in three stages: first the nave and a semicircular apse, then the elaborate cupola over the fifth bay, finally the western porch and the tower over it. The porch is the most impressive legacy of this period; its façade is so serene and classically proportioned that until the nineteenth century all the experts believed it was Roman work. In fact this and other monuments of the same period, like St-Restitut in the Tricastin, owe a lot to the Roman buildings at Glanum, just outside St-Rémy-de-Provence.

Only the lower stage of the tower is original, but the cupola over the final bay of the nave is not only original but unique. Notice how a diminishing series of corbelled arches culminates in an octagon, with the final dome supported on fluted Corinthian columns – a very refined piece of architecture for its period. To the left of the choir is the archbishop's marble throne, and in the final chapel to the left of the nave the flamboyant tomb of John XXII shows him comfortably tucked up in his last resting place. The apse was rebuilt in 1672, and unfortunately the nave has been over-weighted with baroque arches and a serpentine balustraded gallery. The side chapels are equally florid, and the less said about the statue of Our Lady on top of the tower the better.

The far end of the Place du Palais is closed by the **Petit Palais**, a building which was allocated in 1317 to the Cardinal de Via as his official residence, but was taken over on the death of John XXII in 1335 as the archbishop's palace. The coolly elegant façade, with its mullioned windows and crenellated parapets, was added in the fifteenth century. After the Revolution it was put to various unworthy uses, but in 1976 it emerged triumphantly as a home for a major collection of Italian painting. It has taken the place of the Musée Calvet as the most important museum in Avignon, and it includes an adorable Botticelli *Virgin and Child* and a Carpaccio with a typical Italian landscape background. There is an intriguing interior courtyard too, where a line of plain Gothic arcades frames the flamboyant doorway of the staircase tower. Altogether this is not a place to miss, so watch the time – it will shut promptly for two hours at noon, and is never open on Tuesdays.

The heart of the Roman city of Avenio was to the south of the Palais, and it seems appropriate that one of Avignon's chief open spaces, the Place de l'Horloge, occupies more or less the site of the forum. Considerably brightened up in recent years, it makes a good starting point for further exploration. On the right are the pseudo-baroque and neo-classical splendours of the **Theatre** and **Hôtel-de-Ville**, both built in the last century; behind the latter rises the genuinely fifteenth-century clock-tower which gives the Place its name. At its far end, in a side street off to the right, is the church of **St-Agricol** (an imaginary saint who keeps his eye on farmers) with a flamboyant west doorway and a strange-looking semi-detached tower.

Keeping to this side of the rue de la Republique you will come to what is properly called the **Hôtel de Villeneuve-Martignan**, a classic eighteenth-century building with a long low balustraded frontage facing the rue Joseph Vernet. If you were looking for the **Musée Calvet**, this is it, but if you were hoping to find the notable collection of paintings once associated with it, you will be disappointed. In 1988 I found its five gilded *salons* sadly run down and in need of restoration, and a few forlorn peacocks bravely displaying in an overgrown courtyard. The pictures here now are of no account, the early Italian masterpieces having gone to the Petit Palais; there are no Daumiers and hardly an Impressionist to be seen. The best

97

displays are from the original legacy of M. Esprit Calvet (1728–1810), mainly Stone Age implements and metalwork from the Iron Age, though the most surprising single exhibit is a bronze bust of Edgar Allan Poe. I am sure there are plans for a better future.

The greater part of the city lies on the far side of the rue de la République, and with time to spare you may find a few more places of interest. Look first for the **Place St-Didier**, which marks the beginning of the rue du Roi René. Didier (or Desiderius) was a bishop of Vienne who was martyred in the seventh century for exposing corruption at the court of Burgundy. The name is popular in Provence, and his church here is typically Provençal, with a high plain nave running straight on into the apse; its tower might be called a *tour d'esprit*, with its symmetrically arranged groups of three tall bell-openings on each side, an octagonal top stage and a short pointed spire.

To get the flavour of sixteenth and seventeenth-century Avignon, carry on down the rue du roi René past a succession of handsome *hôtels* – one of 1476 belonged to King René himself; the road leads eventually to the chapel of the Penitents Gris. The mediaeval fraternities of Penitents were a curious manifestation, mostly charitable organisations patronized by noblemen and even royalty – partly, one suspects, to foster public relations, and partly as a sop to their consciences. They each sported a different-coloured habit and hood, and the White, Grey and Black orders all had chapels in Avignon. In the sixteenth century both Charles IX and Henri III put on the white hood to process barefoot through the city. The **Penitents Gris** were based in the rue des Teinturiers, at a point where the river Sorgue appears above ground for a short stretch, looking almost like a Venetian canal. The single tower next to the chapel is all that is left of the Couvent des Cordeliers, the Franciscan convent where Petrarch's Laura was buried. Indeed, Mistral declares that he saw her for the first time in the Couvent de Sainte-Claire in the rue du roi René.

Another church you could take in on your way back to the Place du Palais is **St-Pierre**, though unless it happens to be Saturday or Monday you may not be able to get in. Its west end of 1512 is one of the more fantastic mixtures of the flamboyant and Renaissance styles, and the pair of walnut doors are a bewilderingly ornate *tour de force* of wood carving. One reason for stopping here, even if the church is shut, is that the *place* on its north side was once a cloister of St-Pierre, a peaceful and shady oasis on a hot day, where you can find a good meal or a refreshing drink in the intervals of sightseeing.

Like other towns of the *midi*, Avignon has attracted all sorts of literary and artistic figures. First there was Petrarch (though the story of his romantic love for Laura reads better at the Fontaine de Vaucluse), and the Italian master Simone Martini painted here from 1339 to 1344. Froissart knew it well enough to praise both its comforts and its defences, and Rabelais to be disturbed in his revels by its chorus of church bells – 'la ville sonante', he called it. Stendhal, as we know from his *Mémoires d'un touriste*, used to enjoy a quiet moment in the garden of the Hôtel de Villeneuve-Martignan. In the last century Daudet and Mistral, who both lived in nearby villages, would often come into Avignon. Mistral was a pupil (at the age of twelve) at an establishment in the rue Petramale, took his first communion at St-Didier, where he fell in love for the first time with an angelic small girl of the same age – and ran away from school.

Daudet in *Lettres de mon moulin* set his story of 'La Mule du Pape' in Avignon. His rosy picture of life here under the Popes is often quoted because it contrasts so strongly with the disgust of Petrarch – whose words he may never have read. The most surprising expatriate was an Englishman, John Stuart Mill, who retired to Avignon after giving up his seat in Parliament in 1868 and died here five years later – not before he had lent

J. H. Fabre the three thousand francs which set him up as writer and naturalist at Sérignan-du-Comtat.

If you find you prefer staying outside the city limits, that is exactly what the fourteenth-century cardinals found. Fifteen country residences, or *livrées*, were built for them in the west bank town of **Villeneuve-lès-Avignon**. (It is worth remembering that the word *lès*, when spelt with a grave accent, is a preposition meaning 'near'.) The site was strategically important too, especially after the bridge of St Bénézet was built and Philippe le Bel of France had put up the tower which is named after him. In the next century the French kings reinforced their control over the crossing with a huge fortress on 'Mount Andaon', the rocky prominence which matches the Rocher des Doms on the east side of the river. It became known as the **Fort St-André**, after a Benedictine monastery founded there in the tenth century, and its formidable walls still enclose some remains of the abbey.

By far the most important place in Villeneuve – more important even than the Hotel du Prieuré – is the **Chartreuse du Val-de-Bénédiction**. A 'Chartreuse' was a monastic foundation of the Carthusian order, founded in 1084 by St Bruno, who was Chancellor of the diocese of Reims. This was fourteen years before the move to Cîteaux by Robert of Molesme, which founded the Cistercian order in protest against the increasingly lax Benedictine rule, and the Carthusians were the most austere of all the communities of the Catholic church. They were also the most highly organised, as a visit to any of their centres will prove. The name probably comes from Chatrousse, a village in the Dauphiné near which was built the headquarters of the order, the Grande Chartreuse. Our own mediaeval Charter-house, in the city of London, has the same origin; before the school which inherited its name moved out to the Surrey countryside its 'Carthusian' pupils may have considered their regime equally austere.

The Chartreuse of Villeneuve was built in 1356 by Innocent

VI, who succeeded Clement VI as Pope in Avignon, a gesture of respect for the head of the order who had been elected Pope before him but was too humble to assume the office of Christ's Vicar on earth. It took its beautiful name from the site, the Val de Bénédiction at the foot of Mount Andaon, where Innocent VI had lived as a cardinal. It was built on the scale of a small village, cut off from its surroundings by high walls. The elaborate entrance gateway, which now leads off the rue de la République into a pleasant avenue of mulberry trees, was a much later addition.

Today the mood is friendly rather than austere, and the reception point for visitors is immediately under the town's *École de Danse*, as you may hear from the piano music and the tread of dancers' feet above. You will be provided with an annotated plan of the establishment, which is easy to follow and has a recommended route. You come first to the *abbatiale*, or abbey church, of which the apse was destroyed in the Revolution. Still there is the flamboyant tomb of Innocent VI, who was buried here in 1362. Next comes the Little Cloister, a charming Gothic ensemble with a chapter-house and a two-storied office for the Sacristan. From here a long corridor runs along beside the *Cloître du Cimetière*, the most typical and distinctive feature of a Chartreuse.

There are two categories of Carthusian monk, the *Pères* (addressed as 'Dom', short for *dominus*) who live an isolated life in their cells, and the *Frères* who live communally as in other institutions. All down the right-hand side of this cloister are the cells of the Pères, and the first one you come to is open to view – and quite a surprise. 'Cell' seems hardly the word for a comfortable living space on two floors, with a garden below at the back. The austerity, you come to realise, lies in the complete isolation of a *Père* from his fellows, whom he meets only at mealtimes on Sundays and on the feast days of the calendar. During the week his only meal (at midday) is put through a little hatch at the bottom of his private staircase, so there is absolutely no contact with the outside to disturb his solitary life of prayer, study and manual work. The workroom (for carpentry, book-binding or whatever) is on the ground floor, with a little garden outside where he can cultivate both flowers and herbs. Above it is a light and airy study-bedroom with a fireplace, work desk and bookshelves, a bed in an alcove, and a privy with a stone seat – perhaps the only obvious sign of austerity.

At the end of the corridor is a complex of rooms on two floors called a *bugade*, which was in the first place a laundry and has a big fireplace for drying linen. Above it is a little chapel, and cells which could be occupied by sick monks; each has its own squint window through which the occupant could see Mass being celebrated in the chapel, and each has its own privy. There are also cells for prisoners committed there by the Prior, who had judicial power over a community of some three hundred lay bodies as well as souls.

The central purpose of the *Cloître du Cimetière* is what its name suggests, as a burial ground for departed monks. One by one they were buried in this elongated rectangle of hallowed ground, with only a plain wooden cross to mark the spot. God would know who they were. You complete the circuit on the far side of the cloister, coming at the end of the corridor to a cross passage which leads on the left to a little chapel which served the *cimetière*; up a short flight of steps on the right is another almost circular chapel which was part of the original cardinal's dwelling. This has some exceptionally beautiful frescos, painted in grey-green tones by the same Matteo Giovanetti who decorated the chapel of St Martial and the Pope's study in the Palais des Papes. If not on the lookout for this chapel you might easily miss it – it is attached to one end of the Refectory, which had been the cardinal's Tinel, or banqueting hall, now opened only for exhibitions.

Not included in the visit for which you have to pay, though accessible direct from the point of entry, is the *Grande Cloître de St-Jean*, a handsome open space with a rotunda in the middle.

This once covered a large water cistern, known as a *vasque*, from which when it was full the water escaped through holes in the upright stone slabs all round it, and so into runnels which carried it to all parts.

Before leaving Villeneuve you should walk or drive down to the southern end of the rue de la Republique, if only to see the two treasures of the *Musée municipale*, housed in the Hôtel Pierre de Luxembourg opposite the Hôtel-de-Ville. The first is the unique fourteenth-century ivory figure of the Virgin, carved in the round from an elephant's tusk, following its natural curve. The other is to be found on the first floor, the *Coronation of the Virgin* painted by Enguerrand Charenton in 1453 and a minor masterpiece – one of the finest primitives by a French painter.

The ivory Virgin came from the sacristy of the collegial **Church of Notre-Dame** next door. Like St-Didier in Avignon this is a good early example of Provençal Gothic – a style which came much later to Provence than to Burgundy – with the familiar high nave, no side aisles, chapels to north and south. The east end has been totally rebuilt, and is capped by a large fortified tower; the west end is lit by a very high Gothic window – in England we should call it Perpendicular. The church was founded in 1333 by the same Cardinal de Via who built the Petit Palais in Avignon and had a *livrée* here too; the ivory Virgin was a present from him. On the north side is the fourteenth-century cloister, very plain and dignified in a soft grey stone.

The logical place to go next is **Châteauneuf-du-Pape**, though these days the name means a wine rather than a castle. The cardinals could spend the hot summer months in their *livrées* at Villeneuve, but the Popes required something grander and more secure. They built this castle on the high ground between Avignon and Orange as the summer residence of the Papal court, and this site must have been just what they needed. Presumably they also planted vineyards to supply the needs of their table, but Châteauneuf only became known as a top vintage wine of the Côtes du Rhône in the eighteenth century. By that time the château had been reduced to a ruin in the wars of religion, and all you can see after further wanton destruction by the Germans in 1944 is a dramatic fragment on a green and windy hilltop. As Shelley said of the legs of Ozymandias, 'nothing beside remains'.

Yet the Popes, safe within their walls, could survey from their towers the whole of their subject territory – the city of Avignon, the Comtat Venaissin, the Enclave des Papes – as well as the mountains of the Baronnies, Ventoux and Luberon, the plateau of Vaucluse, the Dentelles of Montmirail. Such *grandeur* was no *folie*, and at least today we can share their view. We can also drink to them (if we have the price of a bottle) in the wine made from the modern vineyards which fill the foreground of the view, and (with the same *caveat*) in the Hostellerie du Château des Fines Roches, set among its own vineyards a few kilometres to the south-east. We can do the same in less elegant surroundings at the local Mule-du-Pape restaurant, and toast Alphonse Daudet as well.

A short final sortie of some interest from Avignon takes you out through the north-eastern suburbs along the N100. The road itself is horribly busy, but it leads to a place which is holy ground in modern Provence. Soon after the bridge over the autoroute comes the village of Châteauneuf-de-Gardagne, and just north of that is what Mistral describes as the 'bastide de plaisance' of **Font-Ségugne**. There is nothing of material interest here now, but in 1854 the little château belonged to the family of Gièra, who were hosts on the memorable 'dimanche fleuri, le 21 mai' when the seven founder members of the *Félibrige* met to organise the rebirth of the Provençal language – the 'langue d'oc' of the south – which had long been the dream of Frédéric Mistral. The names of the other six – Gièra, Roumanille, Aubanel, Mathieu, Brunet, Tavan – are hardly known outside Provence today, though Roumanille was Mistral's tutor at his last school in Avignon, and Mathieu was his accomplice in several escapades at Aix-en-Provence.

Only four and a half kilometres further on is **le Thor**, where the church (sometimes known as Notre-Dame-du-Lac) is one of the finest of all in the Provençal Romanesque tradition – though few people stop to admire it. The town suffers from being on a main road, but it has preserved some of its mediaeval dignity thanks to a fourteenth-century town gate which keeps the traffic at arm's length, and there is a quiet corner behind the church where the Sorgue runs in a broad stream under a noble bridge. Le Thor used to be famous for its vineyards, not because they produced a famous wine, but for a grape which was the most popular table variety of its time. Though the Chasselas is still grown and marketed, this corner of Vaucluse is so well watered by the many channels of the Sorgue that far more acres have been planted with fruit trees and laid out as market gardens. The people of le Thor are convinced that the name is another version of *le Taureau*, and they have adopted the bull as the town's symbol. Certainly the solid, humped outline of the parish church supports the fancy, and they say that in spite of standing for centuries with its feet in the water of several underground channels it has never shifted on its foundations.

When you come closer you will see that **Notre-Dame-de-l'Assomption** (or Notre-Dame-du-Lac, as it is sometimes appropriately called) is a masterpiece of Romanesque architecture. The outside, except for the final *lanternon* of the belfry, is pure Romanesque, with the principal entrance from the south. This has a porch flanked by columns and their capitals which are richly and imaginatively carved; the whole is enclosed in a classical façade with flat fluted pilasters to either side and a neat sundial above. If you look closely at the statue over the actual entrance you will see that Our Lady (carved in walnut wood) has a Provençal head-dress. The western entrance is simpler, but still classical in design, with a triangular pediment such as we saw at St Restitut.

The inside is magnificent. One is used now to the high Provençal nave; here it is comparatively short, with very early

Gothic vaulting, and it leads into a choir and apse of great distinction. The tall octagonal cupola over the choir is a brilliant design. Its eight sides each have double interior arches, with columns at all the corners; the *trompes*, or squinches, which convert it from the square, are carved like scallop shells and incorporate the symbols of the four evangelists and the Lamb of God.

If you still have time to spare and like grottos, the one just north of here at **Thouzon** is more interesting than some. It was discovered in 1902 during mining operations in an old quarry, and follows the dried-up bed of an underground river for about 250 yards, with needle-sharp stalactites hanging from its roof. It opens under a low hill with ruins of a castle and a monastery on top. There are plenty of rivers above ground too in this low-lying, almost marshy area. A mile or two further along the N100 is the well named **Isle-sur-la-Sorgue**, where the river Sorgue divides into several channels as it runs in from its source at the Fontaine de Vaucluse. Its two main arms literally encircle the town, and the streams proliferate when both arms divide again, and a smaller fifth channel runs through the town centre, passing close to the church. This is a mainly baroque building, and there is more fun to be had in seeking out the six old water wheels which drove the machinery for the town's weaving and paper industries, as well as for its corn and oil mills. Its outskirts are given over to more modern industries, but in the old town you can still walk along the quays beside water in the shade of plane trees – one of the quays is named after Frédéric Mistral.

Frédéric Mistral, poet of Provence: statue in the Place du Forum

Orange: Roman Theatre

Gigondas: chapel of Sts Côme-et-Damien

St-Jalle: Romanesque west doorway

Church of St-Trinit: south entrance

Abbaye de Sénanque: the cloister

Pont Julien – Roman bridge over the Cavaillon

Left: Early rock burials at St-Pantaléon

Below: Château de Barbentane

Right: The cemetery chapel of St Gabriel

Below: Arles: western gateway of St-Trophime

Opposite: Arles: the cathedral of St-Trophime

Arles: les Alyscamps

Arles: cloister of St-Trophime

7

From Avignon to Arles

If you follow the left bank of the Rhône below Avignon you will find yourself in a countryside and among places which are central to the spirit and history of Provence. Tarascon, Maillane, St-Rémy, les Baux, Fontvieille, Montmajour – the names combine so many strands of its history. Much of it is familiar country, but immediately south of Avignon there is a little patch which few know anything about. The **Montagnette** is bounded to the north by the Durance just before it joins the Rhône; to the south it tapers off to a point close to Tarascon, and its western boundary is the Rhône itself. It rises distinct above the alluvial plain, a mixture of high moorland with intervening belts of broad-leaved woods.

You can approach the Montagnette from either bank of the river below Avignon, and the first place of interest is **Barbentane**, where bishops of Arles and Avignon lived from as early as the ninth century. Their castle had much the same fate as the Château Neuf of the Popes; what people come to see now is the *château de plaisance* built in 1674 by François Puget, a dignitary of the town who was created marquis de Barbentane by Louis XIV. A more famous member of the same family was Pierre Puget, born in Marseille and better known as a sculptor and painter; he may have had a hand in the architecture of the château. You first see its classical façade across the vista of green lawns, parterres and ornamental water, and the sight is guaranteed to put the visitor in a good humour. So are the guided visits, well managed and informative, which you can enjoy at the usual hours during the summer – though in April, May, June and October the château is closed on Wednesdays.

The furnishings inside range from the elegance of Louis XIII to the rococo of Louis XV, but all have been well chosen by the family who have lived here since the place was built. Some of the portraits have a special interest. There is a marvellously frank one of François de Barbentane, with his great nose, and next to it a sweet one of Henriette, who married Louis XIV's military engineer, the Maréchal de Vauban. She was the daughter of the marquis who was ambassador to the Grand Duke of Tuscany in the reign of Louis XV, which explains the Italian influence in a good deal of the décor. The *grand salon* overdoes the rococo theme, with a marble basin fed by spouts issuing on either side of a statue of Venus, but on the whole this is a very civilised family home, in which childrens' toys feature among the antiques.

The *chambre du marquis* on the ground floor has an ingenious arrangement by which his bed is flanked by corner cabinets in panelled wood – one a *cabinet de toilette*, the other a *garderobe* (not to be translated as 'wardrobe'). Both could be serviced from a corridor at the back, which made 'slopping out' a more discreet process than usual. There was the same arrangement in Henriette's bedroom on the first floor, and these hidden passages are a feature of the house, running behind all the main living rooms, so that servants could rarely be seen going about their work. They are still used by the family for strategic retreats during visiting hours.

In the town the church of **Notre-Dame-de-Grace** began as a single-naved Romanesque building in the thirteenth century, but it has been much altered since. Opposite is the **Maison des Chevaliers**, where François Puget lived before he was made a

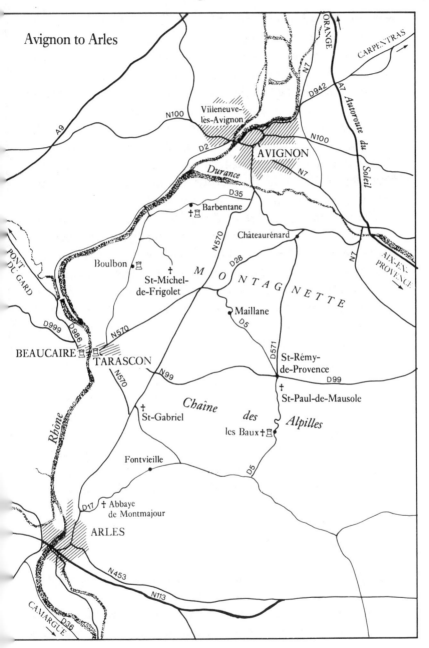

Avignon to Arles

marquis. It had at one time been the Hôtel-de-Ville, and the frontage on the little square is a delight – two wide arched openings at ground level, with a low pillared gallery above, ideal for speech-making or declaring election results.

From Barbentane the D35 runs west as far as the new bridge over the Rhône, then south along the left bank to the village of **Boulbon**. Its few houses are overlooked imperiously by the battlements of a *château-fort* built about 1400 by the counts of Provence to cover their western border at this strategic point. You can climb up to the outside of the main entrance, and though there is no admittance you can see what a dramatic site it is. On the northern edge of the village, up an incline off the main road and surrounded by a large cemetery, is the chapel of **St-Marcellin**. This is a little Romanesque beauty with a charmingly simple west doorway, but it opens its doors only occasionally for a Mass, and notably on 1 June, its saint's own day. Then it plays a part in the celebration of the *saint vinage*, sometimes known as the *procession des bouteilles*. Mistral describes it for us in *Mes Origines*, his most endearing work:

'On the first day of June the men of Boulbon go there in procession, each carrying a bottle of wine in his hand . . . Once inside the chapel the curé of Boulbon turns towards the people and says "Now, brothers, uncork your bottles and pray silence for the blessing". Next, wearing a scarlet cope, he solemnly chants the formula for the blessing of the wine. Then having said "amen" we used to make the sign of the Cross and each took a mouthful. The curé and the mayor clinked glasses together on the steps of the altar, and drank reverently.'

Next day, very sensibly considering that the procession went on through the village refreshing itself as it went, was declared a holiday. If there had been a spell of dry weather which threatened the harvest, they carried the bust of St Marcellin right round the village boundaries, thus conforming with the old saying in Boulbon:

Saint Marcellin
Bon pour l'eau, bon pour le vin

Women were not allowed to take part in the *procession des bouteilles*; as girls they had always been taught that 'water will make you a beauty'.

The wine they blessed and drank was excellent stuff from the *commune* of Frigolet, and this introduces another site in the Montagnette which has a more personal connection with Mistral – though there is no hurry to go there in the heat of the day. It will not be open anyway between twelve and two o'clock, so if you find yourself *en route* from either Barbentane or Boulbon to the abbey of **St-Michel-de-Frigolet**, look for a quiet place for a picnic in the woods. If it should be May or early June you will have a nightingale to sing to you, a cuckoo calling overhead, and swallowtail butterflies cavorting in the clearings. St-Michel is almost level with Boulbon on the far side of the ridge, and to hit the approach road you have to go back a short way towards Barbentane.

The abbey was founded in the tenth century by monks from the much greater abbey of Montmajour near Arles, though most of its original buildings date from the twelfth century when it was ruled by the bishops of Avignon. Nothing is known of its later history until the Revolution, when its lands were sold off and the monastic buildings were deserted. In about 1835 a down-and-out batchelor from Cavaillon bought them (on credit) to set up a boarding school. Among the parents he persuaded to send him their sons was the father of Frédéric Mistral, who thought it was the only way to cure his habit of playing truant from his day-school in Maillane. The move was only partly successful, for Frédéric at the age of nine was happy to run wild with his schoolfellows in the natural playground of the Montagnette. Round the abbey it was all moorland, covered with wild lavender, rosemary and thyme (in Provençale thyme is called *férigoulo*, which explains the name Frigolet). Wild figs and almond trees grew where they could, and there were patches of untended vines. Mistral remembers how 'l'odeur du montagne, dès qu'il faisait du soleil, nous rendait ivres'. It was after two years of this, during which very little was learnt, that his parents decided to send him to a stricter regime in Avignon.

The later history of the abbey is a strange one, and it explains what you find there today. The school survived only a few years, but in 1854 the buildings were bought by one Père Edmond, a member of the 'Premonstratensian' fraternity of Augustinian or 'White' friars. They took their name from the village of Prémontré near Laon in Picardy, where the fraternity was founded early in the twelfth century; its site had been prophetically pointed out – *prémontré* – to its founder St Norbert.

Père Edmond was a remarkable and ambitious man, combining the characters of zealous preacher and practical *entrepreneur*. Within twenty years he had attracted a good hundred followers, built a grand new *abbatiale* and surrounded the whole establishment with crenellated walls. It was so popular with the neighbourhood that in 1880, when the republican government decided to break up the monastic communities, a thousand people took part in a sit-in to prevent the law being enforced. An absurd week-long siege followed, with a whole army brigade encamped outside the walls, taunted at every opportunity by the girls of Boulbon and Barbentane.

One explanation why the Prémontré community became so popular and prosperous was put forward by Daudet in his *Lettres de mon moulin*. The story of 'L'élixir du Reverend Père Gaucher' tells how the cowherd Gaucher (who counted as a lay brother because he worked within the precincts) inherited from his aunt the recipe for a wonderful liqueur distilled from the local herbs. The abbot set him up in a distillery of his own, and the monks marketed the 'elixir' at great profit to the monastery. Unfortunately Gaucher, who had been rewarded with the honorific title of *Père*, became so badly addicted to his own product that he was liable to break out into coarse ditties during Vespers, and therefore qualified for eternal damnation. The abbot's solution was to allow him to celebrate Vespers in his distillery, and to write into the script of the liturgy a special prayer for the sinner which, as it were, absolved him even while he was sinning. This pleasant fable may have been a compliment to Père Edmond's business sense, but it remains true that the fortunes of the abbey changed dramatically during his time, and that an excellent liqueur is indeed distilled from the Frigolet wine and flavoured with the herbs of the Montagnette.

During the first world war the monastery was used as a prisoner-of-war camp, but since then the White Friars have returned, the *loi de St Norbert* prevails again, and – shades of Frédéric Mistral – school parties come here on holiday to study history and ecology. If you find 'Premonstratensian' a mouthful, and the order seems as outlandish as its name, you only need to go to the popular village of Storrington in West Sussex to find it has a home there too, though not in such distinguished buildings.

The principal church, or *abbatiale*, is a nineteenth-century basilica of hideous aspect, gaudy within, badly proportioned without. It does however incorporate the basically twelfth-century chapel of **Notre-Dame-de-Bon-Remède** as an extension of the north transept, though to look at it you would hardly credit such an early date. What happened was that Anne of Austria came here to pray for a 'remedy' for her childlessness, and was rewarded by the birth of Louis XIV in 1638 – quite a contribution by the abbey to the history of Europe. In gratitude the queen presented the chapel with a set of painted and gilded wooden panels which have transformed its character.

Visitors to the abbey are shown round with great courtesy by one of the white-habited friars, but not of course while any of the church offices are going on. The cloister takes us genuinely back to the twelfth century, but best of all is the little former

abbey church of **St-Michel**, which has been beautifully restored. It has all the simplicity and strength of its period, and the
apse has been reconstructed in its original undressed stone. To
the left of the choir is a charming marble figure of the *Vierge
laitante*, where she is giving suck to a baby of appropriate age
and size.

The Montagnette is an anomaly, but the wide and fertile
Rhône valley which encloses it is already narrowing as the bare
rocky chain of the Alpilles comes into view to the south. In the
centre of the triangle of Châteaurenard, St-Rémy and Tarascon
is the village of **Maillane**, famous for only one thing. It was the
birthplace and life-long home of the most renowned man of
Provence since the Roi René. Frédéric Mistral was born here in
1830, and we have followed him through some of his early
schooling. It was the second school he attended in Avignon
which turned his enthusiasm for writing poetry in the Provençal
language into a crusade for establishing it as a national literary
medium. This was because his most admired teacher was
Joseph Roumanille, who shared the same enthusiasm and joined
Mistral and five other friends at Font-Ségune in founding the
fraternity of the Félibrige. The title was pure serendipity. In *Mes
Origines* Mistral tells us that they were at a loss for a name which
would cover their activities, when he discovered a traditional
story of St Anselm in which the Virgin describes the moment
when she found the child Jesus disputing in the Temple with
'les sept *félibres* de la Loi'. Nobody knew quite what the word
meant in that context, but it was immediately obvious to the
seven friends that it described them perfectly, and they seized
on *félibrige* as the collective noun for the association.

If you can find a copy of *Mes Origines* there is no better way of
getting to know this handsome, kindly, generous and dedicated
man, whose memory still just keeps alive the cause for which he
fought. To wade through the long-drawn-out cantos of *Miréio*
or *le Poème du Rhône*, even in the standard French of his own
translation, is a bit like reading the whole of a verse drama by

Shelley or Browning, though they describe a more real way of life, and it was that which Mistral was as keen to record as he was to revive the language itself. We shall see how well he succeeded when we come to the *Muséon Arlaten* which he founded in Arles, but it was for his use of the language that he won the Nobel prize for literature in 1904.

There are three houses in Maillane where he lived at different times, one of which has been turned into a museum with the usual personal relics of his long life – which he ended here in 1914. The little farm of the Mas du Juge, on the road to Graveson, was his childhood home, and for him it always stood for the homely qualities of Provençal life. So did his parents, who recognised their son's talents and gave him so much practical support. It was from Maillane that Mistral set out to take his *baccalauréat* at Nîmes, and to read for his law degree at Aix-en-Provence.

Joseph Roumanille was born at **St-Rémy-de-Provence**, a few kilometres down the road from Maillane. The town is called after St Remigius, and those who remember their Latin might be excused for thinking he was a boatman on the Rhône, but in fact he was the bishop of Reims who baptised King Clovis in 496. He is supposed to have revived a young girl here from the dead, but what he was doing so far away from Reims is not clear – though this typically Provençal town has known many 'foreign' visitors. Gounod came here in 1863 when he was working with Mistral on the opera *Mireille* (adapted from the epic *Miréio*) for which he composed the music; Albert Schweitzer was interned here during the first world war, and Gertrude Stein arrived to do some writing in 1922. On the other hand the sixteenth-century astrologer-physician Nostradamus was a native of St-Rémy, born here in 1503, though he spent most of his life at Salon-de-Provence. The most famous temporary resident was Vincent Van Gogh, but that was as an inmate of the former priory of St-Paul-de-Mausole, which was turned into a mental asylum after the Revolution.

The story of the Dutch painter who captured the aura of Provence better than any other Impressionist, even Cézanne, and whose work now sells for millions, is familiar to even more millions: how he came to Arles in 1888 to try painting in the magical light of the Rhône valley; how he quarrelled with Gauguin, and had bouts of insanity during one of which he cut off his ear and delivered it by hand to an Arlésienne; how he voluntarily entered the asylum at St-Paul and there painted some of his most evocative pictures; how he took his own life in Paris only two months after his release in 1890.

The old priory of **St-Paul-de-Mausole** took its name from the Roman 'mausoleum' a few hundred yards down the road to les Baux. The St Paul of its dedication is the same early father who is commemorated at St-Paul-Trois-Châteaux, and tradition says that a chapel was first built here to shelter the miraculous staff which flowered to confirm him as bishop of the Tricastin. The foundation was dissolved during the Revolution; it has remained true to its sad but useful new calling for nearly two hundred years, and there can be few more peaceful homes for the afflicted.

Nowadays it is called a 'psychiatric treatment centre', with a clinical wing and residential quarters, and you approach it by a pleasant garden walk. On your left you pass a bust of the painter, *sans oreille*. The monastery church of St-Paul has a short Lombardic tower; its façade belongs to the eighteenth century, but inside all is pure Romanesque, well restored, on the familiar Provençal plan; the glass is modern throughout. There is a typical early twelfth-century cloister, small, secret and enclosed. Here Van Gogh was installed, with a small studio on the ground floor and a bedroom in the upper gallery, but its more lasting interest is in the great variety of carved capitals on the pillars of the arcading – in particular I enjoy the one on the south side of a centaur delivering a Parthian shot with a crossbow.

Only a few hundred yards separate the simple twelfth-century monastery, with its poignant nineteenth-century associations, from a site far more ancient and complex. The name **Glanum** comes, they say, from a sanctuary established here for the nature god Glan by a shadowy Celtic people connected with the Ligurians of the Alpes Maritimes. The site itself is a curious one, a narrow but shallow defile leading into the foothills of the bare and barren Alpilles, but it attracted later settlers from the third century BC to the third century AD. The most obvious buildings associated with it are the two splendid Roman monuments on the right of the road beyond St-Paul. One is the **Mausoleum** which gave the monastery its name, and it seems to have been a cenotaph dedicated to the memory of the grandsons of Augustus, Caius and Lucius, whose early deaths upset the emperor's plans for the succession. Its three stages – square base carved with battle and hunting scenes, arcaded main storey and circular top with a continuous Corinthian colonnade – have been wonderfully preserved in the clear Provençal air. Less perfect now are the remains of a ceremonial archway – not strictly an *arc de triomphe* (though it may have commemorated the fall of Massilia in 49 BC) but the gateway astride the road which entered Glanum from the west. It probably dates from a little earlier than the Mausoleum, and its imaginative sculpture suggests a Greek rather than a Roman artist at work.

Crossing the road we come to the main area of excavations which began in 1921 under the direction of M. Henri Rolland. The extremely complex ground plan which he revealed is difficult to follow, even with the help of an excellent leaflet you will be offered at the point of entry. This is because one layer of occupation has been superimposed on another in several different epochs, and what you are looking at are in any case only the foundations of buildings with all sorts of different purposes.

The first excavations you come to belong mainly to the Hellenistic period, when settlers of Greek origin arrived from Marseille, and are of houses built in the typically Greek style with small interior courtyards. Where the valley widens you come to an area which is unmistakably Roman even in its

117

foundations. There was a large forum and basilica on the left, and just beyond it on the right a pair of temples, side by side, which can be dated to the last few decades BC. Further up the narrowing defile you come nearer to the spring which was the source of all this development, as we can guess from the remains of a little temple to the left of the far end of the pathway. It was dedicated during a visit by Marcus Agrippa, minister of works to Augustus, to *Valetudo*, the goddess of health, but it was taking advantage of an earlier Celtic cult site. Agrippa, it is worth remembering, planned the basic network of Roman roads in the *provincia*, as well as the sewer system of Rome, and this would have marked his arrival in the neighbourhood in 27 AD. The *source* itself is approached by a flight of Hellenistic steps, so the preoccupation with *valetudo* seems to have run through all the history of Glanum; its spring water must have had special qualities.

Now we come to **les Baux**, seat of one of the most powerful families in the history of Provence. Their castle was planted right on the edge of the highest ridge of the Chaîne des Alpilles, a limestone outcrop with a fantastically distorted skyline. The first count of les Baux we know about had the Saxon-sounding name of Leibulf, and he lived at the end of the eighth century, but the first great landowner to hold the title was Raymond des Baux in the early twelfth century. His possessions ran to seventy-nine towns and castles, among them Salon-de-Provence, Pertuis, St-Rémy, Mondragon in the Tricastin, and Aix-en-Provence. He married the daughter of his overlord, Count Gilbert of Provence, but this marriage was upstaged by his wife's sister when she married Raymond Bérenger, count of Barcelona and Forcalquier, who controlled an even larger part of Provence.

Although the Baux claimed their descent from Balthasar, one of the Three Kings of the Nativity, and used the Star of Bethlehem in their coat of arms, Raymond was eventually forced to acknowledge his sister-in-law's family as the true counts of

Provence. There was a legend that the Three Kings returned to Maillane at the feast of the Epiphany each year – which commended itself to Mistral's imagination. The Baux remained a proud and important family, and their dashing court life attracted all the best troubadours. They were connected by marriage with the noble house of Orange, and so eventually if distantly with the royal house of England.

The last in the direct line was Alix, daughter of another Raymond, Grand Seneschal of Provence. As a young girl she was made a ward of her uncle the vicomte de Turenne, who took possession of the castle of les Baux. After his death his son Raymond de Turenne defied all authority from this impregnable seat and terrorized the country for miles around by open acts of robbery, kidnapping and sadistic cruelty. He was eventually cornered at Tarascon in 1400, and drowned while trying to escape by river. Alix recovered her title and estates, and after her death in 1426 they passed to René, king of Naples and Sicily, and count of all Provence.

René presented the castle to his second wife, Jeanne de Laval, who enjoyed holding court here, but in 1481 René's nephew left it in his will to the French crown in the person of Louis XI. In the sixteenth century one Claude de Manville was appointed Captain of Les Baux, and his family is remembered in several monuments in the town – particularly the Hôtel Manville, now the Hôtel-de-Ville. They were however obstinate supporters of the Protestant cause, and in 1632 Richelieu had the castle destroyed; he sent the bill for the demolition to the inhabitants and fined them 100,000 *livres* as well. That was the end of les Baux as an inhabited town, but the title – upgraded to a marquisate – was presented by the king to the family of Grimaldi, princes of Monaco. So it has turned out that Prince Rainier's son is now styled marquis des Baux.

When we join the hordes of tourists who stream up and down the steep narrow streets today, between mediaeval and Renaissance frontages adapted to serve as cafés, bars, curio shops and restaurants, we may resent what has happened to les Baux, but we should also be grateful, for this is how Sir Theodore Cook described it in 1905:

'It is a squalid little village that nestles today in the centre of the old robber stronghold . . . The place is a confusion of ruins, grown fragmentary and deserted through the gradual withdrawal of the population from a site destroyed by Richelieu's soldiers . . . a mediaeval Pompeii, a Herculaneum without its lava, set among the scarred boulders of the Alpilles in a melancholy landscape all of cinder grey, as might be imagined in some far-off and extinct planet of the frozen interstellar space.'

Even thirty years ago it could be described as a ghost town, where it was considered eerie but romantic to wander through the ruins in the moonlight, so apart from the plague of tourism the restorers and developers deserve credit for what they have rescued from ultimate decay.

In Cook's day there was a 'Hotel de Monte Carlo' in the village, where he says 'lunch is a perilous adventure, and any other form of hospitality impossible'. Now you can lunch, dine, or stay the night if you can afford it, at M. Thillier's Ousteau de Baumàniere, which in the Guide Michelin claims no fewer than five red knives and forks and three rosettes for cuisine. It also advertises 'demeures anciennes amenagées avec elegance', 'terrasses fleuries', and even a 'club hippique'. Much has changed since 1905.

In spite of everything the site remains unique. In the village itself there are a few quiet corners and one exceptional building. In following the long winding trail up to the ruined castle not everyone finds their way to the Place St-Vincent, which makes room for itself on a separate spur projecting to the west. The **Church of St-Vincent** has three short aisles – they have to be short because the site is blocked by rock to the east, and the resulting building is almost square. The central nave is Romanesque, dating from the time of Raymond des Baux, but the right hand aisle is certainly Carolingian, with two side chapels of the same period; one chapel has a primitive stone altar, the other a baptismal font carved out of the rock. In contrast, the aisle to the left belongs to more sophisticated times, with its late Gothic vaulting and appropriately decorated tombs of the Manvilles. To complete the catalogue of centuries the glass is all modern, designed by the artist Max Ingrand and presented to the church by Prince Rainier of Monaco.

On the opposite side of the square, perched on the edge of the rocky precipice, is the chapel of the **Penitents Blancs**, dating as usual from the seventeenth century and the time of the Manvilles. It was restored in 1936, and some rather bland murals of the Provençal countryside were painted for it by Yves Brayer. From here you are overlooking the Vallon de la Fontaine, which contains not only the Ousteau de Baumanière but the stylish little Renaissance building known as the **Pavillon de la Reine Jeanne**. This in fact dates only from 1581, a century after René's second queen lived here, and even longer after the notorious Queen Jeanne of Naples sold Avignon to the Pope.

To reach the far eastern ridge on which the castle stood, you have to follow the main pathway, the rue du Trencat, uphill all the way to the southern end of the ridge, round the monument to Charloun Rieu, one of the adherents of the Félibres, and skirt the eastern precipice till you get there. You may be disconcerted to find that before you leave the rue du Trencat you have to buy a ticket at the barrier beside the Musée Lapidaire before you can begin the long climb. At the end of it all there are only the gaunt ruins of the thirteenth-century *donjon*, and it needs a lot of imagination to people them with the wealthy, arrogant and pleasure-loving family which lived here for so long. By the end of the fourteenth century they had by all accounts made themselves as comfortable as the Popes in Avignon, and the inventory taken on the death of Alix des Baux sounds like the contents of Aladdin's cave. It is easier to imagine the infamous Raymond de Turenne gleefully precipitating his prisoners for whom no ransom had arrived into space over the sheer cliffs. If you can hold your ground on a windy day the view is unparalleled, but don't go too near the edge.

People used to speculate about the underground passages and galleries which turn parts of the Alpilles into a vast honeycomb. Talk of secret escape routes or hide-outs has proved to be nonsense; the mineral known as bauxite, an essential ingredient of aluminium, is still mined in the neighbourhood, and these are the worked-out galleries of earlier years.

Now back towards the Rhône at Tarascon, a name which resounds with echos of Old Provence. It lies only eighteen kilometres west of les Baux, and once you have left the Alpilles behind there is an easy road through the valley. Stop just before the D33 joins the main road from Arles to Tarascon, and make sure you locate the chapel of **St-Gabriel** – up a steep overgrown path to the right of the road. Among all the little chapels of Provence there is nothing like this. The first sight of its west end as you push your way up past the straggling fig trees and flowering shrubs will make you stop and reach for your camera. Rarely has such felicity been achieved in so small a compass. The plain doorway is framed by a Romanesque archway with a sculptured tympanum; this is enclosed by a classical portico with Corinthian pillars each side, and a little pediment which incorporates a rectangular plaque with more carving and two rows of lettering above it. The whole is enfolded in a lovely wide arch, and the surface of the final gable is broken up by a blind semicircular arch of the same radius; inside this is set an exquisitely decorated *oculus* window around which float the symbols of the four evangelists.

As you come nearer the details of the sculpture stand out. The tympanum presents on the left a naïve picture of Daniel in the lions' den, while to the right Adam and Eve are standing apart in manifest shame on either side of the 'forbidden tree' and a smug-looking serpent. The plaque in the centre of the pediment illustrates the story of the Annunciation and the Visitation; its three arcaded spaces enclose the characters in the story. Thus on the left is the winged archangel Gabriel, whose chapel it is; in the centre is Mary; to the right she stands beside her cousin Elizabeth. The panel looks incomplete, and the stylised 'head-on' portraits suggest an earlier date than the sophisticated detail of the rest of the façade, but the composition is still delightful, with lively-looking birds cocking an eye at you between the curves of the arches. The beautiful lettering proves to be the opening words of the archangel's salutation: 'Ave Maria, gra (tiae) plena', and below them the names of the three characters.

The inside of the chapel is as plain as its façade is elaborate. There are just three Romanesque bays to the single nave, with substantial piers, and the floor rises with the level of the ground beneath to end in a simple apse, semicircular inside but five-sided when seen from without. The only lighting comes from the *oculus* in the western gable and the little slit window in the apse, almost obscured by the rising ground to the east.

Though seldom used today, St-Gabriel was built by and for one of the five corporations of the boatmen of Arles. It would have stood just clear of the marshy swamps which once separated the region of the Alpilles from Tarascon and the banks of the Rhône. Below it the boatmen kept their flat rafts, made buoyant by inflated animal bladders, on which they ferried passengers and goods across the intervening canals, dykes and lagoons. They had plenty of custom, for it was an important link in the overland trade route from Marseille to the Tarascon-Beaucaire river crossing, and it was a bad day for the boatmen when the marshes were drained. Thank goodness their lovely chapel has survived.

Tarascon has ensured its place in the history and folklore of Provence not only because of the magnificent mediaeval castle which commands a vital crossing of the Rhône, though it would have been nothing without it. The crossing itself had existed since earliest recorded times, made first by a ford, then by a pontoon bridge and later by a succession of stone bridges. The rock which is the foundation of the castle rises sheer from the bed of the river at one of its narrowest points. The Romans had built a fort here, but the present castle was built towards the end of the fourteenth century, and it saw the beginning of the last and most splendid chapter in the history of independent Provence.

The turning point in that history came when Beatrice, youngest of the four beautiful daughters of Raymond Bérenger IV of Forcalquier, count of Provence, married Charles, the brother of saintly Louis IX of France – who had already married the eldest of the four girls. Charles brought with him the title of duc d'Anjou, and later acquired that of King of Naples and Sicily; it was his descendant Louis II of Anjou who built most of the castle we see now. Alix des Baux left him the bulk of her personal property and treasures, and when she died in 1426 they were brought for safety to his new stronghold. When his eldest son Louis III died childless in 1434 all his titles – Anjou, Naples, Sicily and Provence – passed to his younger son René. There had been constant skirmishes between the counts of Provence and their powerful neighbours the dukes of Burgundy, and at the time of his brother's death René was a prisoner of Philippe le Bon of Burgundy in his palace at Dijon. He ransomed himself by ceding some of his property in the north to the duke, re-entered Provence in triumph, and on 2 December installed himself in his father's castle at Tarascon.

By this time the substance of his royal titles had lapsed – he had no influence in either Naples or Sicily – but he was happy to keep the style of 'roi' and maintained a palace in Aix-en-Provence, now the provincial capital. The dukedom of Anjou also entitled him to a seat at Angers on the Loire, but he always preferred Tarascon to them both. Like les Baux in its best days it became a centre of the extravagant but civilised aristocratic life of fifteenth-century France – a contrast with that of the rough barons then involved in our Wars of the Roses, most of them still in their grim Norman castles.

Unlike his neighbours in Burgundy, King René was on good terms with Charles VII of France, who with the aid of Joan of Arc had seen off the English claim to his territories. His influence was strong outside Provence, and when peace came he received the English ambassadors in Tours, and betrothed his daughter Margaret of Anjou to Henry VI. Among his descendants (through his younger daughter Yolande) were the dukes of Guise, the Hapsburg emperors and Marie Antoinette of France.

'Le bon roi René', as his subjects and their descendants liked to call him, was a generous and kindly man of many talents. He encouraged writers and artists – especially painters of the Flemish school – and he was deeply interested both in the history of Provence and in the well-being of his subjects. It was he who sent a commission to search for the relics of the 'Saintes Maries' in the crypt of their church on the shores of the Camargue; it was successful in that the bones they found were authenticated by the Pope, and the lower chapel (where the image of the black servant Sara now stands) was built by his order in 1449.

At the same time he founded the Order of the Crescent, as a counter to the Order of the Golden Fleece founded by Philippe le Bon of Burgundy. He celebrated the occasion with the famous 'Tournoi de Tarascon', described by Louis de Beavau, Grand Seneschal of Provence. In the words of Theodore Cook, which catch the spirit of the time:

'People streamed into Tarascon from Avignon, Marseilles, Aix, Salon, Nîmes, Montpellier and Arles, and on the 3rd of June the fun began with a tilt between Pierre Carrion and Philippe de Lénoncourt, who came from Lorraine, and the encounters went on every afternoon from twelve to six. Tanneguy du Châtel, nephew of the famous provost of

Paris, went into the lists with the lovely Honorade de
Pontevès-Cabanes behind him on his charger, but only just
saved her from disaster after the the furious onslaught of
Ferry de Lorraine, who eventually obtained the prize.

René himself brought fresh lances into the arena when
Gaspard de Cossa (brother of Marguerite de Lascaris)
broke his weapon. The jousting ended with a round
between Jean Bézelin and Lénoncourt, after which everyone sat down to a feast provided by Louis de Beauvau, and
the gay company only parted with the greatest regret for
their own homes.'

One of the delighted spectators would have been René's wife,
Isobel de Lorraine, who died at Angers in 1453. For some time
after her death he kept away from the scene of their happy and
lively days at Tarascon, but he was well consoled by his second
marriage to the young Jeanne de Laval. Their portraits are
included in the colourful triptych by Nicholas Froment, known
as 'le Buisson Ardent', which can be seen in the cathedral of
St-Sauveur in Aix.

In contrast to the ruins of les Baux, the castle of Tarascon is
easy to populate with the figures of its past. Seen from the
outside it stands sternly on a low rocky projection, with its feet
almost in the Rhône, a compact and formidable fortress. You
approach it from beside the huge open space created by an
American bombardment in 1944, now gratefully used by tourists
as a car park. The bridge over the moat leads into a sunken open
space, with the main fortress on your left and the other
appurtenances, or *basse cour*, to the right. The walls seem
enormous and frightening as you cross a second bridge to enter
the ground floor of the *donjon*, but once inside the *cour d'honneur*
everything changes.

The space is small and intimate. Round it rise the façades of
royal apartments and rooms of state, well lit by mullioned
windows. The upper storeys are reached by two matching spiral

stairways, entered from either side of the courtyard through shamelessly flamboyant doorways. The queen's chamber on the first floor had a little gallery, or loggia, from which she and the king could look down on command performance by minstrels, jugglers, and companies performing miracle plays – an art form which René particularly encouraged. That we can enjoy all this now is thanks to the *École des Beaux Arts*, who began to restore the castle in 1926 after more than a century's penance as a state prison. The great rooms are bare of furniture, but they have magnificent *cheminées*, and some have seventeenth-century Flemish tapestries on their walls.

Another kind of decoration will remind you of sadder times, for in several rooms there are *graffiti* carved or scratched by prisoners taken at sea by the French in the eighteenth century. The names are all of English or Welsh seamen – Samuel Abigail of Great Yarmouth, Edward Wright of Stockton, Charles Morgan of Newport. John Wallters (*sic*) tells us he was 'Taken in the Constantine Privateer of Bristol on the 19th Day of February Landed on the Island of Minorca the 9th Day of March Brought to Toulon the 28th Brought to the Castle Tenth Day of April 1747'. Lodged in the former *chambre du roi* on the second floor were three poor messmates who may have cheered themselves up a little by scratching on the wall to the left of the door:

'Here is three Davids in one Mess
Prisoners we are in distress
By the French we was caught
And to this prison we was brought.'

Their names appear beside the inscription – David Siday of London, David Howarth of Hull, and a third David whose surname and home port are indecipherable. They were captured in 1778, and we are glad to see that their ordeal was short, for they also record their release in 1779.

More dramatic things happened on the battlemented terrace

above in 1794, when the infuriated inhabitants turned on the local adherents of Robespierre and threw them off the battlements into the Rhône. They would have had a softer landing than the victims of Raymond de Turenne at les Baux, but it seems that they all perished.

One reason for René's popularity was that he had the sense to want his people to have a good time, just as much as his family and courtiers. In 1469 he seized on the ancient legend of the **Tarasque** to inaugurate a popular festival in the town. This was a spectacular monster of the *genus* dragon who in the first century AD used to swim up the Rhône and carry off anybody who happened to be near the river – especially the washerwomen from the river bank, but cattle and children too. The Tarasque was finally subdued, not by a St George in shining armour, but by St Martha, a late addition to the mysterious boatload which landed in the Camargue with the three Marys, and brought Christianity to Provence. She sprinkled it with holy water, put her girdle round its neck and led the now docile beast three times round the town before returning it to the river with orders never to come back. It never has, but to make sure René instituted a fair and procession in which a model of the Tarasque was pulled or pushed through the streets in carnival spirit, and to the cryptic slogan of 'Lagadigadeu! La Tarasco!' – which surprisingly makes the creature feminine. The original scheme was to have two separate festivals, one on the second Sunday after *Pentecôte*, when the dragon was made to lash its tail and grind its jaws as it passed through the streets, the other on St Martha's day, the 29 June, when it was led quietly round the town by a young girl. Now there is only one procession, on the last Sunday in June; the boys hidden inside the *papier-maché* model make it behave in the most unregenerate mood.

One of the difficulties attached to the legend of St Martha is that she was confused in the popular mind with a certain Syrian prophetess who according to Plutarch always accompanied the Roman general Caius Marius on his campaigns. It was Marius

128

who defeated the German tribes who were ravaging the province at the end of the second century BC, and he was credited with divine powers. The combination of two Marthas and a name which was the masculine form of Maria was too much for ordinary people, and the religious version was obviously fostered by the church.

Nevertheless, on the far side of the main street from the castle, you will find the **Église Ste-Marthe**, rebuilt in the twelfth century to hold the body of the saint which had reputedly been discovered in the earlier church, founded in the tenth century. It was consecrated in 1197 – you can see the date carved to the right of the southern entrance – and though that portal is all that remains of the Romanesque building you will find it a very lovely one. Modelled on one of the gateways in the Roman walls at Nîmes, its doors are framed by slender detached columns; overhead a deeply recessed series of concentric arches rest on a classical entablature. An unusual touch is a blind gallery running across the plain wall above, lined with alternate colonettes and pilasters. The sculptures of the tympanum and lintel have disappeared, and the body of the church was almost totally destroyed in 1944 by the American bombers aiming for the bridge, but its mainly Gothic interior has been pleasantly reconstructed.

Enough of sober history and architecture. What about Tartarin? Alphonse Daudet, though he lived at Fontvieille on the road from les Baux to Arles, has never been popular with the Tarasconnais since he created that vainglorious *bavard* and his cronies in two wonderfully funny novels. Yet readers of *Tartarin de Tarascon* and *Tartarin sur les Alpes* may think they recognise in Provence today some of his explosive and credulous characters – a mixture, perhaps, of Walter Mitty and Alf Garnett. Even if the cry of 'Vé! Coquin de sort!' is no longer current in the land, enthusiasm for food spiced with garlic and wine laced with heady argument is still endemic in the Provençal male.

Before passing on to Arles, now only twenty kilometres to the south, we ought to take a look at **Beaucaire**, the French king's bastion which faced the emperor's vassal across the dividing Rhône. Very little is left of the castle begun soon after 1200 by Raymond VI of Toulouse, for like les Baux it was demolished by Richelieu in 1632, and its site was not nearly as spectacular as its rival's across the bridge. However in 1217 Raymond instituted what was to become the biggest international fair in western Europe. Quite a small affair to begin with, lasting only a week at the end of July, it expanded quickly when Louis XI made Beaucaire a free port. During the whole of July it attracted merchants from all over Europe, ships from all the Mediterranean ports, and even schooners from England, trading in every imaginable kind of merchandise. The main site was the open space between the castle and the river, still known as the Champ de Foire, where a new breed of *entrepreneurs* has built a bull ring and a casino. When the railways succeeded the river as the main carriers of trade the fair languished and eventually died.

Though Beaucaire is strictly outside our definition of Provence, it will always be remembered as the home of *Aucassin and Nicolette*, the hero and heroine of the most tender and adventurous of all the love stories told and sung by the minstrels of the south. Best of all, unlike most of the stories in Malory's *Morte d'Arthur*, it had a happy ending, and if you can find either the French version by Bourdillon or the English one by Andrew Lang you may understand the raptures of romance which the mediaeval courts of Languedoc and Provence so much enjoyed, and which Mistral and his friends were trying to recreate – though perhaps they tried too hard.

8

Arles and the Camargue

Arles is the most typically Provençal of the Roman cities on the Rhône, but it can be the most difficult to get to know. Once a royal capital, not only of the kingdom of Provence but of the whole area known as southern Burgundy (which included the transalpine province of Savoy) world traffic now passes it by. The Rhône itself is no longer a major commercial waterway, and though the canal dug by Caius Marius in 104 BC still gives Arles direct access to the gulf and port of Fos, the modern autoroute from Lyon divides at Orange, leaving Arles stranded between the highways to Marseille and Spain. Nevertheless it commands the most southerly crossing of the Rhône, where once a pontoon bridge carried the *via Aurelia* on its way from Italy to Spain, and its position at the head of the delta makes it the gateway to one of the most fascinating natural areas of Europe.

Excavations have found traces of a sixth-century settlement, probably colonised by the same Greeks from Phocaea who founded Marseille in 539 BC. They would have taken advantage of a small rocky outcrop surrounded by salt marshes; indeed the land to the south is now about thirty feet higher above sea level than it was two thousand years ago, and the sea has retreated at least ten miles. The name of the town is probably derived from the Celtic word *arlath*, meaning 'the place of waters', and the

131

Romans knew it as Arelate. They developed it as a rival to the virtually independent city of Massilia, and when the latter sided with Pompey in the civil war the dockyards of Arelate built the galleys which brought victory to Julius Caesar and the destruction of its rival.

In 46 BC it was formally settled by veterans of the sixth legion, and during the next three hundred years it was developed as the most important Roman city beyond the Alps. It was a favourite seat of the emperor Constantine the Great, and when the empire was divided after his death his son Constantine II, born here in 313, took over the Gallic provinces as his share. In the final separation of west and east in 395 Arles became the administrative centre of all the provinces of Gaul, Spain and Britain. It was largely destroyed during the barbarian invasions of the fifth century, and in the eighth it was captured and occupied by the Saracens. When the empire of Charlemagne was divided between his grandsons in 843, Provence and Burgundy were included in the 'middle' kingdom of Lotharingia which went to his eldest grandson Lothaire. This was a curious mixture of unrelated territories stretching from the Netherlands to central Italy, and in less than fifty years it had disintegrated, leaving an independent kingdom of Arles which comprised Provence, the Dauphiné and Savoy. Its first ruler was one Boso, whose sister had married another of Charlemagne's grandsons, Charles 'the Bald', but in 1032 it was bequeathed to the emperor Conrad II; the counts of Provence, now his feudal subjects, no longer lived at Arles.

Church kept pace with State in the early history of Arles. Long before Constantine had his vision of the Cross on the coast south of St-Tropez, its Roman necropolis had been taken over by the early Christian community. Known as the Alyscamps, a southern variation of the Champs Elysées, or Elysian Fields, it received among its earliest occupants the body of St Trophime, the first bishop of Arles. In 597 St Augustine was consecrated as the first English bishop by St Virgil of Arles,

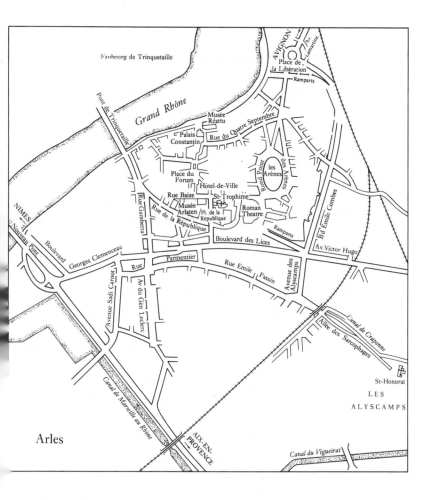

Arles

and both Boso and his successor were elected king by a college
of twenty-three bishops from the southern dioceses. St Trophime came into his own when towards the end of the twelfth
century a great cathedral was built to honour the relics of a man
to whom Christ himself was said to have appeared in his
lifetime. In 1178, soon after it was finished, it witnessed the
coronation of Frederic Barbarossa as both king of Arles and
Holy Roman emperor.

Of all this history, and of the mediaeval centuries which
followed, a good deal remains for the visitor to see, but as I

133

implied in the opening paragraph Arles is a fiendish place to explore. The Middle Ages have left a labyrinth of narrow streets, now frequently blocked by building or demolition works, if not by sheer press of traffic in a complex one-way system. It is no place to drive a car, and once you stray even on foot from the Boulevard des Lices there is no knowing where you may end. This is not just a modern complaint, for both Stendhal ('a hole') and Henry James ('the tortuous and featureless streets of Arles') had caustic things to say about walking abroad here. Above all, avoid Arles during the last week of May, unless you are determined see the great procession of gypsies making its way to les-Saintes-Maries-de-la-Mer. Another event which fills the town at the end of April is the *Fête des Gardians* (the horsemen of the Camargue) but to see this would be worth a little discomfort. It would be pointless to suggest an itinerary to take in the major monuments, so the most sensible thing is to describe them individually in order of general interest, beginning with the earliest.

We must begin with the Roman amphitheatre, or **les Arènes**, to give it its modern French name. For many this is the finest Roman monument in Provence, all the more so because its great oval space is still used for the entertainment of thousands. In the first century of the Roman empire it held more than 20,000 spectators who came to see blood spilt in the classic battles of gladiators or by human victims pitted against wild beasts. The bull-fights of today (some but not all pursued *à l'outrance*) attract nearly as many, and the roar of the crowd is probably no less insistent. However much one deplores the spectacles, ancient or modern, it makes a magnificent arena, and the view northward from the terraces over the red-tiled roofs to the river, or eastward past the abbey of Montmajour to the Alpilles, will colour all one's memories of Provence.

What is more difficult to recapture in imagination is the time when the population of Arles retreated within its solid walls, as though behind the defences of a fortress, when threatened by

Saracen and Norman attacks or the menace of religious war. Even in the more peaceful days of the seventeenth and eighteenth centuries the entire inner space was occupied by buildings – a rabbit warren of houses, alleys, shops and inns crowded so close together that when plague struck (not for the first time) in 1721 there were few survivors. The central area was not cleared till 1825, and when Theodore Cook saw it in 1903 he found the seating and all but the outer walls in ruins. Nevertheless in 1909 the arena saw a spectacle never to be repeated – a performance of the opera *Mireille*, composed by Gounod for a libretto based on Mistral's Provençal epic *Miréio*, and put on as part of three days of celebration in honour of its author on the fiftieth anniversary of its first publication. With considerable irony it was disrupted by the very *mistral* which echoed the name of the poet, but nothing could spoil the warmth of the ceremony held earlier in the Place du Forum, when in the presence of representatives of royalty he received the Grand Cross of the *Légion d'Honneur* from a government minister.

Close by is the **Roman Theatre**. It was begun a century earlier than the Arènes, and would have been used for more peaceful performances of the comedies of Plautus and Terence. In its present state you might mistake it for a Greek theatre, for little survives of the *scena*, and what there is suggests a more refined style of architecture than we saw behind the massive walls at Orange. There is almost nothing left either of the outer arcading which would have enclosed the semicircle of seats and matched the exterior of the Arènes. Practically all the stonework was robbed to build churches and public buildings in the Middle Ages, and there came a time when it was known simply as 'la carrière'. Fortunately when workmen engaged in this 'quarrying' came across the armless statue we know as the 'Venus of Arles' they recognised its value and turned it in to the authorities. The town presented her to Louis XIV, and she has gone to join her sister from Milos in the Louvre. A century later they unearthed the torso of a huge statue of Augustus, which would have stood in the central niche of the back wall of the *scena*, as its counterpart does in the theatre of Orange; perhaps by the first century AD the two buildings were not all that different in style. The emperor's head was found in 1834.

Today the theatre comes to life again for a festival in early July which coincides with the beginning of the bull-fighting season. Mistral would have approved of the revival of *farandoles proven-çales* and other displays in traditional costume, but for most of the year it stands empty and a bit forlorn.

The most extraordinary place in Arles is the **Alyscamps**. Once it was a huge burial ground on the outskirts of Arelate, through which ran the *via Aurelia* on its way to the crossing of the Rhône. Its connection with the early Christian church, and especially with St Trophime (who was said to have had a vision here of the resurrected Christ), endowed it with such sanctity that later bishops, statesmen and princes recorded their wish to be buried here. Even lesser *riverains* of the Rhône would commit the bodies of their relatives to barrels and float them down stream with enough money to buy them a tomb in the Alyscamps, where they could wait in good company for the last trump. Reverence, or at least fear of sacrilege, usually ensured their safe arrival.

In the tenth century the relics of St Trophime were transferred to the basilica of St-Etienne in the centre of the city, and the numbers fell both of candidates for burial and of pilgrims to the site. The lids of the most finely carved sarcophagi were removed by wealthy citizens to decorate their homes, and the plainer stones were re-employed in buildings of all kinds. Then, as the town grew, the site became too valuable to leave undeveloped, and the remaining sarcophagi (now nearly all lidless) were ranged alongside the avenue which led to the ruined twelfth-century church of St-Honorat – the saint who founded the earliest monastic community in France on the Îles de Lérins off the Riviera coast. Finally the railway on its way down from Avignon imprisoned it in a triangle between the main and branch lines and the Canal du Vigueirat.

For us there is the question of how to get there. If you can reach the south side of the Boulevard des Lices from the neighbourhood of the theatre, and follow it eastward as far as the junction with the Boulevard Émile Combes (where you will have a view of the only surviving corner of the mediaeval ramparts) the right turn here is into the Avenue des Alyscamps, from where you have only to cross the railway line to reach your destination. If all this sounds dispiriting, it must be said that in autumn, when the poplars are turning golden and shedding their leaves on the *Allée des Sarcophages*, and when you reflect that you are walking on a section of one of the main trunk roads of the Roman empire, something of its romance can still be felt.

We should now follow St Trophime to his final resting place on the east side of the Place de la Republique, with the baroque frontage of the Hôtel-de-Ville to your left, and on the far side the former seventeenth-century church of St-Anne – now the **Musée d'Art paien**, where you can see the remains of the statue of Augustus rescued from the theatre. The west front of the **Church of St-Trophime** (no longer a cathedral) is one of those masterpieces of sculptured architecture which deserve a long look, and it should be easier once a thorough cleaning and restoring process is finished. Its well proportioned classical format has as its centrepiece a tympanum of Christ in Majesty, seated in a mandorla surrounded by the symbols of the four evangelists. This is a powerful but conventional treatment which recalls a good deal of late Romanesque work in Burgundy. The composition of the lower registers looks stiff at first sight, especially the solemn row of apostles seated on the lintel below, the ranks of the elect processing towards Christ from the left, the damned turning away from him towards a hell which is literally just round the corner to the right; yet if you look closely you will find all sorts of imaginative details which lighten the grand design.

In pride of place to left and right of the entrance are the figures of St Trophime being give his mitre by a pair of angels, and of St Stephen at the moment of his martyrdom by stoning. The latter appears in this key position for the good reason that the first church built on this site was a basilica dedicated to St Etienne early in the fifth century. It was probably built by St Hilaire, who came here from the Îles de Lérins to found the monastery of Trinquetaille on the far side of the river, and succeeded St Honorat as bishop of Arles. His *Life*, written in 461, tells how he cured one of his deacons who had had a foot crushed by a falling block of marble while he was demolishing the proscenium of the Roman theatre. There were no scruples about 'quarrying' a site so conveniently close to the projected basilica.

St Trophime is more difficult to pin down. Trophimus was a name familiar as a disciple of St Paul from the *Acts of the Apostles*, and a number of legends have a figure of this name arriving in Arles in 46 AD, two years before the Saintes Maries landed on the shores of the Camargue, giving rise to a web of pious inventions. Historically the name was a common one in the region, and if we are to accept St Trophime as the first bishop of Arles he would have lived not earlier than the first half of the third century, when the bishopric is first mentioned.

His body was initially transferred in the tenth century from the Alyscamps to the basilica of St-Etienne, and naturally found a home in the new cathedral being built on the site. To accommodate it as well as relics connected with the earlier saint, a crypt was formed under the east end of the cathedral, and pilgrims would come here after first visiting the shrine of St Honorat in the Alyscamps. Although for a time the two saints shared the honours, the name of the local saint prevailed, and that is how we know it now.

The richly decorated west doorway was added at the end of the twelfth-century building programme, and finished just in time for the coronation of Frederic Barbarossa in 1178. The exterior is otherwise unusually plain, and the serenely simple architecture of the nave comes as a surprise as you enter the church. The lofty Romanesque arcades disdain the interruption of carved capitals, and lead the eye up towards a perfectly formed barrel vault. Only in the last few feet are the plain square pillars which support it relieved by short fluted colonettes with Corinthian capitals – a most original touch. The transepts are later by about a hundred years, and the fifteenth-century choir adds lightness and grace to the building. It was during these last alterations that the relics of the two saints were moved to a chamber at the base of the tower.

The **Cloister of St-Trophime** is unusual in being detached from the body of the church, and it has a separate entrance in the rue de Cloître which winds round behind it to the east. It was not till almost the end of the twelfth century that the Chapter of St-Trophime found itself wealthy enough to extend its construction programme to include all the buildings necessary under the rule of St Augustine for the communal life of its canons – who had previously lived in separate houses more casually grouped round the cathedral. This explains why the cloister is not directly connected with the south aisle or transept, and why it was planned on such a generous scale. It encloses a space twenty-eight metres by twenty-five, not a perfect rectangle because the south gallery is slightly shorter than the north. What strikes one immediately is not only its size, but the contrast of styles between the north and east galleries and those to the south and west. The former were the first to be built, so they are Romanesque in both arcades and vaulting. Unfortunately the sources of the Chapter's new wealth were soon diverted to finance crusading activities and as ransom money for prisoners taken by the Saracens, and work on the cloister was stopped.

By the time it began again a hundred years later, the Gothic style had found its way south to the Midi, so that the remaining two sides are completely different in treatment. The happy result is that we have a perfect object lesson in the development from Romanesque to Gothic architecture, while at the same time the combination of the two styles at their best is richly satisfying to the eye. The most striking features of the Romanesque galleries are the solid, square, fluted corner and intermediate pillars with their Corinthian capitals, which would have fitted naturally into some ancient Roman monument, and the slightly asymmetrical arches which support the generous sweep of the barrel vaulting – an effect which leads the eye away from the outer wall towards the arcading and the green lawns of the cloister garth. The Gothic arcading in the other two galleries is simple and uncomplicated, matched by the graceful patterns of its ogival vaulting.

The **Chapter House** opens off the north gallery, the refectory and dorter are on the east side – both completed in the Romanesque period while the money held out. The capitals of every pair of pillars in the arcading are different, most of them telling an Old or New Testament story, and an array of saints decorates the inner faces of the Romanesque pillars. If you climb to the walkway which continues round all four sides you will have the best view of the great central tower of St-Trophime – solidly Romanesque with its well spaced window openings and blind arcading, but given an unexpected subtlety by the simple device of reducing the size of its three stages from bottom to top. I rate it as the finest of the major church towers of Provence, and a visit to St-Trophime is an education in many matters.

The rue Baize, which runs behind the Hôtel-de-Ville, leads to the **Musée d'Art chrétien**. The attraction here is twofold. The museum itself (which is on the site of a seventeenth-century Jesuit chapel) has a collection of fourth-century marble sarcophagi, most of them from the Alyscamps and carved by local artists. From here you can descend to the underground vaulted galleries known as the **Cryptoportiques**. Their purpose has never been fathomed, one theory being that they provided storage for grain, but what is clear is that they formed part of the foundations which supported the buildings of the

Roman forum. The clue to this is the presence of two Corinthian columns embedded in the façade of the now disused Hotel Nord-Pinus, at the south end of what is called the Place du Forum, which belonged to a temple marking the boundary of the actual forum.

The Place, busy as it always is, turns out to be one of the few comparative oases in Arles which could be called an open space. The once popular Nord-Pinus is deserted and decayed, but as a third choice after the fashionable D'Arlaten, a few streets away to the north, and the expensive Jules César on the Boulevard des Lices, you could do a lot worse than choose for your base the Hotel du Forum in the south-west corner. It has no restaurant, but you can eat well at the Vaccarès on the far side of the square. The statue in the centre is unmistakeably of Mistral, with his pointed beard and broad-brimmed hat, and it was unveiled during the 1909 celebrations. A house near the north-west corner is said to have belonged to a Capuchin monk called Père Tranquille, immortalised by his recipe for lettuce soup given in Elizabeth David's *French Provincial Cooking*. The soporific qualities of lettuce were of course discovered to their cost by Beatrix Potter's 'Flopsy Bunnies'.

If both spirit and flesh remain strong, and you can find your way still further north to the banks of the Rhône, you will come to a site known speculatively as the **Palais Constantin**, though all it amounts to are the foundations of a system of baths culminating in an apse built of alternate courses of brick and stone – obviously Roman work, probably of the fourth century and readily identifiable as the *thermes* of a large house or palace. Almost next door, overlooking the river, was the sixteenth-century priory of the Knights of Malta, which after the Revolution was bought by the painter Jean-Jacques Réattu. After his death it was acquired by the city authority, who set it up as a museum for his paintings and for a wide selection of the works of Provençal and other European artists. However the most memorable exhibits in the **Musée Reattu** are a selection of drawings in various mediums by Picasso, presented by him in 1971.

Even if you feel you have seen enough museums in Arles, or have deliberately avoided the others, do leave time to visit the **Museón Arlaten**, whose Provençal name declares its *raison d'être*. It was created by Mistral himself with the money he received with his Nobel prize for literature in 1904, and there is no finer memorial to the poet himself or better illustration of the way of life which he so passionately wanted to preserve, or at least record. The museum is housed in a sixteenth-century *hôtel*, with a spacious courtyard which contains the remains of a Roman market-place and a miniature basilica, but the exhibition proper begins on the first floor with a collection of costumes and embroidery, and a *mise-en-scène* of women at work on it.

You will be welcomed by a nice lady in the soft grey nineteenth-century Provençal costume, picked out in white, just as prescribed by Mistral. She will direct you to a series of other rooms all illustrating some aspect of domestic life, including a model of a Provençal kitchen in a glass-fronted box, and ending in a gallery of traditions and legends with a suitably grotesque model of the Tarasque. The rooms on the top floor make a circuit of the courtyard – not all very interesting, but with the common feature of a tiled floor and coffered ceiling. The best is a fully furnished bedroom with a beautiful double bed in olive wood, carved with dancing figures. Next to it is a room celebrating the foundation of the Félibrige, with a bust of the great man and pictures of various assemblies of the faithful.

From here a short flight of steps leads down to an annexe laid out to illustrate country pursuits, ships and seafaring. Here is a model of the traditional type of cottage built in the Camargue, its thatched roof secured by a white clay ridge, exactly as it can be seen there today. Outside is a (thatched) dog kennel and an observation mast from which the flat Camargue landscape can be surveyed for miles in all directions.

The *chef d'oeuvre* comes just before the exit. Two glass-fronted rooms are peopled with life-size figures: one is of family and friends visiting the scene of a recent *accouchement*, a midwife relaxing by the fire, a cradle at the ready, while the infant is being admired by elegantly dressed ladies; next is a complete scene in a Provençal kitchen-dining-room, the table laid with suitable comestibles and bottles, round which are seated male figures who have come in from the fields for their midday meal. All have the beaky Provençal nose, the thin face pinched in at the mouth, and thick dark hair. No one who has been round the Muséon Arlaten will want to belittle or make fun of Mistral's enthusiasms. The realities of a lost way of life are poignant.

To reach the Camargue from Arles you need to follow the main road bridge across the Rhône, which lands you first on the edge of the suburb of **Trinquetaille**. What now looks like a modern appendage of Arles was once a site of almost equal importance. It was a strategic site, occupying the angle made where the two main river channels divide – the *Grand Rhône* and the *Petit Rhône*. Here were the shipyards which built the galleys for Julius Caesar, here was the monastery founded by St Hilaire, and here was the last fortress of the des Baux family to fall to the counts of Provence.

Little of ancient or mediaeval Trinquetaille survived the allied bombardment of the bridge area in 1944 – in fact only the little Romanesque church of **St-Genest**, which had previously been wrecked in the wars of religion and was restored in 1684 with a new west front. It was built on a site successively used for a Roman temple and a fourth-century *cella* commemorating the martyrdom of St Genès, a scribe who had refused to copy out a decree against the Christians. The rest of Trinquetaille is all modern, including the church of St-Pierre and one of Arles's better hotels, the predictably named Mireille.

The main road to the **Camargue** divides only a mile or so south of Arles. The most travelled branch is the high road to les-Saintes-Maries-de-la-Mer, leaving the Étang de Vaccarès and the vast *Réserve Naturelle Zoologique et Botanique*, which is now the heart of the Camargue, on the left. The other branch, the D36, follows the right bank of the Rhône all the way down to where the salt pans of the Salin de Giraud merge imperceptibly with the sea. If you go straight ahead for les-Saintes-Maries you will arrive there swiftly, but see little of the real character of this 'unique area of wetland' – as the ecologists inadequately call it these days.

If instead you turn left at the junction there will be a further choice of routes very soon. The minor D36B will carry you to the eastern shore of the Étang de Vaccarès, and at la Capellière is the information centre for this part of the *Réserve Naturelle*, as well as marvellous views over the inland sea and the marshes which surround it. If you continue on the major road you will pass (on your right) a side road leading to the *Centre d'Écologie* on the domain of the Tour du Valat. This is a place more for students and researchers than for tourists, but if you carry on to the end of the main road you will find at **la Palissade** a green oasis among the salt lakes. The *Maison de la Nature* was established by the company which runs the salt industry here as a generous gesture of recompense to the ecologists – a fascinatingly informative place where you can walk (with a guide) across the dam road to the Plage d'Arles, or walk down to the very point where the Rhône meets the sea.

It should be clear by now that to see the Camargue properly you need to spend several days within striking distance. To see it thoroughly you would need several weeks. Michelin lists a number of hotels in the neighbourhood of les-Saintes-Maries, of which some are agreeable but none are cheap. For reasons which will appear later you should keep clear of the resort itself, and you may prefer to keep a base back in Arles. The Mireille in Trinquetaille would do very well, though you are unlikely to dine off the equal of the dish of eels consumed by a quartet consisting of Daudet, Mistral, Matthieu and Girvolas which Mistral describes in his story of the *Ribote de Trinquetaille*.

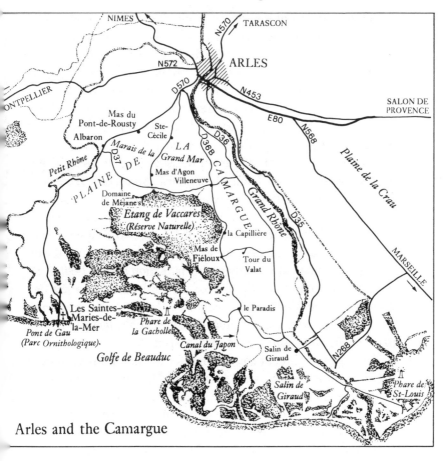

Arles and the Camargue

Before setting out for serious exploration it would be a good idea to do some homework, for this is a world as complex in its history as it is rewarding in its variety. The great triangle of the Rhône delta once extended beyond Arles, with Avignon, Beaucaire and Tarascon as its apex. Two thousand years ago a shallow sea would have covered the whole of the *Réserve Naturelle*, but as dry land appeared more and more alluvial silt was deposited on a prehistoric base of pebbles, leaving half a dozen channels to carry the fresh water to meet the sea. There were woodlands up in the northern apex, and marshy reed-beds in between the fresh water channels; eventually areas of solid grassland dried out. In the twelfth century the indefatigable Cistercians founded communities at Ulmet and Psalmody, and the first steps in cultivation were taken – trees cut down, marshes drained, and a manageable irrigation system begun. By the fifteenth century all but two of the freshwater channels had disappeared, and in the nineteenth the banks of the great and lesser Rhône were raised, and defences built against the sea between Aigues-Mortes and Port-St-Louis.

Now began a time of competition for the natural resources of the Camargue, which is stll going on. The farmers bought up land in the north to rear their sheep, the industrialists developed the salt industry in the south, and the wild life (whose extent and variety was only just being realized) survived where it could. Until 1860 the sheep farmers bred their *merinos d'Arles* for wool. Economic factors made them turn instead to meat production, only to find that their market was eroded by British and New Zealand competition. In any case the long hot summers of the Midi burned the treeless grasslands dry, and from at least the eighteenth century it has been the custom in June every year to transport huge flocks of sheep from the Camargue to the alpine pastures of the north-east, and bring them down again before the first snows fall. The *transhumance*, as it is called, at first involved weeks of trekking on foot for combined flocks which could number as many as 40,000 sheep. Individual flocks could be about 2,000 strong, driven by half a dozen men and led by magnificently horned male goats (known as *boucs*) with distinctive bells round their necks.

Today most of the journey is done by road transport, hundreds of animals being packed tightly into two-decker trucks for as far as the road lasts. Only for the last climb into the mountains are they let out to walk the rest of the way, grazing as they go; anywhere in Haute-Provence you may come across these woolly hordes who have come up for their summer holidays from the Camargue – or from the even more blistering expanses of the Plaine de la Crau on the east side of the Grand Rhône.

Even this tradition is threatened by ineluctable economics, for it involves hiring the summer pastures from their mountain owners. Rents are going steadily up, the cost of transport is rising too, and the area available for grazing even at this height is lessened by afforestation and by the construction of ski resorts, runs and access roads. So down in the Camargue and the Crau large flocks are scarce, and the land once grazed profitably is being turned over more and more to a new industry – rice growing. The climate of the Camargue is at the northern limit for the successful cultivation of rice, but the amount of water instantly available to flood the ricefields makes it an ideal terrain for the purpose. The influx of fresh water also washes out the salt, so that it has become possible to put land down to wheat for a few years in succession.

It can be imagined what effect these changes had on the wild life of the Camargue, just as the growth of arable farming in Norfolk and Suffolk has destroyed so much of value to the environment. Ironically it was the conflict of interest between the farmers and the salt industry which has done most to save the essential qualities of the Camargue. In the 1920s it was observed that a natural *zone d'équilibre* had formed between the salt and fresh water areas, and in 1927 – thanks to the generosity of the major salt company – a *Réserve naturelle* was formed on their land as a kind of buffer state, which included the Étang de Vaccarès and the freshwater marshes which surrounded it on three sides. In 1970 the whole delta was declared a *Parc Naturel Régional*, and in 1972 the World Wildlife Fund assisted the French government to buy the nature reserve at its heart – now the *Réserve Nationale du Camargue*. Pumping stations are in constant action to preserve the precious equilibrium.

The formal establishment of the *Zone* has suited the surrounding landowners, for duck-shooting has become a profitable sideline with about 150,000 duck of many species wintering here every year; the big estates can charge as much as £1,000 a year for a gun. It must be stressed that licensed duck-shooting is not regarded as a threat to wild life – even at Slimbridge the Berkeley family enjoy shooting rights over the land they lease to the Wildfowl Trust on the banks of the Severn. What has been preserved here is the natural habitat of many threatened species of both resident and immigrant birds, and a great variety of wild flowers.

The birds are the real natural wild life of the Camargue. The white horses and the little black bulls are picturesque natives, but no longer wild, for every animal and every acre belongs to a landowner who breeds the horses for riding and the bulls for the popular *courses à la cocarde*. These are mini-bullfights in a small local ring where young men show off their daring and agility in first taunting the bull and then snatching a ribboned cockade from its horns. The bull is led off to rest if he gets tired of the game.

The large estates are each based on a *mas*, or ranch, which employs a team of *gardians* to round up and control their *manardes* of cattle at the appropriate seasons. They are the chief users of the white horses, which they break in and ride in characteristic fashion when going about their duties; when herding the cattle they carry a metal *trident*. The *mas* will subsidise its growing expenses in various ways – letting accommodation, hiring out horses for riding, or organising mounted treks for tourists.

Given that you are prepared to spend several days getting to know something of the Camargue – and it would take a lot longer to do more than that – how do you proceed? Even in the drier areas there are parts you will never penetrate, so suggestions are bound to be eclectic. Most of one day will have to be devoted to the Saintes-Maries and their church, and another could be well spent down at la Palissade, but perhaps it would be best to begin by exploring the eastern and northern shores of the Étang de Vaccarès. To this end the first stop should be at the information centre at la Capellière, where you should find enough guidance to plan ahead, and will have a chance to see some of the terrain on foot. It will not be long before you sight a flock of flamingos, long-legged creatures with ridiculously flexible necks, feeding in the shallows, their plumage a dull and hardly noticeable pink against the sparkling wind-ruffled water. As you come closer they will begin to move uneasily, until by simultaneous consent they rise in a cloud of flapping wings, the under side of each one a brilliant pattern of scarlet and black. This is one of the most familiar sights of the Camargue, but the suddenness of the change is always thrilling.

If you have not already bought a large-scale map – either no. 66 or no. 303 in the *Cartes IGN* series – get one at la Capellière. We assume that you have at least one pair of binoculars between you. Carry on now to the south along the dam road which skirts the *Étang*. A left-hand turn at the Mas de Fiéloux leads to the Tour du Valat and the nearby *Centre d'Écologie*, but if you press on – *étangs* to the right, *marais* to the left – you will pass the improbable site of the Cistercian abbey of Ulmet (no trace now) and eventually reach the point where the dam road takes off into what looks like the open sea – and it can be almost as rough. This is the only way to reach the *Phare de la Gacholle*, a third of the distance along the sea wall known as the *Digue à la Mer* which runs all the way to les-Saintes-Maries. Though that is a way closed to motor traffic, you can in theory leave your car at an established parking place and take to your feet.

You may have already decided that the road you are on is too rough for anything but four-wheeled drive, and that to go further you would avoid the potholes better on a bicycle. A side road from near le Paradis, the D36C, will take you south-east across a typical area of 'la Camargue sauvage' – marshes, meadows, reed-fringed dykes, and a very few trees. It follows roughly the line of the mysteriously named Canal du Japon which joins the Rhône a little way above the salt capital of the Salin de Giraud.

If for the time being you turn back north, or if you come this way another day, the crossroads at Villeneuve offers you a good road along the north shore of the Étang. It leads eventually to one of the most successfully exploited tourist attractions of the Camargue, the Domaine de Méjanes, where there is a golf course, a riding school, a hotel and a *train touristique* for a short trip around the marshes. If all this puts you off, you can leave you car in a *parking* off the road before you get there, and walk down to a commanding viewpoint which projects into the Étang.

If the road looks good enough – and this depends very much on the weather of the previous month or so – you can make your way back to Arles across country, past the Mas d'Agon and the hamlet of Ste-Cécile; or you can continue on the D37 to join the main road at Albaron, another centre of tourist attractions. This is the high road from Arles to les-Saintes-Maries, and it passes the **Musée camarguais** at the Mas du Pont-de-Rousty, where a sheep barn has been converted into a museum of great local interest. It deserves more than a casual visit, not only on the strength of having been awarded the 1979 European prize for museums, but because it offers a three-and-a-half kilometre 'discovery' trail into the country to the south. Although there are no spectacular views over water, this trail is one of the best opportunities for observing wild life and all the comings and goings of the countryside. The visit could easily take up half a day in all, and it can be made every day (except 1 May) from 0900 to 1800 between 1 April and 30 September, and (except on Tuesdays) from 1000 to 1700 between 1 October and 31 March.

I have left to the last the obligatory journey down to the sea and one of the holiest places in Provence. To go over again briefly the legend of the Saintes-Maries, in about 40 AD the Jews of Palestine set adrift a boat without sails, oars or provisions which contained the 'three Marys' – Mary Jacobé (sister of the Virgin), Mary Salomé (mother of the apostles James and John) and Mary Magdalene (sometimes confused with Mary the sister of Martha, who may also have been on board). Rather in the spirit of all those New Englanders who claim descent from the pilgrim fathers in the *Mayflower*, other names were added as the legend took hold. The latest tally, beside these four women, included their servant Sara, Martha's brother Lazarus (whom Jesus raised from the dead), Sidonius (whose sight Jesus restored) and a martyred Roman called Maximius.

This remarkable boatload miraculously survived all dangers and privations to land safely on a promontory to the east of what is now the mouth of the Petit Rhône. After putting up a roughly built oratory in honour of the fourth and greatest Mary, the mother of Christ, they separated to spread the Gospel widely through Provence. Sidonius set off up the Rhône to the Tricastin, where the miracle which restored his sight is remembered in the church of St-Restitut; Martha to Tarascon, where she tamed the dreaded Tarasque; Lazarus to Marseille; Maximius to Aix, though he is remembered now in the nearby cathedral of St-Maximin-la-Sainte-Baume. The Magdalene was said to have ended her days in sad seclusion on the slopes of the Massif de la Sainte-Baume, her body being later transfered to the cathedral of St-Maximin. Only the two other Marys and black Sara remained behind, and after their death their bodies were committed to the oratory they had helped to build.

151

Apart from the mention of an oratory in the sixth century we hear nothing of the site till the middle of the ninth century, when a Carolingian church was begun there. Work on this was interrupted by a Saracen raid, during which the archbishop of Arles – who had timed a visit unfortunately – was carried off and held to ransom. The ransom was agreed, and though the archbishop died suddenly in custody his captors displayed his fully robed body in a life-like position on the shore until it was paid – and sailed away before the truth was discovered.

Next to come were monks from the abbey of Montmajour, who first set up a dependent priory and then, towards the end of the twelfth century, began to build the present church. The times being still dangerous for dwellers on the coast, they made it a massively fortified building and incorporated it in the town walls. A well was sunk in the nave for use during a siege. There are many mediaeval castles less formidable and forbidding, and with its Romanesque machicolations lowering over the almost blank walls – to which the fourteenth century added a crenellated parapet – it looks more like a fortress then a church. Sometimes when the gales from the sea are battering it you might rather take it for a storm-bound ship with its bow thrusting into the waves. Seen from miles away over the flat surrounding country, or from out at sea, its enormous height has something of the unreal look of the tower of Santa Maria Assunta on Torcello, first seen from afar across the Venetian lagoon.

In evening sunlight the outer walls can seem almost golden, but inside the texture of the stone is grim and dark. The plan could hardly be simpler, a single nave of great height ending in a semicircular apse, decorated only by blind arcading supported by eight marble columns. It was modified in the fifteenth century by René of Provence, who had ordained an excavation of the primitive oratory to rediscover the bones of the saints. This done, he raised the level of the choir, leaving a crypt beneath, and above the choir he built a new chapel to contain the relics of the two remaining Marys. The crypt was made over to the servant Sara, whose dark statue in an embroidered dress stands there to be venerated in an atmosphere made torrid by hundreds of guttering wax candles burning day and night. To accommodate more and more pilgrims, who found it a convenient detour from Arles on their way to Spain and St James of Compostela, he extended the nave by two bays to the west.

The pilgrimages continue, but the mediaeval sanctity and mystery of the place has given way to a monstrously inflated tourist industry which has wrecked the litle town, and at times clogs the inside of the church with seething humanity. The cult of the black Sara brings gypsies from all over the south, not only for the great Romany pilgrimage and processions of 24 and 25 May, but as permanent hangers-on to the tourist trade, so that the moment your car pulls up in the car park you will be surrounded by the outstretched and importunate hands of dusky women and children, who even get aggressive if ignored. Things are not so bad if you can avoid Easter, the Whitsun holiday of Pentecôte, and the last week of May, but you should be prepared for an experience which combines the sublime and the sordid.

The main road from Arles, once you are past the Mas du Pont-de-Rousty, is a disappointing approach. You may still glimpse a herd of black cattle grazing in a distant field, but if you see any white horses they will be drooping disconsolately in dusty farmyards, or plodding in single file with a party of tourists on their backs, led by a bored *gardian*. Incidentally they are born with a brown coat, and take four years to grow the adult white one.

You will have to leave the tarmac and go deeper into lonely byways to find the true Camargue. For the stranger this is far from easy, and though in theory a determined cyclist with a large-scale map has the best chance, you may have to settle for one of the established 'trails' connected with the excellent reserve centres. One of the best of these systems – particularly

153

for the bird-watcher – is attached to the *Parc Ornithologique* at **Pont-de-Gau**, off the road only a mile or two north of les-Saintes-Maries. The Parc itself is an admirably laid out and managed 'home' for local wildfowl, and it also includes aviaries – some very big ones – in which you can see three kinds of heron, both little and cattle egrets, bitterns, spoonbills and glossy ibis. Open water is available for assorted ducks and flamingos, while another spacious aviary contains redshank, greenshank, oystercatchers, and (in early summer) ruffs in breeding plumage. Storks fly free to build their nests on top of some of the big cages. All these birds are genuine Camarguais natives, and paths over about eighty acres of marshland give you a chance to see some of them in their natural habitat, as well as a few herds of the little black cattle. The Parc is open from February to November between 0800 and sunset.

No attempt to describe the Camargue can match the accounts given by the two famous spokesmen for nineteenth-century Provence, Frédéric Mistral and Alphonse Daudet. A chapter in *Mes Origines* tells how in the spring of 1855 Mistral joined a cheerful party of pilgrims travelling by wagonette to les-Saintes-Maries from Beaucaire; how they were overtaken by a thunderstorm in the wildest part of the Camargue; how the wheels stuck in the mud, and how the men had to carry the women on their backs through flood water for several miles. Mistral enjoyed this, having chosen to carry the prettiest girl in the party, who was making the pilgrimage to find consolation from the saints for being abandoned by her *cadet*, or boy friend.

It may have been this incident which gave him the central idea for the epic poem he had begun to write in celebration of the old way of life in Provence. Written in the Provençal vernacular which the Félibres had vowed to reinstate, it really consists of a number of disconnected *chants*, or cantos, which describe the customs, characters and landscape of the countryside he knew so well. To give them coherence he works them all into the romantic narrative which was to win him the Nobel prize for literature in 1904 – the story of *Miréio*, or in standard French *Mireille*. Its heroine was the daughter of a prosperous family which farmed just such an estate as Frédéric's father did at Maillane. At the age of fifteen this lovely and innocent girl fell in love with the son of a good man who earned his living by making baskets from the reeds of the Camargue. The boy Vincen, only sixteen himself, had visited the *mas* as his father's apprentice, but was sent packing when Miréio declared her love and refused more eligible suitors. Vincen, after being nearly killed by one of them, sadly withdrew.

The poor distraught girl, remembering how Vincen had told her that the Saintes-Maries would always listen to those in trouble, collected a few belongings and slipped away before dawn one morning to put this to the test. It was late in June, and the rough stony desert of the Crau soon scorched her feet, but she found a young man to ferry her across the Rhône. Then we are told how the sun beat down on the endless plain, with only a few tamarisks for shade, and she sees a mirage of a city beyond a cool lake which fades as she walks on. She toils over 'the burning, yielding heaps of sand, over the salt-encrusted waste, through tall marsh grasses and reeds, with Vincen always in her thoughts'. At last as she skirts the lake of Vaccarés she sees on the horizon the 'tower of the Saints', but collapses from heat and exhaustion. She struggles into the town and sinks down dying on the floor of the church, where her frantic parents find her, and where Vincen has been told to look for her. She is carried to the upper chapel, and has a consoling vision of the two saints before dying in his arms.

Such was the stuff of nineteenth-century romance. Mistral was encouraged to think of himself as another Homer, but *Miréio* seems more like Wordsworth; it was his gift for long-winded descriptive poetry in a strangely sonorous tongue which won him fame in his time. Yet in *Mes Origines* he comes across with an engaging sense of humour and self-mockery – which Wordsworth never had – and he had some lively companions in

155

his young days. Liveliest of them all was Daudet, equally devoted to his native Provence, but never encumbered by the need to write in Provençale. His *Lettres de mon Moulin* may have been written mostly in Paris, but he makes the rich characters of Provence come alive more vividly than Mistral did, and he can put across the moods of the Camargue better than any other writer. One of his *Lettres*, called 'En Camargue', tells of a journey with a party down river in a steamer as far as the Mas de Giraud, from where they are guided to a *cabane* for a few days' shooting. This was a typical hut used by *gardians* or shepherds, comprising a single windowless room, the only light coming through the glass panes of the door, closed at night by shutters. It was heated by a fire of tamarisk stumps, with a short chimney poking through a roof thatched with reeds and secured by a ridge of clay painted white. Outside most *cabanes* there was a tall stepped mast from which the occupant could see what was going on for miles around – even out at sea. His description matches the example we saw reconstructed in the Muséon Arlaten in Arles.

Daudet describes how in one of them a solitary *gardian* lived 'une veritable vie de Robinson', who spent his spare time sitting outside the door and reading the only literature he had – brochures of the chemical remedies for the ailments of horses and cattle. Like Mistral, Daudet uses this character in one of his later published works. *Le Trésor d'Arlaten* is little known and hardly ever read, but shorter and more moving than *Miréio*. Little more than a novella, it tells the story of a young girl disturbed as she grows up by thoughts which she has been persuaded make her unfit to take her first communion. They centre on the figure of an enigmatic *gardian* who lives alone in the Camargue, between the Mas de Giraud and the shores of the Étang de Vaccarés – whose personality and knowledge of herbs give him a strange power over people. Her feeling of guilt leads her to suicide by drowning in the shallow brackish water of the *étang*.

Even today, overlaid as it is and sometimes demeaned by the pressures of industry and tourism, the almost horizonless waste of waters and reedbeds which is the Camargue can still be both beautiful and mysterious. Whether in shimmering heat or under shifting patterns of cloud, the sparkle of windswept water and the rustle of bending reeds – even the sheer desolation of the bare sand spits of the southern shore – make it uniquely compelling.

9

Arles to Aix-en-Provence

If the Rhône valley is the gateway to Provence, then Arles is its southern hinge. From here you can go on down into the Camargue and find the sea at les-Saintes-Maries, or you can slant south-east to the industrial ports of Istres and Martigues on the Étang de Berre, and all too quickly find yourself in the network of autoroutes which serve Marseille and lead on past Toulon to the Riviera coast. A third route, which this chapter will follow, goes due east to Aix-en-Provence, a city which long ago succeeded to the title of 'capital' of Provence, and now fully deserves it.

Again there is no logical sequence of roads to follow – time and convenience will always decide – but as in many apparently straightforward journeys between major towns there are detours leading to surprising and worth-while discoveries. The first objective will be no surprise. As you take the northern road out of Arles towards Avignon, and fork right for les Baux, you will see on the right the great bulk of the fortified tower of the **Abbey of Montmajour**. The abbey is one of the most important and impressive monuments of Provence, though also one of the more sombre.

The low hill on which it stands is a rocky one, like the nearby Mont de Cordes, and it rises like the Isle of Ely from what was

158

once a continuous swamp south of the Alpilles between Arles and Salon-de-Provence. Legend has it that Childebert, son of Clovis and king of all the Franks, founded a monastery here in the sixth century, but in this part of the world legends are difficult to disentangle from myths; there is also a tradition, supported by a spurious inscription, that its founder was Charlemagne himself. There is even a story that St Trophime found refuge here from Arles in the third century, but it seems more sensible to deal with written documents and the stones we can all see.

A ninth-century deed refers to the 'insula Sancti Petri quae nominatur a monte majori', succinctly describing both its situation and the origin of its name. A Benedictine foundation is actually recorded in the tenth century, and the first monks were preoccupied in draining the surrounding marshes to make them a fertile source of livelihood. When they first arrived the only communication with Arles was by flat-bottomed boats or rafts made from inflated bladders, and even when in 1030 the abbé Rambert instituted an annual pilgrimage or 'pardon', which later attracted thousands of people to pray for their sins to be forgiven, they all had to arrive by boat. The revenue from the pilgrimage financed further drainage, but not till the seventeenth century did a Dutch engineer satisfactorily finish the project.

There is little in the complex of grey stone buildings beside the main road which goes back earlier than the twelfth century. The most impressive is the crypt of the abbey church, into which you can penetrate down a gently inclined ramp at the west end. Its function was structural as well as religious, for on the south side the vaulting springs from the rock itself, and the rest of the site was carved out to provide what are really the foundations of the church above. The massive walls enclose a transept, choir, and a circular space surrounded by a unique ambulatory with radiating chapels. There are no pillars, and the light reaches the interior of the rotunda through narrow round-headed windows

Arles to Aix-en-Provence

in the ambulatory walls. The masonry is beautifully cut and aligned, and it shows none of the wear you would expect after nearly eight hundred years.

The church above was begun about 1150 but never finished (the nave has only two bays) and much of its stonework was robbed after the Revolution. What is left is pure twelfth-century Romanesque in style, except for some ribbed vaulting over the crossing which is later by a hundred years. The **Cloister** – more essential to a monastic community than its church – is complete, though only the eastern range is unrestored. The distance by which the north range overlaps the church shows how much of the nave remained unbuilt, and indicates the huge scale on which it was all planned. The arrangement of the arcades looks very much like what we saw in the Romanesque part of the

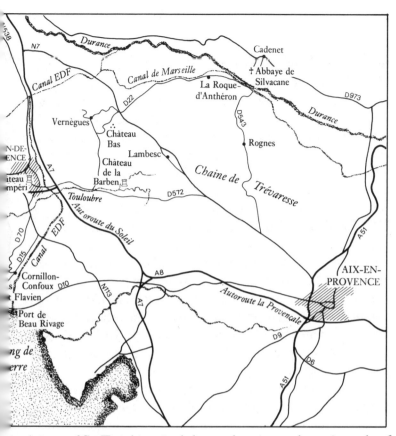

cloister of St-Trophime in Arles, and again much use is made of
fluting on the flat surfaces. The most intriguing decorations are
the animal heads below the corbels of the arches which span the
vaulting. The **Chapter House** on the east side has been well
restored after long neglect; so has the **Refectory** to the south,
which only fifteen years ago was being used as a sheep pen. The
cloister garth has been tidied up too, with its striking well-head,
and from it you get a fine view of the arrogant fourteenth-
century **Tour des Abbés** which dominates the abbey complex.

On the far side of the tower is the oldest and most remarkable
part of the abbey to survive. You may have to wait to see it until
the *gardien* is free from other duties, but the wait is worth it. A
flight of steps and a ramp lead down to the door of the **Chapelle
de Saint-Pierre**, and when the doors opens you pass through a

restored porch into an ancient miniature church lit only by three windows on the south side. Rough though it is, it divides traditionally into nave, choir, and apse, and the arcading is reinforced by short columns with carved capitals. With surprise you find that alongside to the left another nave has been carved out of the rock, and the apse is a dark cavern built even deeper into it. Stranger still is a passage between the two choirs and apses which leads to a nest of grottos which could have been occupied by the earliest monks. A tiny chapel-like enclosure has been fancifully called 'the confessional of St Trophime'.

The principal nave is said to be eleventh-century work, though its southern wall has been reinforced by later exterior buttresses. The columns were re-used from earlier buildings – some may even be Roman – and their capitals, all different, have a combination of geometric and floral designs which go back to the very beginnings of Romanesque sculpture. Earlier still is the Carolingian carving on a pilaster in the passage leading to the grottos, but that too must have come from elsewhere.

Two hundred yards down the road is the **Chapelle Sainte-Croix**, a building as light and lovely as Saint-Pierre is dark and curious. It marks the site of a cemetery of rock tombs which was the earliest *raison d'être* of the 'island of St Peter'. The surrounding swamp was no place to bury the dead, and as the name suggests it was the centre of attraction for those who joined the pilgrimage of the Holy Cross, instituted in 1030. The present building dates only from the end of the twelfth century, like the main church, and its striking arrangement in the form of a Greek cross, or quatrefoil with a short introductory narthex, was probably not connected with the pilgrimage. We have seen the same plan at la-Baume-de-Transit in the Tricastin and at Venasque in Vaucluse, but this is the most sophisticated version of the three. Standing serenely on its own, its great height, clean lines and perfect proportions catch the eye more sympathetically than the big tower up the road.

It almost certainly replaced an earlier building, whose role as a cemetery chapel is declared by the network of graves cut into the rock outside the eastern apse. These are like the rock tombs we saw at St-Pantaléon in the Luberon, and looking at both systems we wonder how these fairly shallow depressions in the solid rock were covered. Stone lids seem ruled out, as none have been found, and wooden covers unlikely, so there must have been a covering of earth, possibly over the whole area. Authorities are curiously silent about this.

For all its interest and historical importance, the abbey site of Montmajour stirs little emotion. There is an empty feeling about the place, which is difficult to people in the imagination with real figures. This must be because nobody has lived or prayed here since the Revolution, and it had in any case been secularized as a mark of disgrace by Louis XVI. Its buildings were plundered in the early part of the last century for stone, a good deal of which went to build the Rhône-side quays at Arles. However Jacques Réattu, the painter who had rescued the priory of the Knights of Malta there, bought and saved from destruction the Tour des Abbés. In 1822 the civic authority of Bouches-du-Rhône bought Sainte-Croix from a fisherman who had used it as a shed to dry his nets. The city of Arles continued a slow process of repurchasing, and finally in 1862 it commissioned an architect called Henri Revoil to begin the long work of restoration which has barely finished now under State supervision. It was – to put it mildly – interrupted in 1944 when the Germans, who had used the abbey buildings as an army store, set fire to them before leaving.

A very short way up the road to les Baux you come to the village of **Fontvieille**, which has always been associated with Alphonse Daudet, the most popular and prolific of Provençal writers. Born in Nîmes in 1840, he was not a native of the village, and on his occasional visits he stayed in comfort with friends at the nearby château of Montauban, rather than in the picturesque 'Moulin de Daudet'. This you can see on its low hill to the south of the road, and it has been turned into one of those little museums by which local communities like to advertise their literary connections. He did make a habit of visiting the mill to listen to tales told by the miller and his customers, but the delightful collection of short stories which he called *Lettres de mon Moulin* was written at his home in Paris and published there in 1868.

Daudet's parents were far from wealthy, and he earned his early living rather unhappily as a schoolmaster – a life he describes in his previous novel, *Le Petit Chose*. He was never committed, like Mistral and his Félibres to recreating a Provençal language, but his feeling for the Provençal character and the way of life of ordinary people is a feature of all his writing. His books describing the adventures and romantic *bragadoccio* of Tartarin, the larger-than-life native of Tarascon, are among the funniest ever written in French, and the short novel about the Camargue called *Le Trésor d'Arlaten* is among the most moving.

Fontvieille depends not only on the souvenir trade brought by Daudet, for it still controls a considerable market in stone and bauxite from neighbouring quarries. Otherwise it can stand on its own as an agreeable small town, and the Moulin makes an attractive subject for photographs on its stony little hill.

If you leave the D17 at Paradou and go south on the D27 you find yourself in a country which is simply the antithesis of the Camargue – the long-dried-up part of the delta between the *étangs* of Vaccarès and Berre called the **Plaine de la Crau**. Here were deposited thousands of years ago the stones washed down and made smooth in their passage from the Alps. Only the sparsest vegetation grows between the stones, though it includes enough fine grass and nourishing herbs to support huge flocks of sheep through the winter. When summer comes the whole plain is parched dry in the scorching heat, so that even today the farmers do their best to find mountain pastures at reasonable rents to embark on the traditional *transhumance*.

The Romans were always preoccupied with water supplies, and with so much water available to east and west it is no surprise to find remains of the aqueducts they built to straddle this almost moon-like landscape. If you take any road across it you may sight some, but the D27 will bring you to the little town of **St-Martin-de-Crau**, which will seem like an oasis in the desert you have been crossing. That is true particularly of the Auberge des Épis, where you will find comfort and hospitality if you need it. Several roads branch off here south and east into the Crau, some only to peter out in a stony wilderness, others leading to the enormous barns in which the sheep are kept during the worst of the winter. In the distance the industrial monuments of Istres make a surreal background to a terrain where the foreground may be occupied by a slowly advancing line of several hundred brown-fleeced sheep.

On now, though, in the direction of Salon-de-Provence by way of the N113, surely the longest and dullest stretch of ruler-straight highway in the south. If after about five miles you feel you have had enough, turn right on the D5 towards Istres, then shortly left for Miramas. This has no more charms than its larger industrial neighbour, but if you pass through it in the direction of St-Chamas you will find on the right of the road the hill village of **Miramas-le-Vieux**. Apart from its view over the Étang de Berre, its standard attractions are the ruins of a thirteenth-century castle and a fifteenth-century church in a pleasant warm-coloured stone, but if you go on down to the cemetery below you will see the little cemetery chapel of **St-Julien**. His statue is over the west door, and the sight of the east end with its humble bell-tower and rounded apse in undressed stone is endearing. Unfortunately both church and chapel are kept locked – not surprisingly considering the number of customers of all sorts catered for in the village restaurants and cafés.

Just past St-Chamas a single-arched bridge once carried an offshoot of the Roman *via Aurelia* over the swift-flowing Touloubre. At either end is a typical example of grandiose but perfectly executed Roman architecture. The two ceremonial gateways which mark the approach to the bridge each have a central arch flanked by fluted pilasters with Corinthian capitals, and crowned by a classic horizontal entablature; you can see exactly how the typical Romanesque church portal developed from such a model. This is the **Pont Flavien**, and there is an inscription on one architrave which announces that it was built by a prefect of the province with the familiar Roman name of Flavius. The *gravitas* of the architecture is a bit unsettled by a pair of stone lions looking outwards from either cornice, bending their front legs to growl at the oncoming traffic. You can still see the wheel-ruts in the roadway as it crosses the river.

We are now on the margins not only of the Étang de Berre but of one of the most highly industrialised parts of France, but the joy of travelling in Provence is that round the most unpromising corner there may be treasures that history has left for us to find. The *village perché* is a Provençal speciality, useless for industrial development and only at risk from tourism if its inhabitants choose. If you follow the D15 from the Pont Flavien as it passes under the Arles-Marseille railway, in a few minutes the red-tiled houses of the enigmatically named **Cornillon-Confoux** will appear up on the left. Confoux turns out to be the name of a nearby family château, and if you make the winding ascent among the pines you come upon a place quite withdrawn from the pressures which afflict even Miramas-le-Vieux. Its centre is the very early twelfth-century church of **St-Vincent**, preserved in its original form with nave, side chapels and apse. The glass is modern, pleasant but not outstanding, the work of Frédérique Duran.

The village square is overlooked by a clock-tower and a mediaeval castle keep, the latter discreetly converted to a hotel; the battlements which encircle the village provide a walkway, or *chemin-de-ronde*, nicely called the rue de Passe-Temps. Spend a little of yours looking at the view, which extends north-west to the Alpilles, north-east to the Luberon, and even as far north as Mont Ventoux. The countryside below, dotted with red-roofed houses and cypresses, supports a mixture of market gardening and vineyards, and you feel you can forget for the moment about Istres and Marseille.

However in Provence you must expect contrasts, and if you leave Cornillon by the quiet tree-lined D70 you come all too soon to the outskirts of **Salon-de-Provence**, administrative capital of the Crau. They are inevitably forbidding, especially if you come in past the railway station, and so is the traffic on its through roads, but the place to make for is the old town, dominated by one of the biggest castles in Provence.

You can enter the old town either from the north by the seventeenth-century Porte d'Horloge or from the east by the Porte Bourg-Neuf, the only remnant of the mediaeval ramparts. Both are served by the fashionable and crowded Cours Victor Hugo, but between the two gateways is a peaceful area of narrow streets, some of them pedestrian precincts, with inviting cafés and restaurants. Close to the older gateway is the **Church of St-Michel**, a picturesque sight from outside, built in a warm golden stone with two tall arcaded bell-towers and a fine western façade; this has a well preserved tympanum featuring St Michael trampling on a brace of young dragons. It was built at the time of transition between Romanesque and Gothic, and the largely Gothic interior is not nearly so satisfying.

At one corner of the winding lane is the Maison de Nostradamus, where the sixteenth-century astrologer and physician lived. He was relied on by Catherine de' Medici for his predictions and by Charles IX for his medical prescriptions, and the house where he spent the last twenty years of his life now contains a small museum illustrating his life, with some contemporary seventeenth-century editions of his major works.

Overlooking all this is the vast **Château de l'Empéri**; in Provence only the castle of Tarascon and the Palais des Papes in Avignon are bigger. The earliest castle here was built in the tenth century, and it owes its name to the time when the kingdom of Arles was annexed to the Empire in 1032. It was rebuilt in its present compass in the middle of the thirteenth century by Jean des Baux, archbishop of Arles, who must have had both grandiose tastes and considerable fears for his own safety. In the sixteenth century Archbishop Ferrier converted most of it into a more comfortable but still prestigious residence.

The elegant north and west wings of the *cour d'honneur* date from this time, but the *cour de l'Empéri*, though damaged by an earthquake in 1909, has some of the oldest work in the castle, including the twelfth-century chapel of St Catherine. Many of the rooms are devoted to a unique museum of French military history from the time of Louis XIV to the end of the first world war. The château, which is approached by flights of steps from the Place des Centuries, is open all the year round at the usual times except on Tuesdays and national holidays.

Before you leave Salon, have a look at the **Collegial Church of St-Laurent** – not difficult, as it stands beside the Boulevard David which is one of the main exit routes to the north. This is a Dominican foundation in the early Gothic style typical of the order. The inside is enormously wide and high, with a series of tall, narrow Gothic windows rather like the one at the west end of the *collégiale* at Villeneuve-lès-Avignon. Yet to left and right of the choir is a pair of perfect little Romanesque doorways in the classical style, looking like miniature replicas of the Roman archways at the Pont Flavien, though there are no lions. Outside, the narrow buttresses and pinnacled tower put it firmly in the Gothic world. It has come a long way from St-Michel in the old town, and somehow you would expect a Gothic character like Nostradamus to be buried here, as he is. Nostradamus was a native of St-Rémy, not a salonnais by birth, but the engineer Adam de Craponne was born here in 1527, and his name survives in the Canal de Craponne which still brings fresh water from the Durance to irrigate this corner of the Plaine de la Crau.

Before moving on to Aix, which is now only fifteen miles away, there is another rewarding detour which covers two profound and still tangible influences on Provence, the Roman and the Cisterician. First though, if you have a taste for seventeenth-century French *grandeur*, drive the first few miles along the still pleasant D572 as far as the **Château de la Barben**, off the road to the left up a rather rough lane. Based on an early mediaeval fortress first mentioned in 1063, its former owners included the abbey of St-Victor in Marseille and King René of Sicily, count of Provence. He sold it to the head of the noble Provençal family of de Forbin, who held it for the next five hundred years. Considering all that happened between 1400 and 1900 no wonder it has a bewildering mixture of styles and features, including a staircase of the time of Henri IV, gardens laid out by le Nôtre, tapestries from Aubusson and Brussels, and the room which Pauline Borghese decorated in Empire style, with a wallpaper by the painter Granet who has a museum named after him in Aix.

This said, visitors must be warned that the present owners have rivalled if not outdone the proprietors of Woburn and Longleat in developing quite different attractions. Part of the outbuildings have been turned into a 'vivarium', where exotic fish and reptiles from southern Europe are on view, and (on the far side of the road) a large *Parc zoologique*. The effect of this is that the grounds, especially at weekends, are swarming with people and the car park crammed with cars. You should heed the warning notices not to leave anything you value in your car.

You will appreciate more than this the détour I have suggested, which takes you a short way back on your tracks, then northwards along a green country road (the D22) towards Vernègues. Just outside the village bear right for the vineyard estate of **Château Bas**. This must be an idyllic place to live and work, for the seventeenth-century *château-ferme* is surrounded by trees, and behind it are green lawns and a swimming pool. Yet the eye turns immediately to the woods beyond, where on the lower slope of a scrubby hill they frame a substantial lump of masonry set off by a group of tall fluted Corinthian pillars. No

169

doubt about it, this was a Roman temple which must have been as grandiose in its time as the château of la Barben. The noble columns and beautifully carved acanthus-leaved capitals put to shame their twelfth-century imitations, and they must have formed the portico, or *pronaos*, of a temple on the lines of the Maison Carrée at Nimes. The foundations are massive blocks of stone cut into clean rectangles, and the one surviving section of wall is wonderfully tailored to its full height.

To complete a composite picture typical of Provence, a lot of the masonry was re-used in the eleventh century to build a Romanesque church, most of it contained within the body of the temple, but with a choir and apse protruding to the east. It was consecrated by the bishops of Arles and Apt, but some time later the nave was demolished, leaving only the tiny little chapel walled off to the west, with a pair of windows looking in at the remains of the temple. If you walk round to the east you will see the unusual sight of a Romanesque apse built of huge clean-cut Roman blocks of stone. The doorway on the south side was a sixteenth-century development. Christianity may have won the spiritual clash of cults, but I suspect that the foundations of the Roman temple will last another two thousand years – unless they are robbed to make a nuclear fall-out shelter. The real continuity of the site lies in the château itself, for this is just the situation where you would expect to find a Roman villa managing its farmland and vineyards, though with a heated bath system rather than a swimming-pool.

In the eleventh century a small party of *religieux* settled on a low eminence above the marshy land bordering the left bank of the Durance, across the river from Cadenet in the Luberon, and equidistant from Salon and Aix. Being subject to the all-powerful abbey of St-Victor in Marseille they dedicated their chapel to its patron saint. As at Montmajour they set about draining the marshes and building roads, and they welcomed visitors to their monastic quarters. In 1145 St Bernard passed this way on a mission to Languedoc, and persuaded them to join the expanding Cistercian order based on Cîteaux in Burgundy.

Two years later a party of Cistercian monks arrived from Morimond, the second 'daughter' of Cîteaux, and thanks to a grant of land from Raymond des Baux and donations from Raymond Bérenger, count of Provence, and from the cathedral chapter of Aix, a new monastery was begun to which they gave the lovely name of **Silvacane**, or 'forest of reeds', for the land round about was still a waste of marshes.

This was the origin of the youngest and loveliest of the 'three Cistercian sisters' of Provence, though le Thoronet and Sénanque had still to be completed. In spite of many disastrous changes of fortune over the centuries, the buildings have lost little of their moving simplicity and charm. You can reach Silvacane easily in twenty-minutes from Château Bas by the road which follows the Canal de Marseille to the village of La Roque d'Anthéron.

As a Cistercian foundation the abbey was laid out according to the strict rules of the order, though the fall of the ground on the north side made it necessary to follow Sénanque in placing the refectory alongside and parallel to the cloister. The church itself follows the uncompromising plan of a plain wide nave with side aisles, leading to a transept with only slightly protruding wings, from each of which two square-headed chapels extend to the east, on either side of the equally plain sanctuary apse. All the glass is plain.

In common with all Cistercian architecture, which was inspired by the Platonic philosophy of mathematics and music, the proportions are beautiful; yet it has a shy, even feminine grace not obvious at Sénanque. Difficult to analyse, it comes perhaps from its creamy stonework, its tentative but telling decorative touches, and especially from the way the light falls from the windows of the central apse. The alignment of these is the most beautiful I know in church architecture – just a row of three Romanesque lancets, the middle one very slightly the tallest, and above them a breath-takingly simple eight-lobed *oculus* set deep in the wall. The morning light falls on the plain stone altar, and on the few steps which rise from the floor of the nave. The west end is lit in the same way through larger windows which let in the evening sun.

The body of the church cleverly disguises the fact that (again because of the fall of the land to the north) the floor of the north aisle is quite a bit lower than that of the nave, while the south aisle is higher by about the same amount. The discrepancy is concealed by the low wall between the nave and the north aisle, which appears to match the rise to the south while actually concealing the drop to the north. The feeling of lightness is helped by the slightly broken arches of the barrel vault and the ribbed groins of the crossing, and also perhaps by the treatment of a typical Cistercian feature in which the supporting pilasters end about six feet from the floor, and are carried on imposts which recede by softly moulded steps into the face of the main pillars. It seems amazing that such apparently fragile beauty has survived the damage it suffered in attacks by brigands, from natural disasters, in religious conflicts and over long periods of neglect.

The church must have been finished about 1230, and the rest of the monastic buildings added in the course of the same century. Restoration of these is still incomplete, and the refectory has almost subsided down the bank to the north. The cloister, a relaxed and gentle place, was still waiting when I saw it last for repairs to the damaged arcading of its southern and eastern ranges. The Chapter house is particularly gracious, with delicate ogival vaulting springing from two central columns, one of which has a twisted 'barley-sugar' shaft. The *chauffoir* of the monks looks comfortable, with a large fireplace, window seats and shelves for their books. The central space of the cloister is planted with lavender and shaded by a cypress, and there is a battered *lavabo* intended for the monks' ablutions but (judging from the number of coins thrown into it) now treated as a wishing well.

The west end of the church is shaded by a huge and ancient plane tree, nightingales sing in May and June, and there seem to be happy spirits abroad in Silvacane – on our last visit we found a violet-eyed cream-coloured kitten scampering about the nave, but there were no other human visitors that morning.

Only fifteen miles separate the peace of Silvacane from the exhilarating frenzy of Aix-en-Provence, and that is typical of the country. The road south through Rognes and over the Chaîne de la Trévaresse makes a picturesque transition, but very soon you will be battling with the traffic of a city where you will need to keep all your wits at the ready.

10

Aix-en-Provence

Aix is so much a city of the present that it would be a mistake to spend too much time writing about its past. One look at the map shows why it has always been and still is the heart of Provence, though never its largest city. So many roads, and now a complex of autoroutes, enter from all points of the compass, and depart scattering their traffic to all parts of what was the Roman *provincia* of Transalpine Gaul. It became the first centre of Roman activity away from the coast when the consul Caius Sextius Calvinus founded a settlement of Roman colonists after defeating the local tribesmen (the Saluvii) and destroying their *oppidum* at Entremont, just outside the northern limits of the city. He had found there the thermal springs so sought after by Roman valetudinarians, and the settlement became known as Aquae Sextiae. 'Aix' is the same contraction of the Latin *ad aquas*, meaning 'by the waters', which you find in Aix-les-Bains and Aix-la-Chapelle.

Within twenty years the Roman camp associated with the settlement was the headquarters of Caius Marius when in 102 BC he defeated the biggest threat to Rome since Brennus and his Gallic horde captured the city (but not the Capitol) in 391. A combination of German tribes, the Cimbri and the Teutones, whose migrating armies had been roaming the country for some

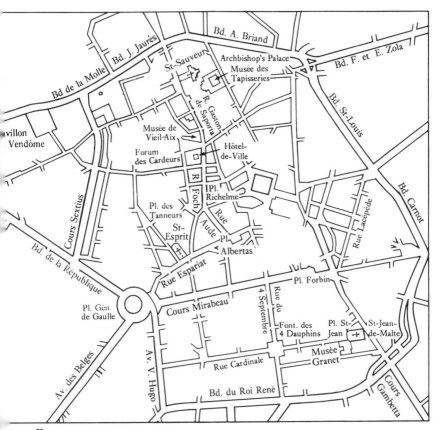

-en-Provence

time, were threatening to invade northern Italy when the
masterly tactics of Marius at the battle of Aquae Sextiae all but
annihilated the Teutones. Not only did this, and his subsequent
victory over the Cimbri at Vercellae in Lombardy, remove all
threats to Rome from the north, but in the course of the
campaign Marius had organised the Roman army on professional lines so efficiently that Julius Caesar found a ready-
made instrument for his later conquests, which established
Roman supremacy over western Europe for the next five
hundred years. The scene of the battle of Aquae Sextiae has
never been firmly identified, but the village of Pourrières on the
eastern slopes of the Montagne Sainte-Victoire is the most
likely.

We have seen how Arles, connected to the sea routes by river
and canal, became the earliest commercial centre of Provence,
and its royal capital. In the early Christian era Aix was upstaged
in the pilgrimage business by its neighbour St-Maximin, which
had the priceless relics of St Mary Magdalene, and by the
Saintes-Maries in the Camargue. In the early Middle Ages it
was no more than an important cathedral town, and not till the
fifteenth century did it come into its own as a home for the arts
and learning. That it did so then was due mainly to the
personality and activities of René of Anjou, titular king of Sicily
and Naples but substantively count of Provence. Having been
turned out of his southern kingdom by Alfonso of Aragon in
1442 he transferred his court to Aix-en-Provence, and divided
his time between his palace in the town and his castle at
Tarascon.

Though the reign of 'le bon roi René' has always been
thought of as a golden age in Provence, and however mistily
romantic that idea may be, he was certainly more enlightened
and more popular in his lifetime than most mediaeval autocrats.
During the seventeenth and eighteenth centuries it was the
continuing social prestige of Aix which attracted noble families
and rich merchants to build their town houses, or *hôtels* here.

176

Thereafter, while Marseille grew into the most important maritime city in France, and Toulon the largest naval base, Aix was still the home of artists and men of letters. Above all it was a university town, and to have a university founded in 1409 puts it among the oldest in Europe.

Although the Thermes Sextius, an eighteenth-century establishment in the north-west quarter, keep alive the idea of Roman baths as a way of relaxation, they play no part whatever in the life of a city which recognizes no need to relax. Thanks to its university population it has kept its youth – a place where anything and everything can and does happen, unrehearsed and at great speed. Before and after their times of work the students mount their mopeds and snarl their way through the already teeming traffic in search of food or other diversions. Or they gather in groups to argue, laugh, and play silly games on each other. Once I saw a serious-looking young man released from his studies leap-frog his way down a fifty-yard row of iron bollards meant to keep cars from parking on the pavement; to my relief he made it without injury. You do not as a rule hear much abuse of portable radios, but I have heard an impromptu musical performance on accordion and bamboo pan-pipes beside the tables of an open-air café. Unfortunately dogs seem equally uninhibited, to the detriment of the pavements – poor things, they have little choice as the wheels flash by in the road.

You will have gathered that Aix is no place in which to drive a car unless you have to, and unless you have nerves of steel. There are a few municipal car parks, but none in the centre of the town, where pavement parking is the custom, if not the rule. If you see a space take it in a flash before someone else does. This raises the question of where to stay, for once you have found a safe resting-place for your car Aix – at least the interesting part – is small enough to explore on foot from a conveniently placed hotel.

Of the top hotels, the modern Paul Cézanne is on the noisy ring road, too far from the centre of things, and has no *parking*.

The Pigonnet is quiet but even further away. A new hotel called the Augustins has been made out of the former convent of that name, and is conveniently placed off the Cours Mirabeau. It advertises a garage, but in my book it cannot compete with the long-established Nègre-Coste, right on the north side of the Cours, which has a huge and well guarded private parking area behind, spacious and comfortable rooms and an obliging staff. Le Manoir has also recently modernised the site of a fourteenth-century priory, a surprisingly peaceful and secluded spot in the rue d'Entrecasteaux off the Place des Tanneurs in a busy part of the old town; it qualifies as a 'relais de silence'. In a more modest class the Cardinal, in the rue Cardinale to the south of the Cours, is comfortable, quiet and welcoming, but you have to take your chance of finding a parking space in the road outside.

The **Cours Mirabeau** is one of the most famous streets in Europe, and it deserves to be. The wide boulevard is shaded by double rows of plane trees on each side, and the space between the two carriageways is marked by three islands, each with one of the distinctive fountains which are such a feature of Aix and of several other provincial towns in Provence. The Cours runs roughly east and west between the Place General de Gaulle, with its three great spouting fountains, and the irregular little Place Forbin, in front of which a statue of King René, holding a bunch of the muscat grapes he introduced to Provence, presides over a particularly moss-encrusted fountain. If you are first entering the Cours by car, always do so from the Place General de Gaulle, as the *sens unique* makes it impossible to reach the Place Forbin from any convenient point on the ring road.

The two sides of the Cours Mirabeau are strikingly different in character. The north side is overlooked and overcrowded by cafés and other tourist enterprises, and on Saturday or Sunday nights walking down it is no fun; it attracts all sorts, conditions and races, sometimes disconcerting in their behaviour. Yet on a weekday or a Sunday morning, with the sunlight filtered by a thick cover of green leaves, the Cours can look magical. The south side is always quieter, and is lined by a series of eighteenth-century *hôtels* which are protected as ancient monuments from any development other than as banks or respectable commercial premises.

The whole area behind the Cours on this side follows the tone set by these *hôtels*, and contrasts utterly with the haphazard mediaeval development to the north. It was laid out on a classical grid plan in the seventeenth century by Cardinal Michel Mazarin – not the *éminence grise* who haunted the court of Anne of Austria, but his brother who was archbishop of Aix. The name of the central street of the grid, the rue Cardinale, makes a double play on the Latin word *cardo*, which meant the hinge or pole round which things turn, and so described one of the axial roads in Roman town plans. As you would expect, the streets of this quarter are quiet, the houses sedate and dignified. At its geometrical centre, where the rue Cardinale meets the rue du 4 septembre, is the **Place des Quatre Dauphins**, where the most engaging fountain of them all spouts water from the mouths of four cheerful dolphins, each facing a 'cardinal' point.

The eastern end of the rue Cardinale is marked by the tall tower of the church of **St-Jean-de-Malte**, originally the thirteenth-century chapel of the Knights of St John and the first Gothic church to be built in Aix. It is closed on Wednesdays, but provided no restoration work is going on you can see inside on mornings and afternoons during the rest of the week.

On the right of the Place St-Jean is the **Musée Granet**, itself housed in the former *commanderie* of the Order, and named after the painter friend of Ingres who was born in Aix. The museum is a heterogeneous assembly representing all sorts of cultures, from Celto-Ligurian finds on the Plateau d'Entremont to a collection of French and Flemish paintings of the fifteenth to the twentieth centuries, most of it contributed by Granet himself. It includes a self-portrait by Rembrandt (possibly original), but otherwise nothing stands out except two pictures by Ingres – his brilliant portrait of Granet, dated 1807, and his large-scale 'Jupiter and Thetis' of 1811. The surprise is to find nothing by Cézanne, easily the most famous artist who worked in Aix. You will find his *atelier* preserved in the Avenue Paul Cézanne, tucked away in the northern parts beyond the inner ring road; it contains mementos of his working life, but again none of his paintings. The inescapable truth is that they are now too valuable for a provincial museum to hold or acquire.

The old town lies north of the Cours. To find your way about it is far from easy, but much more rewarding than it is at Arles. This is a prosperous town brimming with confidence, but never garish; it has style as well as *élan*. Even if you miss your way in the tortuous system of streets, something interesting will catch the eye, and the scale is so small that you will not be lost for long. Your hotel will usually provide you with a street map, and I suggest one basic route which takes in most of the best things and is easy to follow on the map.

Near the west end of the Cours Mirabeau, the rue de la Masse leads off it past the new 'Augustins' hotel into the rue Espariat, the narrow but exclusive shopping artery of the old town. Leaving behind you the flamboyant *clocher* of the Augustinian priory, with its elaborate Provençal ironwork crown, you are faced by the classical façade of the church of St-Esprit. Turn right, and after a hundred yards or so you come to the cobbled **Place Albertas**, an unforgettable miniature of eighteenth-century town life, surrounded on three sides by the uniform façades of the former Hôtel d'Albertas, with a handsome (though later in date) fountain at its centre.

Film directors find the Place Albertas an irresistable location for period productions. I shall always associate it with a day when it was occupied by a typical television crew filming a scene from the life of the comte de Mirabeau, the extraordinary reprobate known as 'l'Ouragon', who seduced the rich young heiress of the de Marignanne family, and brazened it out when her father returned to find Mirabeau's carriage standing outside the door of his *hôtel*. The episode being shot showed Mirabeau appearing *en déshabille* on the balcony of a house in the Place, while grooms and flunkeys gaped, the carriage horses stamped and snorted, and M. de Marignanne shook his fist at his daughter's paramour.

The father insisted on a marriage, which took place at the church of St-Esprit in 1772, but refused to support the couple, so that Mirabeau ran up enormous debts with the tradesmen of Aix, for which he was eventually committed to the island prison of Château d'If outside the harbour of Marseille. In spite of all this, and though not born in Aix, he has been treated as a favourite son (hence the Cours named after him) on the strength of his later career as a revolutionary orator in the National Assembly; he joined the throng of citizens who demolished the Bastille after its storming in July 1789. Though not perhaps a typical Provençal career, it does show some recognisable traits of character.

At this point you should turn left up the rue Aude and continue by the rue Maréchal Foch into the Place Richelme, where the daily fruit and vegetable market is held. This is one of the most colourful you will see anywhere, with some stalls selling cheeses and herbs, and a separate fish market occupying the opposite corner on some days of the week. French markets, and this one in particular, should be a lesson for our shabby equivalents. All the produce comes fresh from the country, and the stalls are set up in the early hours of the morning. When midday strikes from the sixteenth-century clock tower across the road they are immediately dismantled, their goods are carted away, and the whole Place is swept clean and hosed down. By 12.30 there is not a scrap of refuse, paper or plastic to show there had been a market. A little further up on the right the tricolour flies from the façade of the **Hôtel-de-Ville**, built by a Parisian architect between 1655 and 1670. The wide *place* opposite is a popular venue for meeting and animated discussion, with café tables set out on the far side.

The rue Gaston de Saporta will now take you on to what has

probably been your goal from the start, the cathedral of St-Sauveur. However, before moving on in that direction, it is worth turning left on the far side of the Hôtel-de-Ville into the **Forum des Cardeurs**, a long sloping rectangle with a big modern fountain at the top, and otherwise – astonishingly – empty as a rule. The lower end is sometimes used for fairs or exhibitions, and at the top the tables of a café and an excellent *al fresco* restaurant are set out, but this unexpected breathing space in a tumultuous city is something to relish while you can.

The first major frontage on the left of the rue Saporta is that of the **Musée du Vieil Aix**, in one of the finest of all the old *hôtels*, built in 1668. It belonged to the family of Estienne de Saint-Jean, the last member of which converted it to a museum. It is still privately administered, with no civic support and therefore no large resources, but it has assembled a wonderful collection of local treasures. The lower rooms have an exhibition of *santons*, the doll-like creations peculiar to Provence which illustrate every aspect of social life in the costumes of the past; they were widely used in displays of the story of the Nativity at Christmas, and some of them are mechanically animated to move as puppets. There is a good collection of the *faïence* which used to be made at Moustiers-Ste-Marie – much better than any of the stuff you can buy there now. A fine stone staircase leads to the first floor, where there is a most interesting series of *gravures* by Jean Valéry Cornillon which show women employed on the daily occupations of the last century. The sedan chair on display belonged, we are told, to a prominent numismatist of Aix, and there is a travelling trunk with a combination lock, false bottom and secret hiding-place for jewels.

Further up the road on the right is a passage-way which leads to the **Musée des Tapisseries**, occupying a large part of the former **Archbishop's Palace**. The museum has been overshadowed during July for some years now by the Aix music festival which is held in the Palace courtyard. This has become increasingly prestigious and popular, especially now that the whole area has been roofed in against the elements; on one disastrous night a few years ago an opera performance was disrupted by a thunderstorm. It seems appropriate that a musician as unorthodox as Darius Milhaud should have attended the same Lycée in Aix as Cézanne and Zola.

In 1849 an architect surveying the roof of the palace found some bundles of material which turned out to be eighteenth-century Beauvais tapestries, probably hidden there in haste at the time of the Revolution. There were three separate lots, all now exhibited in the splendid apartments created for the archbishops of the seventeenth and eighteenth centuries. The most eye-catching are the nine scenes from the life of Don Quixote, brilliant in colour and execution. Four others represent Russian *divertissements* involving lively gypsy-like characters, and the remaining six are *grotesqueries* from designs by Bérain.

The Palace was naturally built adjacent to the **Cathedral of St-Sauveur**, in fact separated from it only by the cloister. The western doorway of the cathedral opens directly on to the rue Laroque, and is itself one of its great attractions. The two tall wooden door leaves were carved in walnut by Jean Guiramand, a master from Toulon, in 1504. They show in high relief the figures of four of the Old Testament prophets and twelve sibyls – the sibyl, or pagan prophetess, was a favourite subject for Renaissance artists who enjoyed the freedom it gave to portray seductive feminine forms and dresses. To prevent damage from weather or criminal sabotage, the doors are kept behind shutters which can only be opened by the sacristan – who naturally expects a *pourboire* for doing this, and will usually wait till a small crowd has collected.

The same precaution is taken with what is regarded as the cathedral's great treasure, the painting by Nicolas Froment known as the 'Buisson Ardent', or 'Burning Bush'. It was commissioned in 1475 by King René, and the central panel of a triptych is based on the scene where Moses sees a bush (here a little plantation of trees) which burns without being consumed, at the heart of which is the Virgin and her Child. In the lower part Gabriel appears to Moses (depicted as an unusually patriarchal shepherd watching his sheep) to announce the virgin birth symbolised by the unconsuming flame of the Holy Spirit. In the two wings of the triptych are the figures of the two royal patrons. A solid-looking René kneels to the left, to the right his slight young second wife Jeanne de Laval – rare examples of realistic contemporary portraits in a religious setting. Saints and church dignitaries form a background, carrying symbols appropriate to each. A familiar sound in the nave is the creaking of the leaves which tells you when the sacristan is opening up the triptych to reveal the picture, which is charming in its detail and vivid in its subject and colouring.

Though it is fashionable to dismiss the architecture of St-Sauveur as a muddle of styles from different periods, it seems fairer to say that it remains what it has been almost throughout the Christian period, a dignified and friendly place of worship to which different ages have contributed what then seemed the best. What we find the most arresting contribution today originated as early as the fourth or fifth century – a Gallo-Roman **Baptistery** which has an octagonal baptismal font sunk in the floor, surrounded by tall Roman columns of an even earlier date. Some say that they came from a second or third-century temple of Apollo on the same site, and there is no doubt that early Christian builders were happy to re-use both the sites and the materials of their heathen predecessors. The floor of the baptistery is sunk almost a metre lower than that of the nave, and the feeling of mystery and age is enhanced – perhaps anachronistically – by the dim light filtering down from a central cupola which was only added in the sixteenth century. One feels that a baptism here must have been a more than usually solemn occasion, though of course the total immersion it provided was for adults rather than infants.

The later history of the site is certainly complicated. We know nothing of the earliest cathedral, but some time in the eleventh century the cathedral Chapter built themselves a new church (dedicated to Notre-Dame) between the baptistery and a small oratory known as the Sainte-Chapelle. In the following century the need to serve the growing population of Aix led to the building of the parish church of Corpus Domini to the north of the baptistery, with an entrance on the street. In 1285 the then archbishop decided to replace Notre-Dame and incorporate Corpus Domini in a new Gothic cathedral dedicated to the Saint-Sauveur, which superseded all the Romanesque and earlier elements. Building went on till about 1350, and it was 1513 before the façade was finished. The tower in its present form took just as long to complete, and the flamboyant upper stage only received its final pinnacles in the early sixteenth century.

The tower makes its presence felt when you sight it from far down the rue Saporta, but the best view of it is from the **Cloister**, which is dated about 1190 and belonged to the earlier church of Corpus Domini. After the solemn muted atmosphere of the baptistery it always seems a release to walk round into the cloister, where sunlight and shadow make marvellous patterns on the stone. The most uniformly harmonious of the great Romanesque cloisters of Provence, it differs from all the others in not having its arcading broken up into separate bays. The rows of twin marble columns march uninterrupted round each side of a perfect square, an arrangement only possible because there is no heavy stone vaulting to be supported. Elsewhere the barrel vaults over the galleries need strong intermediate pillars to take the weight of the transverse arches, but here there is only a light wooden ceiling all the way round, and the architect made good use of the opportunities that gave.

Even the corner pillars are not that massive, and are all differently treated: one has elaborately carved panels on its four sides, one is surrounded by neat colonnettes, in another the colonnettes have got themselves into a marvellously fluid twist, while the one in the north-east corner has a life-size statue of

St Peter, holding upright his traditional key of office. The eastern range has wavy moulding on the underside of its arches, and the capitals of the northern range are carved with scenes from the life of Jesus, from the Annunciation to the Descent from the Cross. The effect throughout is of lightness and grace, with a few eccentric touches typical of Aix.

There will always be new things to discover here, and no writer can cover them all. One place it would be easy to miss is the chapel of the **Catholic College** in the rue Lacépède, not one normally open to the public. Its lofty Renaissance interior has an exceptionally good acoustic, which makes it a favourite setting for chamber and instrumental concerts, so look out for any advertisements or advance publicity. If you call at the *Office du Tourisme* in the Place General de Gaulle, they should be able to tell you what the chances are of getting in during your stay.

The rue Lacépède will stir the memory of anyone who knew Aix in the 1970s or early 80s, for at No. 9 the brothers Henri and Gérard Charvet used to conduct one of the most delightful and intimate restaurants in the Midi – quite properly awarded its rosettes by Michelin. Now its discreet frontage on the street is closed, dark and grimy, and nobody knows what has happened to the brothers and their elegant womenfolk. Rumour says they are in New York, but perhaps one day the two open fires at either end of their civilised and enticing dining room will be lit again, and guests will be savouring a *ragout de langoustines* and digesting their dinner over a generous glass of cognac, *age inconnu*.

In the 1660s Provence was governed by Louis, cardinal of Vendôme, on behalf of Louis XIV. He was a grandson of Henri IV, and he decided he would like an informal summer residence on the outskirts of Aix. In 1664 he commissioned the architect la Rivière (whose real name was Matisse) to build what is known as the **Pavillon de Vendôme**, standing in its own grounds on the south side of the rue de la Molle as it leaves Aix in the direction of Avignon. Perhaps its isolated position gives it an advantage over the other *hôtels* in the town, and you can argue that the proportions might have been better without its top storey, but you will seldom see a perfectly restored seventeenth-century residence of this quality in such agreeable surroundings.

The interior furnishings are all of a piece with the period and just as satisfying, and the double staircase leading to the upper floors is magnificent. The baroque central doorway has an elaborate frieze supported by a pair of the head-and-torso figures known as *Atlantes* (after the titan Atlas, who according to one myth was compelled by Zeus to carry the world on his shoulders). They became a favourite architectural device in the neo-classical period, usually marked by an expression of anguish as they clasp their heads with one hand and try to hold up their nether garments with the other. The well muscled pair here were the work of Claude Rambot, the sound of whose name may evoke thoughts of the late twentieth century. The attraction of the pavilion for a classical artist is obvious, and in 1730 it was bought by Jean-Baptiste Van Loo, a member of a distinguished family of Dutch painters, who was born in Aix and whose work you can see in one or two churches in the city. He lived here for the last fifteen years of his life. You can spend a pleasant hour or so in the house and grounds, away from the crowds and the traffic, and the historical video laid on for visitors on the ground floor is a good one as they go.

Now that the Charvets have gone you will find the city centre short of really good restaurants; in the more popular class fashions change from year to year, and the best move is to consult the receptionist where you are staying – few hotels have their own restaurant. At the time of writing (a necessary warning) one eats nowhere better, at a more reasonable cost and in a more civilised ambiance than at les Petits Ventres in the Place des Tanneurs.

There are two places easily reached from Aix which have different claims on your interest. The **Château de Vauvenargues** is known today chiefly because Picasso is buried there, having bought it in 1958. You can see what attracted him: the cubic symmetry of its four faces and its short chimney-stacks popping up through the fan-like patterns of its Provençal tiling, floating as it does on a little green hill in a sea of trees which pass through the seasons in every shade of green, brown and gold; and the unapproachable privacy it secured for a public man when he needed it. It may also have amused him that the owner of Vauvenargues is entitled to the style of marquis – at least it failed to deter a notable one-time communist.

This is a Renaissance not a mediaeval building, and its title once belonged to a man whose history and character could hardly have differed more from Picasso's. Luc de Clapiers, second marquis de Vauvenargues, was born in Aix in 1715, a thoughtful and retiring man who lived to be only thirty-two. During a short life he wrote so profoundly and eloquently about the human condition that he is now thought to have contributed more – and certainly it was earlier – than did Rousseau to the philosophy of the Revolution. He was a friend not only of Voltaire but of the elder Mirabeau (respectable father of the republican rake) but unlike Picasso the Spaniard he was far too introverted to be claimed as a true son of the south.

Unfortunately the nearest one can get to the château is the terrace which overlooks it from the village of Vauvenargues. The road across the intervening valley is barred to visitors who do not have an *entrée*, for Picasso's family want to keep private at least the place where he chose to be buried. However, this should not deter you from taking the eastern exit road from Aix which runs below the northern slopes of the Montagne Sainte-Victoire, passing through Vauvenargues on the way. It makes a lovely outing, especially in autumn, as the road winds up and down among the trees; by turning right near a hamlet called le Puits de Rians you can complete a circuit of the Montagne before returning to Aix. At its far south-eastern corner is the village of Pourrières, which most authorities now believe was the site of Marius's victory over the Teutones – more because the terrain matches his tactics than for a fanciful idea which connects the word *pourriture*, or 'rot' with the thought of rotting corpses.

From here the road back to Aix follows the southern flank of the Montagne, which is as steeply dramatic as its northern slopes are gentle and green. The sight of its bare wrinkled limestone crest, etched against a Provençal sky, so fascinated Cézanne that he must have painted it a dozen times on his major canvases alone. There is a comparatively easy climb to the top of the ridge from Vauvenargues, which takes about two hours and joins the line of the Grande Randonnée GR9. This walkers' highway runs between the Croix de Provence and the Pic des Mouches at an average height of about three thousand feet, with a much steeper descent to the south at either end. If you do the circuit by car, you would be wise to avoid the weekend, when the whole of Aix seems to have the same idea. As you near Aix on the homeward run you come to a popular stopping place, the village and château of **le Tholonet**, which in less crowded conditions is worth a visit. It was built in the seventeenth century, like so much of Aix; during the summer festival the château is floodlit, and there are concerts in the grounds.

Finally we end the chapter more or less where it began, at the **Plateau d'Entremont**, which occupies the high ground north of Aix in the angle between the N7 and the A51 autoroute. In one sense Entremont is to Aix what Glanum is to St-Rémy, the Celtic settlement which was there before the Romans came. The similarity ends there, because the actual sites are different in character and had quite different later histories.

Glanum lies in an accessible and undefended valley, and was continuously occupied first by the Celtic or 'Glanic' tribes, then by Hellenistic settlers from the coast, then by the conquering Romans, and was only abandoned after the barbarian invasions of the late third century. Entremont on the other hand was a typical fortified hill town such as one finds further north at Alésia and Bibracte in Burgundy, but it knew no life after it was destroyed by Sextius Calvinus in 125 BC. A larger and more varied site than Glanum, with a fine view down to Aix, its ruins have so far been only partially excavated. What has been brought to light shows that the Saluvii were part of an advanced and artistic Celtic civilisation which was never entirely snuffed out by the Roman conquest. Many impressive sculptures and articles of domestic use from Entremont can be seen in the Musée Granet – which might be worth a second visit when you are back in Aix.

For all its drawbacks and eccentricities, Aix-en-Provence is one of the special places of Europe. Speak to anyone who has been there once, and the talk will be of 'do you remember . . . ?' and of 'next time we go . . .'. After two visits most people will become addicts of a city where nobody feels old, and few are.

11

Arles to Bandol

What I am suggesting here is a route which again takes advantage of the key position of Arles at the head of the Rhône delta, but this time takes a direct line to France's south-eastern seaboard and the Côte d'Azur. Inevitably it will bring you very soon to Marseille, a seaport and city so international in feeling and history that you may find it difficult to fit in with your ideas of Provence. We shall test that when we come to it, but in the meantime the roads which lead there have some interesting byways.

The main road from Arles to Marseille, an uncompromising dual carriageway, takes you again over the arid stony expanses of the Crau. To your right is the main channel of the Rhône, with all its attendant canals and *étangs*, ahead is the Golfe de Fos, surrounded by oil refineries. Not yet an autoroute, the road passes through Fos-sur-Mer, with its hopeful 'Plage du Fos', and on to Martigues. Here it does become an autoroute, which crosses the Canal de Caronte by a spectacular viaduct which would have astonished the bridge-builders of Avignon, but if you want a glimpse of what is left of the one-time fishing port of Martigues you should take the escape road to the left which is signposted to Istres.

The name **Martigues** – in old Provençale *Mouartaigues* – has

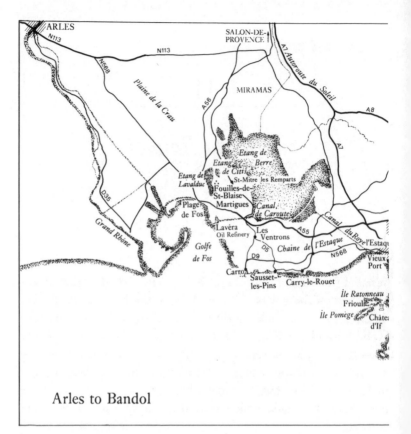

Arles to Bandol

reversed the syllables more easily recognised in Aigues-Mortes
('dead waters'), the fortified town in the western Camargue
beyond the Petit Rhône. The port faces the Étang de Berre, the
huge inland sea connected by the Canal de Caronte to the Golfe
de Fos. The canal divides into two main channels at its eastern
end, so that Martigues is split into three separate *quartiers* –
Ferrières to the north, Jonquières to the south, and the Île
Brescon occupying the middle ground between the two water-
ways. Until 1581 they were independent towns, each with its
own *mairie*, parish church and town walls, and even in the
eighteenth century they were treated as separate *bourgades* with
their own town bands and distinctive colours. To this France
owes the tricolour, for in a triumphant revolutionary march

192

through the streets of Paris the three contingents from Martigues were chosen to head the procession with their blue, white and red banners – the proper sequence of colours for the French flag.

So much of the old town was built either beside a canal or facing the Étang de Berre that even now, when the huge petrochemical plant at Lavéra is threatening their rear, the waterfronts of Martigues have kept a lot of their charm. The rows of little stuccoed houses, with their brightly coloured shutters, are reflected in the still water just as they were when the artist Felix Ziem arrived from Burgundy in 1840 and never tired of painting them – as a visit to the museum here will show. Corot was a later admirer, and Augustus John had a house here where he entertained his English friends. One of the best views is from the bridge over the side canal of St-Sebastien on the Île Brescon.

There is another good reason for turning aside into Martigues, for if you take the road which leads on north through Ferrières towards Istres, you will find this the easiest way of reaching the archaeological site of the **Fouilles de St-Blaise**, a more important one than Entremont and more imposing than Glanum. Soon after passing below the hill town of St-Mitre-les-Remparts you will see a sign directing you to turn left for the excavations. They occupy a substantial bluff between two *étangs*: the main site overlooks the Étang de Lavalduc, while the twelfth-century chapel of St-Blaise is on lower ground facing the Étang de Citis. Here you can leave your car before entering the remains of a major Hellenistic town – provided you come on the right day at the right time. Only from 1 July to 30 September can you be sure of admission in both mornings and afternoons. At other times the system is that on Mondays, Wednesdays and Fridays it opens only in the afternoon – and of course never on Tuesdays.

This was a wonderful place to build a town. Surrounded by pine woods, and with plenty of natural greenery, it was protected on two sides by sheer limestone cliffs; ramparts were hardly needed except where the slopes are gentler to the north and east. Like most natural sites it was undoubtedly occupied in prehistoric times, but its first historical connection was with Etruscan traders who came in the seventh century BC to barter their north Italian wines for salt from the sea lagoons. Trade increased when the Phocaean Greeks established themselves at Marseille, and later finds include pottery from Asia Minor as well as from Etruria.

The most prosperous period was to come, when a well-organised Hellenistic city (called apparently *Mastrabala*) took shape during the third century BC, protected by a superbly engineered system of ramparts, which are easily traced today. So is the street plan of an upper and a lower quarter, with some quite big houses, workshops and storage cellars. Yet its life was short, for the Romans captured it in 125 BC after a siege which must have lasted some time, judging by the number of sling bullets and shot fired from catapults which have been unearthed from inside the ramparts. Unlike Glanum it was not a site which the Romans – who needed easy access rather than fortifications – were keen to develop, so we hear no more of it until the fifth century AD, when it must have provided a refuge during the barbarian invasions. You can see places where the Hellenistic walls were built up with inferior stonework, and there are foundations of two early Christian churches within the *enceinte*. Too near the coast to avoid the attentions of the Saracens, it was sacked in 874. By this time it was known as *Ugium*, from which the name of the *étang* below has been ingeniously derived: 'Lavalduc' is said to be a corruption of 'la vallée d'Ugio'!

Part at least must have been rebuilt by the eleventh century, when we find it called *Castelveyre* (the equivalent of the Italian *castelvecchio*, or 'ancient castle') and the ramparts were extended to enclose the **Chapel of St-Blaise**. This was referred to in a Papal bull of 1156 as Notre-Dame de Castelveyre, but the cult of St Blaise caught on here during the Crusades. He was an Armenian bishop, but the story attached to his martyrdom in 316 would have gone down well in Provence. He had befriended a poor old woman by persuading a wolf to return her a piglet it had killed, and while he was in prison awaiting execution she brought him a dish of brawn she had made from the piglet.

The chapel is a simple Romanesque building in rough stone, not unlike the cemetery chapel at Cornillon–Confoux. It has a short nave, entered through a rather battered doorway on the south side, and a semicircular apse which still has its original heavy tiles supported by stone brackets. Near the west end you can see the foundations of an earlier church, probably the one dedicated to St Pierre, which was destroyed by the Saracens and rebuilt in the eleventh century. In 1390 the marauding followers

195

of the infamous Raymond de Turenne from les Baux sacked Castelveyre, and its inhabitants finally deserted it for St-Mitre-les-Remparts.

You can equally well reach St-Blaise and Martigues from Salon-de-Provence by way of Miramas and Istres, but in either case Marseille will be the next objective on your way east. Some might call it an obstacle rather than an objective, and few travellers will be staying there for more than a night – waiting perhaps for the car-ferry to Ajaccio in Corsica, or en route for some North African resort. Yet Marseille is more recognisable as part of Provence than the miles and miles of internationally polluted coastline between St-Tropez and Monaco.

There is no hurry to get there, unless you have a boat to catch, or are addicted to travel by autoroute. By way of the A55 and A7 you can cover the forty kilometres from Martigues in twenty minutes or less, but there are pleasanter ways than that. In the first place take the southern exit from Martigues by the D5, which should be signed for Carry-le-Rouet and crosses the autoroute almost at once. It will take you across an arid limestone ridge called the Chaîne de l'Estaque, interrupted briefly by a transverse valley running down to the port of Lavéra – a valley now being saturated by housing developments.

At les Ventrons you have a choice. The right-hand fork takes you across the valley, up the stony waste of the Chaîne, then down to the seaside village of Carro, still just recognisable as a fishing harbour. Or you can keep to the main road up to the head of the valley, over the top of the Chaîne, under a major dual carriageway, and down to the straggling seaside resort of Sausset-les-Pins. From here the D5 winds along the coast to **Carry-le-Rouet**, which is not a bad place to spend an hour or two, especially if you have planned to lunch at l'Escale, a magnificent restaurant from whose terraces you can look down on a genuine fishing harbour and enjoy an early view of the real Mediterranean. These places along the coast will always be crowded at weekends, but the pine-clad hills drop so steeply into the sea that there is not a lot of room for the kind of development which has ruined so much of the Riviera coast.

After le Rouet the hills encroach still closer on the sea, so that the main road has no option but to strike inland to rejoin the ridge. From it a few minor roads fall steeply down through the hills to the deep rock-lined inlets known as *calanques* – marvellous places in fine weather for small yachts to put in for swimming and skin-diving. After Ensuès-la-Rédonne, a substantial village in a sheltered hollow with vineyards and olive plantations, you join the N568 which turns south again over the Col de Pas, then suddenly dives through a tunnel to the sea.

A more spectacular route still was taken here by the underground **Canal du Roye**, the exit from which can be seen to the left of the road if you stop and walk under the railway. This extraordinary piece of engineering involved a tunnel seven kilometres long under the Chaîne de l'Estaque, and was wide enough to allow barges of more than 1,000 tonnes to ply between the Étang de Berre and the sea approaches to Marseille. Unfortunately it was blocked by a landslide in 1963 and has never been reopened. The main railway from Arles to Marseille also has to burrow through the rock for a short distance before emerging beside the increasingly commercial harbour of l'Estaque. That this should have been a favourite haunt not only of Cézanne but of Braque, Dufy and Derain is surprising, though the Provençal light they wanted is still astonishingly clear all along this coast.

Perhaps the most bewildering experience of this drive is waiting for you when you join the A55 to be hustled along behind the quays where the big ships and ferries lie, then suddenly into a tunnel from which you emerge on the far side of the **Vieux Port of Marseille**. If you still have your wits about you, keep right (for *centre ville*) as you reach the next junction, and you will find yourself on the Quai de la Rive Neuve, the south side of one of the most wonderful harbours in Europe. To appreciate it properly you need to make your way round to the

197

north side, the Quai du Port, from where you have the famous view over the crowded waters to the hill where the enormous statue of the Virgin – Notre-Dame-de-la-Garde – watches over the heart of Marseille.

The Vieux Port is no longer a commercial harbour. Its rows and rows of pontoon jetties provide moorings for countless private yachts – a forest of masts and a kaleidoscope of many-coloured hulls. Yet its busiest occupants are still the little one-man fishing boats which you can see and hear phut-phutting out to sea in the early morning, and back before sunset. The three sides of an almost landlocked harbour are all different in character. The respectable side is the **Quai du Port**, where you may, if lucky, find meter parking for your car while you have a drink in one of the quayside cafés. Halfway along it is the old Hôtel-de-Ville, with a baroque façade dating from 1674. Across the head of the harbour is the wider expanse of the **Quai des Belges**, where at any time of day you will find an astonishing variety of human races and colours, mostly engaged in different ways of parting tourists from their money.

This is how Daudet described the scene which met the intrepid Tartarin on his first excursion from Tarascon:

'Shops full of strange confections, smoky huts where sailors were cooking their meals, stalls selling pipes, monkeys, parrots, ropes and canvas; fantastic piles of nautical bric-a-brac. . . . Sellers of mussels and clams squatting and crying their wares, sailors passing with pots of tar, steaming stewpans, and great baskets of squids to wash in the chalky waters of the fountains. Everywhere a prodigious jumble of merchandise:- silks, pigs of iron, planks of wood, ingots of lead, cloths, sweets, carob beans, rapeseed, liquorice, sugar-canes.'

He summed it up as 'L'Orient et l'Occident pêle-mêle', and it seems as good a description today, though now the Africans steal the show. Faces ranges from *café-au-lait* to ebony, and the most colourful are the ebony-skinned men in bright cotton robes who set out their cheap jewellery on rugs to beguile the tourist. Only the traditional morning fish market remains a purely Marseillais mixture of commerce and entertainment.

To the south the **Quai de la Rive Neuve** has always had a more sinister feeling about it. The buildings are run down, the cafés more scruffy, and the streets behind look as if they may be harbouring all sorts of disreputable premises. This was their reputation in the past, and though it may be an exaggeration now, I would rather not – as a foreigner – walk there after dark.

To continue what can be only a sketchy tour of Marseille *centre*, its essential axis is the street known as **la Canebière**, the long straight artery for traffic, business, leisure and entertainment which leads from the Vieux Port to the Palais Longchamp. This superbly uninhibited building in nineteenth-century neo-classical style is based on a curved Ionic colonnade from which flights of balustraded steps descend on either side of a spectacular Provençal fountain; the water is the end product of a canal which links Marseille with the River Durance. The name of the street is said to be derived from the word *chénevières*, meaning the plantations of hemp which provided the raw material for all the ropes needed in a port. The irony is that cannabis resin is misused for a different purpose here today, along with other more dangerous drugs.

At each end of the colonnade is a wing containing a major museum. To the right is the *Musée d'histoire naturelle*, which specializes in exhibits from the Mediterranean natural world, both animate and inanimate. To the left is the *Musée des Beaux Arts*, an outstanding collection in a land which loyally recognises its painters, sculptors and architects. It has a strong Provençal content, and it reminds us that Marseille produced two artists not as well known elsewhere. Three rooms are devoted to the painter-architect Pierre Puget, whose visionary designs for the city in the seventeenth century were as revolutionary as those of Wren for London – and even less regarded at the time. A later genius was Honoré Daumier, the sculptor-draughtsman whose caricatures were the scourge of the court of Louis-Philippe. The Impressionists are there, though not in such force as further along the Riviera coast, and the greatest French architect of the twentieth century, le Corbusier, is remembered not so much here as in the **Cité Radieuse**, the area he designed for modern living behind the Corniche Kennedy.

The murals on the staircase landing are by Puvis de Chavannes. One of them depicts Marseille as a Greek colony, reminding us how widely the ancient Greeks colonised the shores of the Mediterranean before the Romans arrived. In about 600 BC a party of Ionian Greeks from Phocaea on the coast of Asia Minor established an enclave here which became known as Massilia, as well as other trading posts up and down the coast between Arles and Nice. While Roman colonies were usually imposed as military establishments, the Greek trading instinct was more pervasive, and this is what gives life to modern Marseille. When the Romans created their new *provincia* of Transalpine Gaul they treated centres like Aix and Narbonne as colonies under a provincial governor, but they allowed the Massiliots to keep their own constitution and government as 'friends and allies of the Roman people'. They paid for a bad mistake in backing Pompey against Julius Caesar in 49 BC, thereby losing maritime and commercial supremacy to Arles, but they continued as a free people into the Christian era, with a university which kept alive Greek learning and arts in the western world. Not surprisingly we find the earliest Christian foundations in Europe appearing along this coast, and Massilia was the natural gateway to the Rhône valley by which their evangelists reached the hinterland.

Marseille today is hardly a Christian city. Every religion under the sun must be represented on its quays and in its streets and alleys. The statue of Notre-Dame-de-la-Garde which presides over it is more in the spirit of Athena on the Athens acropolis, whose flashing helmet and spear were both a symbol of power and a beacon for ships at sea. You will find no great cathedral where Mass has been celebrated under Romanesque vaults for seven hundred years. Only the tiny remnant of the old cathedral of **Notre-Dame-la-Major** survives from the twelfth century, insignificant in the shadow of its monstrous nineteenth-century successor, with its pseudo-Byzantine domes stuck on top of a pseudo-Romanesque exterior of black and yellow brick. If you make your way up to the limestone spur where the piously named architect Espérandieu built his basilica, tower and statue, you will find more of the same date and style, only redeemed by the views which Notre-Dame commands over land and sea.

There is one notable survival. Behind the dubious frontages along the Quai de la Rive Neuve (and easily reached from there) there rises what looks like a mediaeval castle – a group of crenellated towers and battlements which in fact conceal one of the oldest of Christian shrines. In the third century a Roman officer was canonised as St Victor after his martyrdom here at the hands of the Romans. In the early fifth century a Romanian monk called Cassianus (popularly known as Jean Cassien), who had travelled in the east from Bethlehem to Egypt and Constantinople, settled in Marseille and founded what was to become the most influential Benedictine monastery in the Midi, the **Abbaye de St-Victor**. Its base was a palaeo-Christian cemetery which included a grotto in the rock which held the relics of St Victor. Alongside this Cassien built a small basilica church, in a space surrounded by rock tombs and sarcophagi, and entered through a large classical *atrium*, or narthex.

All this now forms the crypt of a Romanesque church built in the thirteenth century and extended to the east a hundred years later under the protection of these formidable walls, which turned it into a fortified church like the Saintes-Maries in the Camargue. In the last thirty years investigators of the crypt have revealed and dated sarcophagi from the second and third centuries (the earliest is a touching little one intended for a child) so there is no reason to doubt that St Victor's is among

201

them. Even St Lazarus and St Mary Magdalene are associated in legend with the catacombs, but there were enough genuine remains from the early Christian period to excite the archaeologists. The ordinary visitor can only marvel at such antiquity.

Off the easternmost point of the city, the Pointe d'Endorme, is a group of islands of which the two larger ones enclose the subsidiary port of Frioul. The smallest is the most notorious, for on it François I built the **Château d'If** as part of the sixteenth-century defences of Marseille. It was never put to the test from outside, for during the wars of religion it has turned into a state prison for the thousands of Huguenots who fell foul of the state. Personalities immured here included Louis XIV's mysterious prisoner, the 'Man in the Iron Mask', and the young Mirabeau as a debtor to the tradesmen of Aix. Even better known is a fictional character, Dumas's Count of Monte Cristo, who actually managed to escape from this grim fortress. Seen from seaward its walls and towers are blank and almost windowless, barely distinguishable from the white limestone rock on which they are built. There is no vegetation for shade or shelter, and it looks like a place where you would fry in summer and freeze in winter.

This is a city not to linger in, perhaps, but one which can never be ignored when writing about Provence. It was through Marseille that civilisation first entered the south of France, and the arts have always flourished here alongside its commercial successes. The Marseillais have the reputation in the rest of France for enterprise verging on a zany kind of recklessness, and as a naturally warm-hearted people prone to unpredictable violence. Where else even in Italy could an outburst by a dissatisfied opera audience have ended in bloodshed? It still lives by the sea and its traffic, and the sight of the Vieux Port at sunset or in the early morning light is not easily forgotten. You may be lucky enough to find accommodation with a balcony overlooking the Quai du Port, but otherwise the nearest you can stay in comfort and peace is at the Grand Hotel Genève, in the

St-Restitut: southern façade

Venasque: church of Notre-Dame

Opposite: Notre-Dame d'Aubune

Abbaye de Sénanque

Château-Bas: Roman temple

Opposite: Château de Bargème

Borie in field

Cotignac: *l'heure de midi*

Castellane: *le marché*

Haute-Provence: from the Col d'Allos

St-Julien-le-Montagnier: *une partie de boules*

Haute Provence: near le Lauzet-Ubaye

rue Reine-Élisabeth behind the Quai des Belges.

On leaving Marseille you will again have to decide whether you want to speed eastward on the autoroute or take a more leisurely road to Bandol which keeps closer to the coast. This alternative allows you an easy and pleasant exit from the south side of the Vieux Port without tangling with the main traffic routes. Turn south on the Corniche Kennedy, which will give you a glimpse of le Corbusier's Cité Radieuse on the Boulevard Michelet, and eventually takes you past the **Château Borély** in its busy public park on the southern outskirts. The château is a discreet eighteenth-century mansion named after the family of rich merchants who built it. Furnished throughout in contemporary style, until recently it held some important collections of French art and archaeological treasures – the plum being one of Egyptian antiquities put together by a nineteenth-century dignitary called Clot Bey. These are now being transferred to the more secluded and recently restored **Hospice de la Vieille Charité**, designed by Pierre Puget, north of the Vieux Port. They are being replaced by a museum of decorative art.

Once free of the suburbs the D559 climbs to the Col de la Gineste before beginning a slow descent from another long limestone ridge; the ridge itself is occupied by a military camp. If you come this way in spring or early summer you will find the rock faces above you brightened everywhere by clumps of rich red valerian, brilliant against the chalky background. As your road crosses the valley above **Cassis** you look down on the first of many harbours where the fisherman has been elbowed out by the yachtsman. Wine-making too has given way to cement production, and though the town still attracts holiday-makers the more discriminating will be looking for access to a whole series of little fjord-like *calanques* which bite into the coast west of the bay. Yet not so long ago Cassis was celebrated by Mistral in *Calendau*, his encomium on Provençal life and customs, and it was a happy discovery for Fauvists like Derain, Dufy and Matisse.

Next you come to **le Ciotat**. This is a much bigger town, with the inevitable sea-front development, even more yachts in its harbour, and a shipyard which still builds and repairs large tankers. The name is derived from the Latin *civitas*, or city state, and there are signs of dense Roman and pre-Roman occupation – even grave finds from the late Neolithic Age. A third-century Roman freighter was found in the harbour, with busts of emperors and a leaden bath-tub among its cargo.

Coastline development continues at les Lecques, which is the sea-front for the misleadingly named St-Cyr-sur-Mer, after which the road drops steeply down into **Bandol**. It may seem unfair to pick out Bandol as an exception from the depressing tide of development which has swamped the coast, but it has many redeeming qualities. Except around the harbour front, its hotels and villas are well spaced out, there is plenty of greenery, and the long sandy beach west of the harbour is not too crowded except at weekends. It was the first stop for literary refugees from Nazi Germany in the 1930s, among them Brecht, Feucht-twanger, Toller and Zweig. Thomas and Heinrich Mann made it their home for a time.

One of the advantages of Bandol is as a base for exploring the hinterland, and fortunately there is a hotel one can unreservedly commend for the purpose. It too has a literary and artistic background, for the Ker Mocotte stands on the rue Raimu, a quiet backwater above the main part of the town. It was formerly the Villa Clementine, home of the actor Jules-August Muraire, *alias* 'Raimu', who created the part of the baker in *La Femme du Boulanger* – the film script adapted by Marcel Pagnol from a story by Jean Giono, another great Provençal writer. The walls of the hotel's reception rooms are covered with Raimu's contemporary posters; its informal garden terraces overlook the best of the beaches and are shaded by pines and tamarisks. The food is good, and Bandol wines are some of the best in the department of Var, where we now find ourselves.

There are two circuits, manageable in a day, which you can

make from Bandol. They combine some lovely scenery with a few intriguing stops by the way. Both start in the same direction, taking the D559B which turns north from the east end of the town beyond the harbour. It will be signed for le Beausset, and whichever way you go after this you should on no account miss a place marked on the map as **le Beausset-Vieux**. To reach it you join the N8 for a short way south towards Toulon, turning right when you see it signposted, and pursuing a series of steeply twisting *virages* till you reach a projecting spur just over 1,000 feet high. There, with views all round which take in everything from the long white mane of la Sainte-Baume to the north-west and as far south as Bandol and the sea, is a perfect little *ensemble* recreated from buildings first put up in the tenth century.

The site had been a place of refuge at the time of the barbarian invasions, and again during the Saracen raids of the eighth and ninth centuries. After the final defeat of the Saracens in 973 by William the Liberator, members of his family built a small *château-fort* up here, and in 1164 the archbishop of Marseille added the chapel of Notre-Dame de Beausset-Vieux to serve as a parish church for the small population which still gathered around the fortifications. Gradually the people began to drift away to the more fertile country in the plain below, and in 1506 the parish responsibility was transferred to what is now le Beausset. Apart from annual pilgrimages to the chapel the place was deserted, and in 1615 Richelieu had the château dismantled. The chapel survived, but in spite of a visit by Napoleon in 1792 it was sold three years later by public auction and fell into disrepair.

During the last century there were periodic attempts to restore it, prompted by the part its statue of the Virgin was thought to have played during cholera epidemics in 1849 and 1865, but it was a losing struggle, and by 1961 after two world wars the whole site was in ruins. At Easter that year the *curé* Lucien Baud began a campaign to restore it worthily and thoroughly, a process which has been continued ever since by volunteers who have been working every Saturday throughout the year, and is now triumphantly complete.

Thanks to Richelieu there is little left of the fortifications except for a few sections of the tenth-century ramparts. The short square *donjon* on the north side is a modern addition, and the building west of the chapel is a reconstruction which serves as a reception area for visitors. All the new work has been finished in the attractive light local stone, and roofed, like the chapel, in Provençal tiles. The chapel is a small Romanesque treasure, one simple nave faced with the original rough stone-work, barrel-vaulted and lit only by two little windows on the south side, ending in a semicircular apse of the same width. In the sanctuary an altar has been built up of three superimposed millstones, and on a bracket behind stands the gilded wooden statue of the Virgin which is the object of enthusiastic pilgrimages at Easter and *Pentecôte*, and more especially on the feast of the Nativity of the Virgin (7–8 September). A niche to one side contains a seventeenth-century Crucifixion in wood, which was once a wayside Calvary. In 1936 it miraculously survived a forest fire, losing only the fingers of Christ's right hand.

The statue of the Virgin also has a history. It was carved in the workshops of Pierre Puget in Toulon in 1712, and replaced the ancient wooden one which had been removed to the new parish church in le Beausset, and which had been burnt there in 1794 by revolutionary zealots. The Puget statue then went underground, hidden by parishioners, until she could safely be restored in 1802. Evidence of the devotion she inspires can be found in a strange vaulted upper chamber which has on its walls a unique collection of *ex voto* pictures of the nineteenth century which record the survival or recovery of their donors from a variety of accidents and illnesses – which the pictures illustrate vividly. There is even a rack of discarded crutches and a child's surgical boot.

Another stairway to the left of the chapel entrance leads to a gallery where a *crèche provençale* has been created – a collection of *santons* surpassed only by the one in the Musée du Vieil Aix, though on a much smaller scale. Traditional doll-like figures, dressed to represent every *métier* of Provençal life, are visiting the crib of the Nativity in a miniature landscape; the realism includes a stream of water which can be made to flow by pressing a switch. Some of the *santons* are two hundred years old; some were made by the grandmother of today's principal *gardienne* – who is a lady of charm and distinction. Finally, on a downward slope beyond the east end you will see a cross delineated on the ground by pebbles. It marks the site where bones disturbed during several periods of restoration – many of them belonging to victims of local warfare – were reburied and left to rest in peace. Le Beausset-Vieux is today both peaceful and exhilarating, transformed by the patient work of careful hands – 'un joli petit coin', as the lady in charge charmingly understates it.

Nothing on the rest of this first tour has quite the same appeal, though the scenery is marvellous and the wild flowers overwhelming. In summer the rocky hillsides are lit up by clumps of valerian, Spanish broom and white cistus; the roads are lined by mauve cistus and purple thistle in full bloom; the verges are bright with blue flax and all kinds of other small flowers. To enjoy the best of it, rejoin the N8 and continue north past le Beausset as far as a junction with the D402 on your right. This passes uncomfortably close to an *autodrome*, or motor racing circuit, but carry on regardless till it meets the D2, turning right for Signes and Méounes-lès-Montrieux. Méounes is a pleasant country town typical of the lower Var, where the café of the Hotel de France, shaded by the plane trees of the Place de l'Église, may tempt you to stop for half an hour on a hot day.

To the south of Méounes are two older sites you may think of visiting, Montrieux-le-Vieux and the **Chartreuse de Montrieux-le-Jeune**. The names sound interesting, but of the former there is nothing left but some fragments of mediaeval walls, and you should be warned that the Chartreuse, apart from a seventeenth-century cloister, was rebuilt in 1850. The site is a pleasing one, and to reach it you walk for ten minutes up a leafy lane beside a running stream, but the Carthusian order abhors public attention and admits visitors only to the crudely decorated chapel of Ste-Roseline.

Instead you may prefer to continue on the D554 through Garéoult, and just before Forcalqueiret turn right for Rocbaron; as you turn you have a dramatic ruined castle on the skyline to your left. From Rocbaron the Grande Randonnée (GR9) provides a wonderful route for walkers across the Barre de Cuers to Belgentier in the valley of the Gapeau, but the nearest thing for those in a car is to take the narrow D40 to your right – a most beautiful road which winds its way along the flank of the mountain and down to Cuers, where it joins the N97 for Toulon.

At this point you will want to escape quickly from a nightmare of autoroute intersections, so take the first opportunity and turn right for Solliès-Toucas, from where you can embark on a cross-country drive of twenty-seven kilometres through the fabulous scenery of the Forêt de Morières-Montrieux and the Plateau de Siou-Blanc. The road qualifies only as a *route française*, but there is nothing wrong with the surface, and after the steep initial climb to the plateau the gradient is gentle; you hardly realise you are well over 2,000 feet up before rejoining the D2 west of Signes. From there you can return to Bandol by the way you left it, through le Beausset.

A second or alternative circuit will take you further afield, and though its main objective is one of the holy places of Provence that is by no means the only reason for undertaking it. To begin with, instead of going through le Beausset again, soon after passing under the autoroute you can keep left for **le Castellet**. This was where *La Femme du Boulanger* was filmed, and though the autoroute now comes very close, and it has attracted a large number of French commuters and second-homers, it still has the character of a Provençal *village perché* and quite a good restaurant.

Then take the minor D26 as far as its junction with the N8, and carry on in the direction of Aubagne. Ignore a sort of Disneyland 'Parc d'attractions', and look north to where the cliffs of the Saine-Baume massif block the sky ahead. The road climbs to the Col de l'Ange, beyond which you keep right for Gémenos. This is a small town with a seventeenth-century château, now the Hôtel-de-Ville, and the starting point for a breathtaking drive which takes you up behind the summit ridge of the Massif. It begins modestly through the trees, and arrives first at a remarkable institution called the **Parc de St-Pons**. This is a natural valley, cleverly adapted with shady walks by rushing streams, and here and there an open sunny space designed for picnics – which are elsewhere forbidden.

You can leave your car by the entrance (though do lock it and take valuables with you if you can) and walk for perhaps twenty minutes up the valley, at the head of which a path circumvents a flurry of sparkling waterfalls to reach a deserted Cistercian convent, almost hidden under tall beech trees. The buildings are in ruins except for the church, which has an impressive Romanesque façade, unexpectedly capped by a crenellated watch-tower. While the park is open all day every day (except Tuesdays) the church is kept locked, and it would take a special application to the Mairie in Gémenos to unlock the door. The visit is worth it just for the freshness and the sounds of running water under the trees – which besides beeches include maples, ashes and hornbeams, and Judas trees with their purple flower clusters in spring.

Now begins the most exhilarating part of the day, as the road twists and turns up the southern flank of the Massif to the Col d'Espigoulier. Under the Provençal sun the stony slopes gleam with a tapestry of wild flowers – everywhere the valerian, the broom and the cistus, with little pink alpine plants in the rocky crevices. Above you all the time are the jagged outlines of the limestone crags. Eventually the road flattens out as it reaches the plateau, and you run down to the hamlets of la Coutronne and Plan d'Aups. You are now looking up at the north flank of the Massif, quite different in aspect from the south side. The flowers have gone, and instead there is a thick green forest of deciduous trees which climbs almost to the skyline. These are all trees commoner in northern climates, sheltered here from the southern heats and benefiting from rain when it falls over the higher ground to the south.

The road continues over level ground to the area known as **la Sainte-Baume**, which you may find crowded with coaches and people, cafés and restaurants. It all stems from the legend of the Saintes-Maries. You may remember that two of the occupants of the boat which made landfall in the Camargue were St Maximin and St Mary Magdalene, who made their way to the Roman colony of Aquae Sextiae. There they preached the gospel to such effect that St Maximin became the first bishop of Aix-en-Provence. 'La Madeleine' however decided to retire to this remote mountain, and according to tradition spent the last thirty years of her life in complete seclusion in a grotto just below the summit of the ridge. The name Sainte-Baume ('holy balm') refers to the 'alabaster box of precious ointment' with which she had anointed Jesus.

It was probably Jean Cassien, founder of the abbey of St-Victor in Marseille, who first made the connection with a particular cave among many on the mountain, and despatched a party of monks to guard this precious site. Naturally it attracted pilgrims from as early as the fifth century, though there was a period of about two hundred years when it was believed that the saint's relics had been moved for safety to the church of the Madeleine at Vézelay in Burgundy. In 1279 Charles d'Anjou, brother of St Louis, claimed to have rediscovered them in the cathedral of St-Maximin, and the pilgrim trade resumed in even greater strength. Everybody came – kings, popes and nobles from all over Europe, as well as a tide of ordinary pilgrims which has never ceased to flow. About 1300 the Dominican order, which has taken over the control and supervision of the site, built a *hôtellerie* to accommodate the pilgrims. It or its successor was destroyed in the Revolution, and the building which goes by that name now is a nineteenth-century replacement; it was again the Dominicans under Henri Lacordaire who revived the cult. Further development in 1968 turned it into a spiritual and cultural centre, especially for the young.

The actual shrine is a cave just below and to the south-west of the peak of St-Pilon – the name refers to a classical column which used to stand there, now replaced by a chapel – at nearly 3,000 feet. It adjoins a terrace with a white marble statue of la Madeleine, from where the views are marvellous – though they are even better from the top of St-Pilon. To reach the cave calls for only such fortitude as is right for a pilgrimage. After passing the *hôtellerie* you will find a notice which points the way to the grotto, a walk which follows the line of the GR9 and takes about an hour. The notice warns you that the temperature inside the grotto is only 12° C., and though that may seem enough for a northerner, it recommends you to take something warm to put on when you get there – sensibly, because the sudden change can be a bit of a shock. The site is open every day between 0800 and 1800.

To finish the circuit which began at Gémenos, follow the D80 down through Nans-les-Pins, a *station de vacances*, to Châteauneuf, where there is a luxurious and secluded hotel. Turn left there on the N560, and if you want to avoid autoroutes pass under the A52 to Roquevaire and under it again to Gémenos on the N396. You could however avoid a very busy intersection by taking a minor road loop through the village of **St-Jean-de-Garguier**, where there is a seventeenth-century chapel with another large collection of *ex voto* pictures, some of them five hundred years old. The snag is that the chapel and its museum are open only on weekend afternoons. From Gémenos you will know your way back to Bandol and the sea.

In between these two longish drives you might like to make a shorter expedition to the **Calanque du Port d'Alon**, a little inlet and harbour on the coast a few miles to the west. You can do this by car, taking the main road back towards St-Cyr and turning left about six kilometres out. Avoid a later right turn to le Deffend (which is a developed area) and go on till you reach a sheltered bay with a simple café-restaurant at its head. There are cliff paths through the trees which follow the coastline in either direction; indeed you can walk here all the way from Bandol if you prefer – a lovely coastal walk which takes about two and a half hours, and passes the Plage des Engraviers where you can swim.

12

Bandol to St-Tropez

Eastward from Bandol all roads lead to Toulon, but such is the variety along this coastline that all kinds of distractions are possible for connoisseurs of serendipity. One source is the peninsula south of Sanary-sur-Mer, which ends in the rocky headland of Cap Sicié. Even before you reach the peninsula, and within a few hundred yards of the A50 autoroute, is a fascinating little Romanesque chapel, **Notre-Dame de Pépiole**. It takes a little finding, but if when still in the outskirts of Sanary you take a left-hand turn on the D63 for la Seyne, look for signs on your left which will guide you up a narrow approach road to the chapel.

You first see it across a pleasant domestic landscape of olives, vineyards and cypresses, so that you hardly realise that the cluster of red roofs ahead of you is anything other than a small farm. Its unique character was first appreciated in 1965 when Dom Celestin Charlier, a monk from the nearby abbey of Maredsous, began to celebrate church offices in the neglected chapel covered with unsightly stucco. During the next ten years he and those whom he regarded as his parishioners set about restoring this remarkable place, and building a two-storeyed extension as a place of retreat for himself and other seekers of peace. Stripping away the rough-cast rendering they revealed

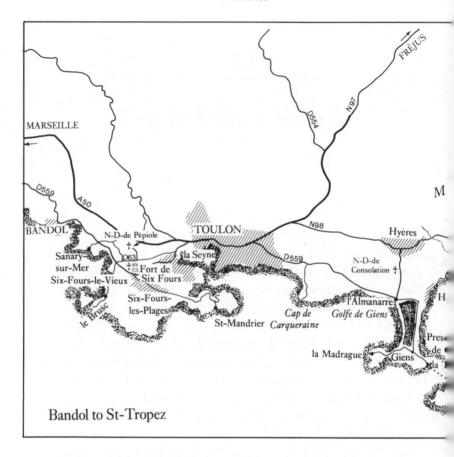

Bandol to St-Tropez

and restored (within and without) the warm stone surfaces of a church of three aisles, each with its broad semicircular apse, lit only by tiny windows set haphazardly in the irregular masonry. The chapel was reopened for regular services in 1967, and on Sundays and feast days the bells ring out from its two *campaniles* (major and minor) across this peaceful oasis.

No one knows its origins. An uncertain reference in a document of 1144 is the earliest we know, but the style of building must put it no later than the tenth century, and perhaps a good deal earlier. Evidence from tombs and a funerary jar

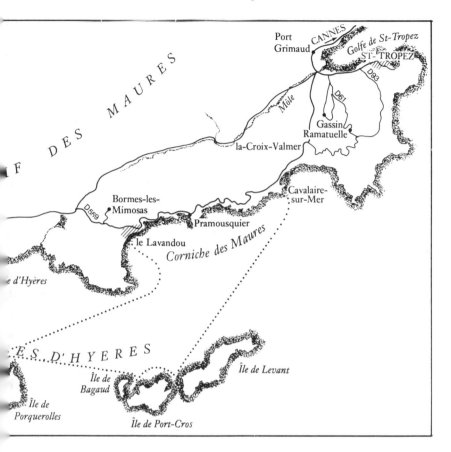

takes us back to the early Christian era, and a strange rock outside the southern entrance is thought to have had a heathen, even a sacrificial role. Inside, Christian paraphernalia have been stripped to a minimum, one stone altar in each apse, and a wooden figure of the Virgin and Child behind the northern one – said to have been carved from rowan wood in the sixteenth century and hidden by a local family at the time of the Revolution. By stripping back the walls and vaulting to the basic stone the restorers have revealed some impressive early building technique, and the modern glass in the little windows displays

215

another of Dom Charlier's talents. His first idea was to fill them with bottle-glass of different tints, but then he taught himself the skills of a master glazier to achieve something more decorative. He lived to see the whole work finished, and is buried near the east end of the chapel which is his earthly monument.

To reach the rest of the peninsula you have to go back to the D63, turning either left or right to rejoin the D559 from Sanary. Its centre is the entirely mis-named Six-Fours-les-Plages, which has neither ovens nor beaches, but is a dreary ribbon of commercial development leading to the smaller peninsula of St-Mandrier which commands the entrance to Toulon harbour. Avoid that, and off the southern loop of the main road look for a turning north which leads up to the village and fortress of **Six-Fours-le-Vieux**. The old *village perché* has been almost submerged by what is now a huge military fort, but in the shadow of its battlemented walls is a quiet courtyard closed at one end by the collegial church of **Saint-Pierre**, which began life as part of a priory attached to St-Victor in Marseille.

The hill above is said to have been first fortified by the Phoenicians around 600 BC, and there was probably a Christian chapel down here in the fourth or fifth century (of which some traces have been found), but the Romanesque core of Saint-Pierre dates from about 1020–40 and is a larger and more refined structure than Notre-Dame de Pépiole. It too has been undergoing restoration, only just finished, which has revealed a beautifully balanced east end – crossing, choir and two side chapels. The original nave was broken off half way across its last bay to make way for a late Gothic replacement, built in 1608 by an architect from the Borély family of Marseille. The contrast is not only in styles, but in the materials used, for the hard grey limestone of the east end gives way suddenly to the gentler pinkish stone favoured by Borély. A confusion of styles is obvious from the outside too, with two Romanesque doorways – the smaller one with an oddly unbalanced arch – a Gothic window and a short stumpy bell-tower.

To the south of the urban ribbon of Six-Fours, one road leads to le Brusc on the west coast, which is a rather untidy gaggle of villas overlooking what was the Greek harbour of Tauroentium, while a narrower and more adventurous one crosses a wooded hillside to the highest point of the peninsula, which the seventeenth-century chapel of Notre-Dame-du-Mai shares with the remains of a watch-tower. From a height of more than a thousand feet the view is tremendous, taking in a great sweep from the harbour of Toulon to the Cap de Carqueraine, with Giens and the Île de Porquerolles away to the east.

If you know Corsica you may be struck by the similarity of the vegetation and rock formations along this part of the coast – not surprising given that Calvi is less than 150 miles south-east of Toulon. It was at Calvi in 1794, then a naval port under attack by a British fleet, that Nelson lost an eye. A year before that Napoleon had bombarbed the British out of Toulon, where Admiral Hood had been supporting the royalist cause, and earned himself promotion from captain of artillery to brigadier-general. This superb natural harbour was called *Telo Martius* by the Romans, and the waters of its bay bred the shellfish known as *murex*, from which they (and the Phoenicians before them) manufactured a scarlet dye.

It was Louis XIV who turned **Toulon** into the biggest naval base in Europe – as it still is, despite some rough treatment during the last war. In 1942 the Vichy admiral scuttled sixty ships of his fleet to deny them to the Allies, thereby blocking the entrance. In the allied attacks of 1944 the old harbour was destroyed from the air, and the Germans blew up the rest of the installations before surrendering to General de Lattre de Tassigny. Even now Toulon harbour retains a good deal of glamour, though in spite of Puget's Hôtel-de-Ville the same can not be said of the city.

The aim of most travellers will be to find the quickest way through (there is no way round), and this is not easy, for the A50 gives up just behind the harbour, leaving one stranded in a maze of inadequately marked streets. If you want to continue along the coast, the A57 is no use to you, so you must keep heading east and hope to find direction signs to either Hyères, Carqueranne or Giens.

Hyères will not generally be recognised as the earliest of the Riviera resorts, but its mild winter climate made it popular with the English in the eighteenth century. Queen Victoria stayed here once, and R. L. Stevenson loved it. The sea has receded almost three miles since its harbour received St Louis on his return from the seventh crusade in 1254, and he must have been glad to see it. There is a partly Romanesque church dedicated to St Louis, whose first act on his return was to pray there, and the Knights Templar used the thirteenth-century chapel of St-Blaise as their *commanderie*.

Halfway between Hyères and l'Almanarre on the Golfe de Giens is one of those places which illustrate the heart-warming local enterprise with which France threw off the ugliest memories of 1944. On the map the name of a chapel to the west of the road is given as **Notre-Dame-de-Consolation**. The earliest chapel we know of on the site was dedicated to St Michael and mentioned in a document of 1062. The story goes that 'une noble dame', wanting to give thanks for the safe return of her son from the crusade – he had landed at Hyères in 1254 with St Louis – rebuilt it with a new name. The date at least is about right, as it was built in the same transitional style as the parish church of St-Louis in Hyères.

It was a natural focus for festivals and processions in honour of the Virgin, and in the last century a neo-Romanesque façade was added, and a bell-tower crowned by a bronze statue of the Virgin. If its origins were romantic, so was its situation on a commanding hill-top overlooking Hyères and a long stretch of coastline to the south. Its position in the end was its undoing, for in 1944 the Germans commandeered it as an army post, and in spite of their promises not to damage the fabric the allied landing in August between Toulon and Fréjus gave them the excuse to blow up the tower – which of course demolished the rest of the building as it fell. The date was 15 August, the feast of the Assumption of the Virgin Mary, and the appalling explosion was heard during ceremonial Vespers in the church of St-Louis. After the war urgent appeals were made for the state to fund its restoration, but it was not till 30 November 1952 that the first stone was laid of a new chapel 'de la Consolation'. What you see today was carried to a triumphant conclusion three years later in the modern French style, uniquely suited to this kind of enterprise.

From afar you see what looks like a tall narrow watch-tower, surfaced in rough stone, flanked by lower buildings on either side. To the left are doors leading into the chapel, to the right a reception and information centre. The front face of the tower is filled by a huge wooden cross, and as you approach you will see at its foot a lovely elongated statue of the Virgin and Child. This is one of many captivating examples of modern sculpture by M. Lambert-Rucky; note especially a sequence of scenes carved in relief over the chapel entrance which tell the story of the Virgin from Annunciation to Assumption. The interior is vaguely Romanesque in plan, but there are beautiful and superbly apt decorative details which catch the eye wherever you turn.

The modern stained glass, designed and made by the *maître verrier* Gabriel Loire, is the most thrilling I have ever seen. His design and colouring is dazzling and constantly exciting; his use of the spaces provided by the architect is brilliantly judged. Almost the whole of the south wall of the nave is taken up by a window divided into narrow vertical panels by thin stone mullions. The lower part shows a sequence of historical scenes, from the departure of the crusade of 1248 and the return of St Louis in 1254 to the occasion in 1883 when the original statue of the Virgin was miraculously saved in a fire. Up above are shown the Saintes-Maries arriving by boat in the Camargue, a group of locally born saints, and the central figure of Notre-Dame de Consolation, light streaming from her golden crown and robes. When the sunlight strikes through the glass the whole church is filled with an extraordinary radiance. Every panel is alive with movement and fresh colour – this is the kind of work which deserves to last for centuries.

Close by, commanding an airfield and beyond that a panorama stretching to the sea and the offshore island of Porquerolles, is a monument to members of the French Naval Air Service killed in the last war. Notre-Dame de Consolation is herself a memorial to the spirit of the whole French people.

South of l'Almanarre and Hyères-Plage two narrow causeways connect the coast with the Presqu'Île de Giens, enclosing an area of salt flats and dividing the Golfe de Giens from the Rade d'Hyères. All through the summer the waters on either side bristle with many-coloured sailboards, while the causeways carry visitors to the holiday resort of **Giens**, surprisingly green and pleasant, with a ruined château on the heights above the village. The peninsula – really an island with a causeway approach – is aligned mainly east and west. The western end, known as la Madrague, is remote and hardly yet developed; the main road runs to the south-eastern extremity, where the comically truncated Tour Fondue overlooks a busy little harbour where ferries leave every hour half hour for Porquerolles, the nearest of the Îles d'Hyères – sometimes called the Îles d'Or because of the way their rocks light up in the evening sun. The Greeks called them the *Stoechades*, a name which botanists will connect with *lavendula stoechas*, a species of wild lavender found here – and more appropriately at le Lavandou.

Porquerolles is the most visited. A roughish road system runs through its pine woods, and it has one excellent and a few reasonable hotels. Its beaches are on the north side, for the south coast has only precipitous cliffs which come to a point at Cap d'Arme. The furthest east is the Île de Levant, a bare island which is divided – apparently peaceably – between the navy and a colony of militant nudists. The most interesting and beautiful is the one in the middle, the Île de Port Cros, which is a thickly wooded national park, and in Le Manoir has an outstanding small hotel. Most exclusive is the uninhabited Île de Bagaud, a protected nature reserve which you can visit only with a guide. If you are tempted to look for accommodation on either of the two nearer islands you will need to book a long way ahead, and it would be wise to pick a time either early or late in the season.

The low outlines of the Îles d'Or will be in sight to seaward as you travel towards le Lavandou. To landward are the towering slopes of the **Massif des Maures**. Geologically this and the offshore islands form one of the oldest land masses on earth. It extends into what is known as the Massif de l'Esterel beyond Fréjus, and is made up of a single block of porphyry, in which red and violet rocks mix with anthracite, schist and green serpentine. The name 'Maures' comes from the Greek word *mavros* meaning black, though in modern Greek it can also describe red wine. Little of the actual rock is visible, for the southern slopes are covered by an impenetrable forest of umbrella pines, cork oaks, Spanish chestnuts and holly. Few roads cross it in any direction, most of them hardly more than tracks. Only close above the main road do the red-tiled holiday villas peer through the pines, though more appear every year.

Le Lavandou is a lovely name for what was once an attractive and flourishing fishing village. Now it has gone the way of all the Riviera communities which offer a sheltered harbour for yachtsmen and a sandy beach for sun-lovers. The sound of its inland suburb, Bormes-les-Mimosas, is attractive too, though they say the old village of Bormes only adopted its tailpiece to emulate Juan-les-Pins. Here more expensive villas proliferate among flowering trees, and it would be churlish to compare it with the brash development along the coast. There is even a surviving village with ordinary simple shops.

The road divides a few miles before le Lavandou, and you may prefer to continue on the D98 which takes the inland route to St-Tropez along the valley of the Môle. If you choose to stay within sight of the sea you will have to brave the traffic along the busy corniche road, whose attractions are fast disappearing. A big problem for the itinerant visitor is to find a lodging other than those laid on by travel agents, or in the kind of hotel which devours your money without offering even a whiff of regional life. A surprising exception is to be found (or was in 1989) at **Pramousquier**, where the Beau Site appears above the road on your left. It has the kind of simple comfort more usual in an inland village, and its position at the head of a small peninsula means that from close by you can walk down to a quiet sandy beach. An encroaching rash of villas may soon bring more people, but one hopes no more sophistication.

Pramousquier, if it survives, would be a good base for exploring the hinterland of the Massif des Maures – a rewarding venture in spite of the difficult terrain. For the present it would be more appropriate to end this chapter at St-Tropez, whose reputation on the Côte d'Azur these days rivals that of Cannes and Antibes. The road follows the corniche past the lovely bay of Cavalaire before turning north to cut off the peninsula of Ramatuelle and reach the head of the Golfe de St-Tropez. You may be past the village of **la-Croix-Valmer** before you remember the reason for its name. What happened here in 311 changed the history of Europe almost literally in a flash. Following his return from Britain in 308, during the civil war with his rival Maxentius, the emperor Constantine the Great was passing this way when he saw in the sky before him a cross of light, and heard the words 'In this Cross you will conquer!' Next year Maxentius was finally defeated outside Rome, and Constantine made a solemn public profession of Christianity.

Now for **St-Tropez**, once one of the loveliest and now the most sadly abused of Riviera harbours. Beween the wars, and perhaps right up to the 1960s, it must have been an enchanting place, and even today the intense blue of the sky which encircles this unassuming headland, with its crown of red-tiled houses and its perfect natural harbour, ensures it a magic quality, however superficial. A site like this is bound to have a history.

The Greeks called it Athenopolis, the city of Athena; Brigitte, the modern Aphrodite, would be a more suitable patroness today.

St Torpes was a Roman officer martyred under Nero in 68 AD. His headless corpse was said to have arrived from Pisa in one of those mysterious boats which drifted about the Mediterranean in the first century AD, shared only with a dog and a cock; his head remains as a relic in Pisa, where he was beheaded. In later times the harbour attracted enemies rather than pilgrims or tourists, and St-Tropez was repeatedly attacked and destroyed by Saracens and raiders from the north African coast.

In the Middle Ages the Knights Templar undertook to guard the coast and its widespread communities, but when their power and authority declined the Seneschal of Provence persuaded a group of wealthy Genoese families to sponsor a new harbour with appropriate defences. In 1538 François I built a citadel to support his campaign against Savoy. The next significant intrusion was by the neo-Impressionists, followed later by Colette, who lived on the Baie des Canoubiers for thirteen years between the wars. Paul Signac was the first painter to arrive in 1892; many followed to set up their studios in the town, and this was the basis for its reputation at the turn of the century – an artistic reputation kept alive by one of the best art galleries on the south coast.

Not far from the huge modern car park (where you should promptly leave your car), sandwiched between a chain of ghastly cafés and the quays of the old harbour, is the **Musée de l'Annonciade**, on the site of what was once a chapel of that name. It has a fine collection of paintings, beautifully hung and lit, which represents mainly the post-Cézanne generation. There are no really great pictures, but a few stand out. The two Utrillos are in a class apart; there is a Matisse drawing which catches the eye; interiors by Vuillard, and a set of watercolours by Dunoyer de Segonzac of St-Tropez in winter. There are some telling local scenes by Camoin – look for his game of *boules* in the Place des Lices – and some strange impressions of London by Derain. Among several pictures of uncertain merit by Albert Marquet there is an interesting view of the Vieux Port in 1905; you can see the same view out of the window to the left, rebuilt after the Germans blew it up in 1944. There was an extraordinary happening in July 1961, when more than half of the collection was stolen in a midnight raid, uninsured, only to be recovered within a few months.

The Annonciade is not the only attraction left, though. The famous harbour, it must be admitted, is full to bursting with 'yachts' which have no sails to hoist even if their owners knew how to hoist them. A view of their massed sterns provokes only curiosity about which is the biggest and how much each cost. The real yachts, some of them very handsome ships, lie at anchor usually in the roads outside. The quays which surround the Vieux Port, once friendly, then fashionable, now neither, have surrendered to the tourist – at least during the summer.

Yet as so often happens when herds take over the most accessible parts of a town or countryside (witness Venice and the Lake District) they leave unvisited other parts of equal interest. Though the back streets of the *vieille ville* are surprisingly seedy and run down, there are some attractive mediaeval corners, and you will find a real fish market at the Place des Herbes behind the Quai Jean-Jaurés. The climb to the citadel is worth it for the view, though a visit to the parish church shows only how God has given way to Mammon. The real centre of St-Tropez is still the Place des Lices, very much as it looked in the picture by Camoin, though if you sit down to eat or drink you will pay for it, dearly.

A first visitor may be surprised to find there are no beaches at St-Tropez. There are plenty round about, though, not only on the shores of the bay but on the eastern side of the big peninsula to the south. The two little hill towns here, Ramatuelle and Gassin, have become dormitories, but Ramatuelle still has some mediaeval charm. You can make a round tour of the peninsula by taking the D93 turning off the main road into St-Tropez, though beyond the Col de Collebasse there is a hair-raising descent to la Croix-Valmer.

In 1964 a development company commissioned the architect François Spoerry to design an exclusive residential area at the western end of the bay, aimed perhaps at reproducing the canal frontages of Martigues, and suited mainly for yacht owners. The houses of **Port Grimaud** are all individually designed, with private quays on a network of canals. There are no streets, and internal communication is only possible by boat; the result is a sort of concrete Venice – but so unnaturally still as to seem moribund. You can stay at the Hotel Giraglia, but the price of a room will be beyond most mere visitors.

13

The Massif des Maures and the Îles de Lérins

In such intractable terrain routes have to be chosen carefully, without trying to cover too much ground in a day. You can wander round this wild and beautiful country and hardly meet another car on the way, but the roads are steep, narrow and twisting – and often roughly surfaced. I can only suggest two main objectives and the easiest ways to reach them.

Supposing you have a base on the coast, perhaps at Pramousquier, my first suggestion would be a day's expedition starting at Bormes-les-Mimosas and aiming first at Collobrières, a town which takes advantage of the meeting of two mountain streams just above it, and the resulting river the Réal Collobrier which runs through it. The road north from Bormes makes a glorious beginning to the day, winding but well surfaced. It climbs to the Col de Babaou (surely a Saracen name) through scenery still much resembling Corsica – a thick covering of cork oaks and Spanish chestnuts on the hillsides, mauve and white cistus in the clearings and a wonderful range of wild flowers on the verges.

Collobrières when you reach it seems surprisingly sophisticated, but its secret is that it almost rivals Apt as a producer of sweetmeats – and naturally of *marrons glacés* in abundance. The river runs through the middle of the town, spanned by a single-arched mediaeval bridge, but its chief feature – apart from some extensive *allées de boules* – is an elegant eighteenth-century Hôtel-de-Ville in the Place de la Liberation. This reminds us again that the main allied landings in August 1944 took place on the coast between Hyères and St-Tropez, and it evidently took no time for the liberating troops to reach Collobrières. The Place which commemorates this is beautifully laid out with plane trees and a fountain – not a bad place to stop for mid-morning refreshment.

The more serious business lies ahead, so pick your way carefully out along the D14 in the direction of Grimaud, twenty-three kilometres to the east. After three kilometres turn right, and right again after about the same distance. Your objective now is the **Chartreuse de la Verne**, which should be sign-posted, but you must be prepared for some rough going. Take it slowly, and after what will seem a long six kilometres you will be rewarded. A 'Chartreuse', as you will remember from Ville-neuve-lès-Avignon, is an enclosed community of the Carthusian order, run always on exactly the same routine and with an unvarying layout – the most efficient of all monastic regimes. What marks this out is its position. There is no other habitation within miles. Its ancient walls occupy a matchless site, sheltered on three sides by thick woods but with the view to the south open all the way to the sea and the Îles d'Or.

Just as all Benedictine foundations recognise Cluny and St Hugues as their fountainhead, and the Cistercians regard the arrival of St Bernard at Cîteaux as their inspiration, so the only founder of the Carthusian order was St Bruno. From the wealthy diocese of Reims, where he was the Chancellor, he retired in 1084 with six companions to the seclusion of what became known as the *Grande Chartreuse*, in the Dauphiné mountains near Grenoble. Almost a century later a party of monks left there to found a new house for the order in the heart of the Massif des Maures. They had been encouraged to do this

The Massif des Maures and the Îles de Lérins

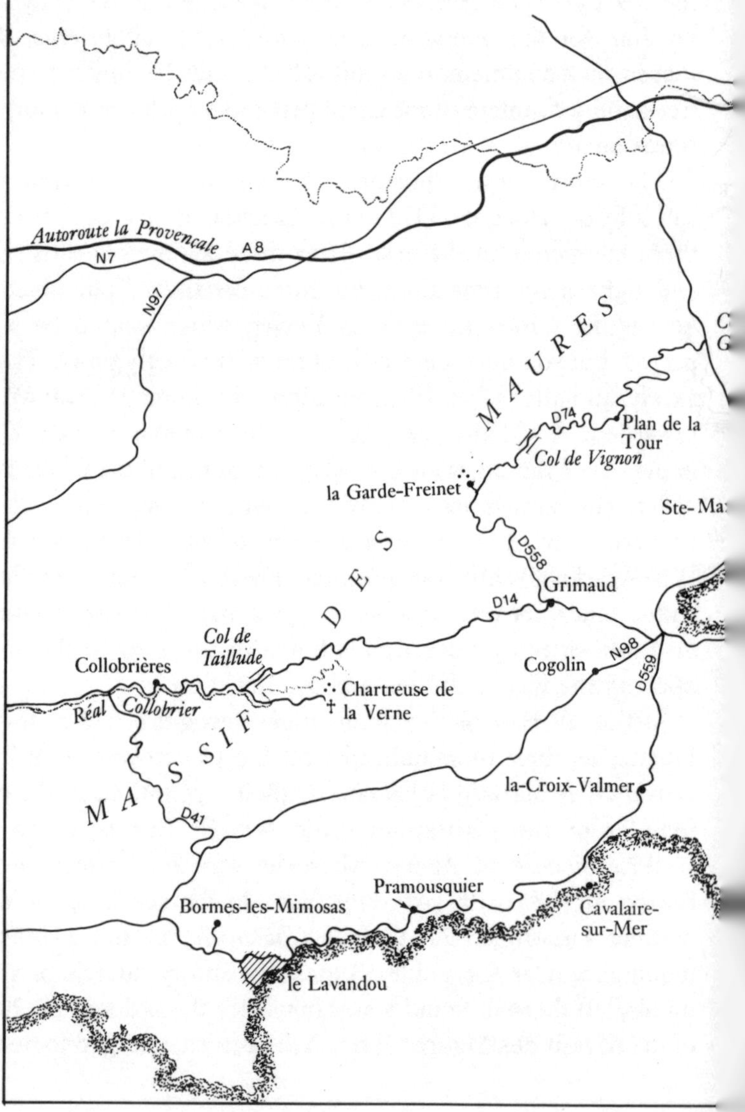

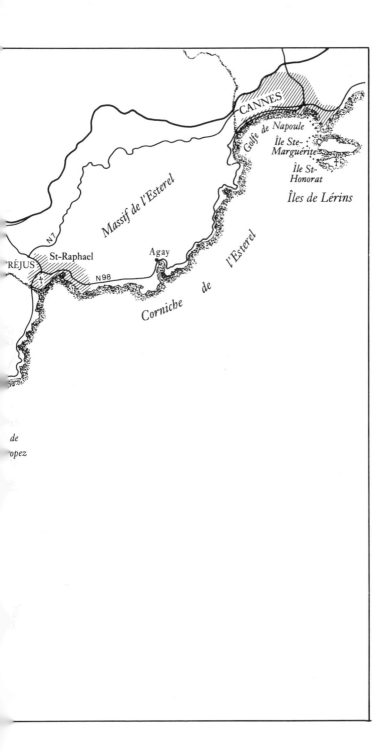

by the bishops of Toulon and Fréjus, and it happened that the site they chose was cut in two by the boundary between the two dioceses.

Like many long-accepted local names, 'de la Verne' has been given some far-fetched derivations, but the simplest and most appropriate connects it with the Latin noun *ver* meaning 'spring', and its adjective *vernalis*, or 'green'. As usual there is a tradition, and a quite likely one, that there had been a temple here to Diana, goddess of the woods. The first priory church was consecrated in 1174. Later history is difficult to establish, as all its records were lost at the Revolution; we do know that it was destroyed by a forest fire in 1271 and again in 1318, while in 1577 it was the victim of a savage assault by the Huguenots in the wars of religion. After the Revolution the monks left the Chartreuse for Italy, and the property and its contents were sold off in two lots which recognised the line of division between the two dioceses. Not till 1921 did the state recognize how important the site was, when it was classified as an historic monument. Still nothing was done to restore the fabric until 1961, when the Department of Water and Forests took it over and sanctioned the work undertaken by an association of 'les amis de la Chartreuse'. Finally in 1983 a small monastic community returned to give it spiritual life again.

No wonder it is today a confusion of architectural styles, from the early Romanesque fragments of the twelfth-century priory to some imposing Renaissance doorways and a lofty eighteenth-century church with the remains of its cloister. Notice how in the later periods dressed blocks of a blue-grey local granite were used to outline the doorways, arches and pediments, in contrast with the rough stonework of the older walls. Even before that the distinctive green serpentine of the Massif had been used to point up features like groins and friezes.

The layout of the Chartreuse is extremely complicated, and fortunately the efficient association of *les amis* provides both a clear plan annotated in English and an illustrated booklet in the

Art et Tourisme series. As at Villeneuve the centre of the community was the big oblong rectangular cloister, with monks' cells arranged along the galleries to east and west. The middle ground was always used as a burial place, where each monk was laid to rest by his fellows in an anonymous grave with only a plain wooden cross to mark it. Here the far or northern end has been laid out as a garden, and thanks to the patient restoration still going on you can see better than anywhere else how and where secular activities were carried on – in stables, cowsheds, kitchens, cellars, oil press, bakery and forge. An hour spent here makes clear that the Carthusians were not only self-supporting – they had to be – but the most highly organised religious community of them all.

Yet the first and last impression of the Chartreuse de la Verne is a romantic one. Seen from outside, the high fortress-like walls show up in the sun like a great golden Ark stranded on its green Ararat; inside, the little community of brothers is constantly at prayer or private work. In a way one hopes that restoration will never go so far that it impersonalises these abandoned buildings, petrified in their last inhabited state like the streets of Pompeii.

In theory you could now set off along the remainder of the D14 towards Grimaud and St-Tropez; the road over the Col de Taillude and along the crest of the Maures is stunningly beautiful, but punishing for the driver, so by the time you have bumped your way back to the junction you will probably settle for an evening aperitif in Collobrières before returning to base.

Another day may find you back in St-Tropez, or passing that way *en route* for Fréjus. If so, you can arrive more easily at **Grimaud** by way of Cogolin on the N98, and this is a mediaeval town of much interest and character – not to be confused with the *ersatz* Port Grimaud at the head of the bay. You will be right to associate the name Grimaud with the Grimaldi of Monte Carlo, inheritors of the fortress village of les Baux. It owes both its name and its importance to the victory of William of Provence over the Saracens in 973, when he captured their last stronghold, or *fraxinet*, known today as la Garde Freinet, standing high in the hills to the north of Grimaud. The Saracens had established several of these pirate strongholds in the Massif, and the Christian world only roused itself to deal with them when they kidnapped the abbot of Cluny as he was returning from a visit to Rome. They demanded an inordinate ransom for him, whereupon the emperor Otto ordered his vassal William to rid the country of this menace. His success earned him the title of 'Liberator', and he awarded the lordship of the area to one of his knights, Gibelin de Grimaldi.

In the next century the Knights Templar established a *commanderie* here as part of their accepted task of guarding the coast – and the pilgrimage route to Compostela – against pirates of all kinds; you can walk along the arcaded rue des Templiers to what is left of their headquarters, a foursquare tower with blank walls. Number 22 in the street was the birthplace of His Excellency Gabriel Ollivier, Minister Plenipotentiary of the Sovereign Order of Malta, whose family was first established in Grimaud in the sixteenth century. He lived from 1908 to 1981 and became a sort of folk-hero of the place, responsible as honorary mayor for the upkeep of its secular buildings. There are signs of civic pride all round, with pretty gardens and small open spaces which have been inaugurated by various local bigwigs.

There are other mediaeval streets to wander in, and the town is overlooked by the ruins of a substantial castle, but the most interesting place is the Templars' church of **St-Michel**, dated 1020 and now restored to the pure Romanesque style of its origin. It stands to the south of the *commanderie*, and you enter the single nave down a flight of eight steps. It has only two bays, with blind arcading and lancet windows – for which the glass was made by Jacques Gautier in 1975. A plaque behind the statue of the Virgin to the right of the entrance tells you that the high altar was rededicated in July 1964 by the bishop of Fréjus and Toulon (by then a combined diocese) in the presence of His

Excellency Gabriel Ollivier. If the church is dark you can illuminate it by feeding one franc to a slot on the left as you come in. You can stay in comfort here at the Côteau Fleuri, and eat well at M. Girard's traditional Provençal restaurant, les Santons.

You will enjoy the climb northwards to **la Garde-Freinet** through more of the same rich scenery; there are even lines of mulberry trees beside the road. Stern notices forbid you to pick up the fallen chestnuts, which are a valuable crop in these parts. The town when you reach it is chiefly marked by a hundred-yard series of *allées de boules*, where championship games may be under way as you come in, but you ought to go a little way beyond it for a view of 'Fraxinet', the ruins of the last Saracen fortress to fall to the armies of Provence.

If you are still a glutton for scenery you can tackle the mountain road over the Col de Vignon and through Plan de la Tour to the Col de Gratteloup on the D25. There is a swift descent from there to Ste-Maxime on the coast, which is a more traditional kind of resort than some of its neighbours. You may prefer to reach it more orthodoxly by returning to Grimaud and rounding the Golfe de St-Tropez, but beyond Ste-Maxime the corniche road skirts the last of the Massif des Maures to reach **Fréjus** at the foot of the wide valley of the Argens – a river which has travelled a hundred kilometres through the low-lying Centre-Var from its source near St-Maximin.

The euphonious scramble which produced the name Fréjus from the Roman *Forum Julii* is no surprise in Provence. Its position both at the feet of this strategic valley and astride the *via Aurelia*, the principal highway leading through Gaul to Spain from northern Italy, made it an important town when the empire began to consolidate under Augustus. The value of its harbour was recognised by Julius Caesar in his Gallic campaigns, and Augustus used it as a base before and after his victory over Mark Antony at Actium in 31 BC; yet by the seventh century the old harbour had silted up, and when they built the railway to Nice it ran right over it. The general route of the *via Aurelia* can be easily followed now, as the same line is taken by the Route Nationale N7, supplemented more recently by the A8 autoroute as far as Aix. Some lengths of it will be obvious from their straightness, other points can be picked out where a Roman bridge still crosses a river.

'The actual Roman remains at Fréjus are scanty. A few sections of wall and bases of towers survive, and you can see where the road entered through the Porte de Rome and left by the Porte des Gaules, both fairly well preserved. Between them ran the *decumanus maximus*, or main street, cut as usual at right angles by the *cardo maximus*, the 'hinge' of the grid plan. The amphitheatre, or *arènes*, was one of the biggest in Gaul and seated about 10,000 spectators, but it was built too close to the course of the river Reyran, which used to flow into the sea separately from the Argens. Both rivers were subject to serious flooding, and it was only in 1828 that the amphitheatre was dug out of a mass of alluvial mud, only to be buried again during a disastrous flood in 1959 which changed the course of both rivers and caused the death of four hundred people. It was rescued again, but only a limited restoration has been possible and it remains sadly ruinous. The theatre has been excavated to the north of the *decumanus maximus*, which seems to have been the most prosperous quarter, but it had been so badly plundered for building material that not much was left above ground.

It is more as a mediaeval city that Fréjus captures the eye and the imagination, though this aspect is concentrated in the *quartier episcopal* in the south-east corner of the old town. There is the thirteenth-century cathedral with its twelfth-century cloister and its (probably) fifth-century baptistery, and the Bishop's Palace built by Pope John XXII at the beginning of the fourteenth century before he left for Avignon. As so often in southern Provence one is conscious of being very close to the origins of European Christendom. Forum Julii was a bishopric as early as 374, and it was not till 1957 that the diocese was made subject to Toulon, and what was left of the Palace became the Hôtel-de-Ville.

The best view of the **Cathedral of Notre-Dame** is from the Place Formigé, but it is an oddly composed one. What looks rather like an apse at the west end turns out to be the upper stages of the baptistery. There is no formal western entrance; instead you enter from the south through a sixteenth-century doorway, which gives access on a lower level to a magnificent Romanesque narthex. This supports a three-stage bell-tower, which rises from an almost flat tiled roof. The real apse is concealed from the south by the Hôtel-de-Ville. Though architecturally a muddle, the warm pinkish sandstone in which it is all built gives it a kind of unity.

The internal plan is curious too. The principal nave is early Gothic, much restored, but alongside it to the north what looks like a side aisle is really the nave of a separate and earlier church dedicated to St Etienne; the west end of this dates from the middle of the eleventh century, and it was extended to the east about 1100. None of this has a lot of character, and one is drawn back to the narthex to wonder at the height and elegance of its four cardinal arches. From here one moves westward into the baptistery, an octagonal chamber lit by five windows, with recessed apses at four of the corners. Unlike the Aix baptistery of St-Sauveur it has kept its cupola, which is supported at the eight angles by granite pillars with marble Corinthian capitals, six of them undoubtedly Roman. A feature not to be seen at Aix is the *dolium*, a circular cavity beside the baptismal pool, lined with terra cotta, which would have contained liturgical oil for anointing the initiates.

Opposite the doorway by which you enter the cathedral is a flight of steps leading up to the cloister, and into a much lighter atmosphere – almost frivolous after the solemnity of the baptistery. Pairs of white marble columns support the arcades, which run continuously round the four equal sides. Restoration in 1925 included a well-head in the centre, round which a garden of *lauriers roses* has been planted. Instead of the usual vaulting the galleries have painted wooden ceilings. During restoration work in the cathedral there has been some uncertainty about conditions for visits. Normally you need a guide to see the baptistery and cloister, and he will also reveal the Renaissance panelling of the doors of the southern entrance. Remember that in any case the museum – off the north gallery of the upper cloister – will be closed on Tuesdays, and the cloister with it.

In the spring of 1988 important excavations began at the western end of the Bishop's Palace, right up against the south wall of the cathedral, and some interesting finds will no doubt be transferred to the museum. While we were watching the work going on, a lady excavator handed up a lovely bronze clasp in the form of a lizard which she had that moment found. She confirmed that they were working on a large Roman town house, as part of a campaign to save more of the town's history from the developer. Only a few days before, the French press had reported that the mayor of Fréjus had found it wise to leave for Corsica after authorising a new road (in which he was said to be financially interested) through the area of the Roman baths.

Fréjus and **St-Raphael** now form a continuous township, and, though Fréjus was originally far more important, St-Raphael has a long history too. It began as a dormitory suburb for wealthy Romans from Forum Julii; when peace returned to the coast after the rout of the Saracens from Fraxinet, William the Liberator gave it a status and a name by dedicating a church here to the warlike archangel Raphael. The Knights Templar added one of their typical fortified churches in the twelfth century. In the later Middle Ages the cathedral city naturally predominated, but as its harbour silted up St-Raphael became the more important port. Yet it was still little more than a fishing harbour in 1799 when Napoleon landed after his defeat at the battle of the Nile – and indeed when he re-appeared under guard on his way to his first exile on Elba.

If one emphasises the past in St-Raphael rather than the present, the irony is that its simple attractions in the nineteenth century contributed a good deal to the modern development of the Côte d'Azur. In 1851 the *Figaro* correspondent Alphonse Karr retired to Nice and began to write back enthusiastically to Paris about life on the Riviera. Ten years later Nice had become too crowded and fashionable for him, and he retired further along the coast to St-Raphael. It would be wrong to blame him and the friends who visited him here – Maupassant, Dumas, Gounod and Berlioz among them – for what has happened since; it was a long time ago.

The Esterel Massif is geologically an extension of the Massif des Maures, and even more rugged and impenetrable. Somehow the *via Aurelia* must have crossed it, perhaps by combining sections of the modern routes followed by the N7 and A8, and taking advantage of the valleys of the Argentières and the Reyran. To enjoy the scenery you have a choice between the N7 and the corniche road, of which the latter is the spectacular choice, though the road is squeezed so narrowly between mountains and sea that the view is limited to the next cape ahead and the horizonless sea below. Only at Agay do the cliffs draw back a little to allow more than a strip of habitation.

Beyond lies Cannes, and here I maintain that Provence comes to an end. Fréjus and St-Raphael at least are still in Var, while Cannes belongs to the *département* of Alpes-Maritimes, whose coastline as far as Nice, Monte Carlo and Menton is now an international fairground which has all but abandoned its roots in the history and culture of the land we have come to see. True, there is at Cagnes a museum of Mediterranean art and natural history; at Antibes and Vallouris you will find Picasso in flood, and a diet of Cocteau at Menton, but the one is a Spaniard, the other a northerner. At St-Jean Cap Ferrat there is a collection of treasures assembled in Paris and brought down here by a Rothschild baroness. Nice is a city with a history and a character of its own, but neither is Provençal. Only in the **Îles de Lérins**

237

off Cannes is there a site so ancient and so seminal in its influence that we must visit and write about it with enormous respect.

There are two islands, Ste-Marguerite and St-Honorat, the latter called after the man who is looked on as the founder of western monasticism. We have come across him in Arles, where he was claimed, perhaps fancifully, as its first bishop, but the legends which connect him with these islands have more substance. He was born in Roman Trier as Honoratus, the son of a Roman official and a boyhood friend of the future western emperor Gratian. He and his brother Venantius became Christians and went off with an older man called Capresius on a pilgrimage to Rome. Disillusioned by what they found there, and equally convinced that the service of Christ called for more than a solitary hermit's life, they returned along the coast as far as Forum Julii, where the bishop was a powerful personality called Leontius (St Léonce in his French form). He persuaded the little party to stay in the neighbourhood, and they began preaching to fishermen from a grotto near Cap Roux, one of the most dramatic headlands of the Esterel. From there they could see to the north-east the two islands which the Greeks had called Lero and Lerina, where they thought they might realise their ideal of a community which would pray and work for God in simplicity, brotherhood and peace.

Neither island was inhabited, which suited them, but the smaller one which they favoured was overrun by snakes and thought to be uninhabitable in any case because it had no water. This did not deter the Romans. The early Christian fathers were often credited with eradicating snakes, which had always been symbols of the underworld and the powers of darkness, and his education had taught Honoratus something of engineering. They soon found an underground spring, which in later times proved copious enough to supply a monastery of 3,700 monks and lay brothers. Here they say was founded the first truly monastic community on lines which became familiar in the west: a regime common to all, separation without isolation, a simple life in which work and prayer were regarded as almost synonymous, where religious scholarship flourished, and where above all the Eucharist and other offices of the church were celebrated by the whole community.

The date given for the foundation of the monastery known as Lérins is 410, so it has to be seen in the context of the earliest cathedral in Fréjus and its surviving baptistery. There were links with figures like St Germain of Auxerre, who came over to Britain to support the church here, St Patrick and his mission to Ireland, and St Loup who as bishop of Troyes in 451 fought off Attila the Hun. Lérins came under Benedictine rule in 575, and for a time in the tenth century Cluny and Lérins were ruled by the same abbot. During the flowering of the monasteries in the early Middle Ages, gifts of money and land were showered on Lérins, till the abbey and its rulers became one of the major powers in Provence, temporal as well as spiritual. The town of Cannes – *portus Canis* in those days – was only one of its possessions along the coast. Inevitably worldly decadence set in, and at the same time the monastery came under attack by the Mediterranean powers, who began to look on these islands off the Golfe de Napoule as strategically important.

In 1786 there were only four monks left where there had been nearly four thousand; Louis XVI removed its title, and two years later the Pope summarily dissolved it. The island and its buildings were bought up privately in 1791, and for some years it was the home of a well known actress of the *Comédie française*. At last in 1860 it was bought back for the church by the bishop of Grasse, who gave it to the Cistercian community who had just returned to Sénanque. Twenty years later Sénanque was disbanded by the anti-clerical law of 1880, and the main body of its monks joined in rebuilding Lérins.

A regular ferry service leaves from outside the Gare Maritime in Cannes for both islands. The island of **Ste-Marguerite** is named after the sister of St Honorat, who is said to have occupied it with a party of equally dedicated women. They were never allowed to set foot on the men's island, but there is a good story that St Honorat promised to visit his sister when the almond trees were in flower, but God saw to it that they blossomed once a month throughout the year. Apart from tourists, Ste-Marguerite makes a popular excursion for those who live in Cannes; Aleppo pines, evergreen oaks and eucalyptus trees provide a pleasant shade for picnics. Near the landing stage on the north coast is the military fort built to the orders of Richelieu in 1635, and later enlarged by Vauban for Louis XIV. Built originally for defence, it was later used as a prison and entrusted with Louis XIV's victim in the 'Iron Mask'; he was in the personal charge of the Governor, M. de St-Mars, who took him with him when he was transferred to run the Bastille.

St-Honorat is naturally more interesting because of its history, though the monastery buildings put up at the end of the last century are conventional and dull examples of the neo-Romanesque. This hardly matters, as ordinary visitors are kept at arm's length, but it was a pity that nobody gave a thought to preserving something of the past. Fortunately elsewhere in the island two small chapels have survived which go back to the earliest days. They seem to have been used by *réligieux* detached from the main community, and are both architectural oddities.

The path leading westward from outside the monastery arrives at the **Chapel of St-Sauveur**, a small octagonal chamber with its east face interrupted by a semicircular apse, looking rather like a miniature baptistery. That was what Prosper Merimée thought it was, and he believed it could be as early as the one at Fréjus; nowadays, though it is obviously pre-Romanesque, scholars looking at it more closely have suggested a date not much before the tenth century. In any case the cupola was replaced in the eighteenth century, when the nicely calculated symmetry would have appealed to restorers in the Age of Reason.

Towards the eastern and more wooded end of the island the

Chapel of la-Trinité seems to have a different story to tell. Its irregular masonry and the clutch of apses at the east end may remind you of la Pépiole and other very early Provençal chapels. The interior plan is again symmetrical, but here I think we are on safer ground in giving it an early date. From inside you can see that its three apses are arranged in a trefoil, not as the culmination of separate naves or aisles. This suggests a Byzantine influence, and so does the construction of the cupola over the centre of the trefoil, not unlike the one in the mausoleum chapel of Galla Placidia in Ravenna – and she died in 450. We know that many fugitive monks from the east came to Lérins before the end of the seventh century, and would have brought architectural expertise with them. However the plan is not a simple Greek cross, for the place of a fourth apse to the west is taken by a short square nave with an entrance on the south side. The stonework looks rough, apart from some dressed blocks at the western corners, but in good condition thanks to careful repair work done in 1938.

The most impressive building on St-Honorat now stands on the cliffs which command the sea to the south. In 1073, made desperate by the continued attacks of Saracen and other pirates, the abbot Aldebert II began to build a fort behind whose walls the monks would be safe to carry on their prayer and at least some of their work. Of this original *donjon* only the north and west walls are left; the entrance was about twelve feet above ground on the north side, reached by a ladder which they could pull up once the last monk was inside.

During most of the next few centuries there was still a danger from the sea, and the monks felt they needed to develop their refuge on a bigger scale, so the building was gradually expanded into a *monastère fortifié*, where a full monastic regime could be kept up behind the defences. There were five floors to accommodate the monks' living quarters, the refectory, the library and a chapel. It was arranged as a hollow square, and the space in the middle became a cloister with two storeys; it is said that the fine white marble columns of the upper storey were presented by the Genoese as recompense for the damage they had done during a siege of the monastery.

From the upper gallery you could reach the chapel of Sainte-Croix, where the bones of the founder and other saints were preserved, but it was the romantic situation and the range of amenities provided for the monks which attracted the actress Sanival de Saint-Paul, whose father bought it for her in 1791. She must have given some wonderful parties here, but now the walls stand only two storeys high, and in a crumbling state. Though there are vineyards on the island it seems doubtful if we shall ever see 'Château St-Honorat' on a wine label.

14

Haut-Var

With relief we leave the overcrowded coast to drive up into the heart of eastern Provence. This is a land few people know, and no one would want to popularise it with undiscriminating travellers; the safeguard is that there are no great monuments or shrines, no spectacular gorges, no magnets for gourmets. The Haut-Var is just a very beautiful part of the world at all seasons, and the ancient hill towns where so many of its people live are calm and happy places. If you need to relax, this is where to do it.

The drive north from Fréjus on the D4 is lovely all the way, one of the loveliest in Provence. The first few villages – Bagnols-en-Forêt, St-Paul-en-Forêt for example – have not escaped colonization from Fréjus, but the new houses are built in traditional designs and discreetly scattered among the trees which give rise to their names. The woods line the road without hemming you in, and as it drops down from the col north of Bagnols they give way to more open and flowery slopes.

The capital of this area is **Fayence**, a dignified provincial town, upstanding on its hill. It has a big fifteenth-century church and some scanty remains of a once solid castle, but a more distinctive feature of these Var towns is the tall clock-tower, usually with an elaborate basket of ironwork on top, which

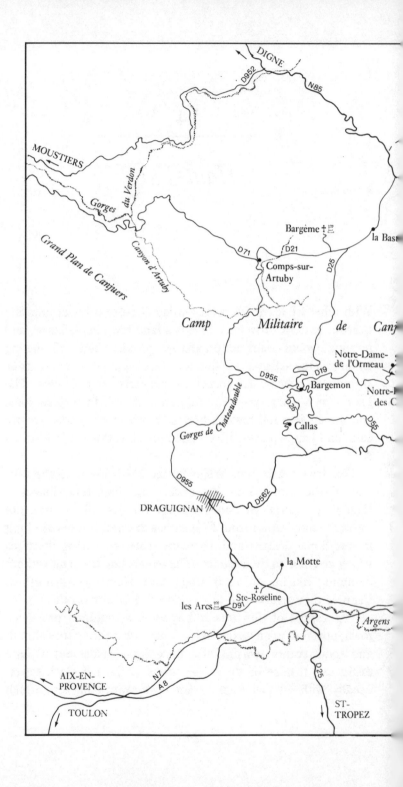

Haut-Var

Col de Valferrière

Mons

ALPES   MARITIMES

Route Napoléon

D656

D96

St-Cézaire

Cabris

GRASSE

NICE

NICE   Callian

N95

Puits de
Jaubert

Lac de St-Cassien

Siagne

NICE

aul-
orêt

agnols-
a-Forêt

48

CANNES

ANTIBES

Île Ste-
Marguérite

Île St-Honorat

Massif de l'Esterel

N17

ST-RAPHAEL

l'Esterel

N98

de

ÉJUS

Corniche

de

seems to have replaced the parish church as a source of civic pride. For all that, you will more immediately enjoy the civilized atmosphere of the place – plenty of parking spaces, attractive little cafés and restaurants, and a number of coolly splashing fountains. The terrace below the clock-tower has a low wall set with a range of enamelled tiles which identify all the physical features in a wide half-circle of the view to the south.

Fayence has no hotel worth considering as a base, but there is one just outside the town to the west. The Moulin de la Camandoule (an old olive-oil mill) is on a byroad which leads to one of several little 'pilgrimage chapels' which you may stumble on in these parts. This is **Notre-Dame des Cyprès**, whose name explains itself at first sight, and which is an outstanding example of the genre. It was once part of a priory known to have been occupied by Benedictines from Lérins in 1030, but its foundations are Roman, and the evidence of tombs and coins found there proves Roman occupation from the early Christian era. Bigger than most of its kind, it was adopted in the thirteenth century as the parish church of Fayence – 'Nostra Dame des Cypressos', as it was called in a deed of 1225. This explains why the earliest church in the town was not built before 1400, by which time it was thought inconveniently far away for regular services.

Attempts were made by various orders to capitalize on the site by attracting pilgrims, and the big arched porch was added at the west end to shelter them on arrival. The substantial tower was built in 1688, with a flying buttress to the south to take the pressure off the wall. At the foot of the outer walls of the nave there are niches – two to the north, three to the south – and there is some argument whether they were for burials, or more probably just convenient places for pilgrims to wash before entering the church after their travels. There is running water close by from which basins could be filled.

To see inside you will have to ask the *curé* of the parish church at Fayence to lend you the key, so it is best to be prepared before you come. The nave looks surprisingly high, its floor being a foot or more below the level of the porch. All is obviously well cared-for after its restoration in 1938; the only drawback is a huge baroque marble *retable* which blocks the Romanesque nave, and the gallery at the west end would have been added later. All around is a peaceful countryside of vineyards, pasture and cornfields; they still use bullock-carts to carry away the hay crop.

If you now rejoin the D19 and carry on in the direction of Seillans you will pass close by another of these chapels, **Notre-Dame de l'Ormeau**, which has a similar character and history. Once the parish church of Seillans, it is mentioned under the same name in 1155, but it has no elm to shelter it. Had there been one it would have gone the way of all elms by now, but the name comes from a legend that a primitive statue of the Virgin was buried during the Saracen invasions in the roots of an elm tree in a nearby field. Two hundred years later, the story goes, a farmer turned it up with his plough – a miraculous find which gave it miraculous properties.

There is no sign of it now, and the inside of the chapel has not been as well treated as its neighbour of the cypresses. Though built on the same Romanesque lines, its walls are still plastered over and hung with crude pictures and *ex voto* offerings. On the other hand the marble *retable* here is dated 1574 and very much finer. The western porch is later and clumsier, but to the south a genuine Romanesque porch supports a sturdy little tower. Water runs past the east end, and there is another niche, probably for washing purposes, in the south wall.

Seillans is another hill town, smaller than Fayence, less sophisticated and even more delightful to wander in. Its mediaeval fortifications have lasted better – a line of ramparts and a so-called 'Porte Sarassine'. Below the ramparts there are narrow winding streets between tall houses, running in confusing directions and some of them quite steeply stepped. The street lighting should be a lesson to other provincial towns –

old-fashioned lanterns on iron brackets projecting from the house walls. Guarding the entrance to the Grande Rue is a fearsome iron image of the Tarasque, with a sharp spiny backbone and threatening jaws, but you suspect he is only putting on a show, for the people are very friendly, and the atmosphere is one of cheerful relaxation in a town of quiet corners and café tables set out in the shade of plane trees. The church is said to date from the eleventh century, but the only bits remaining which could possibly be as early are the apse and the square pilasters which carry the vaulting. Everything else inside has been altered in the last two centuries according to the taste of the time, but the tower is a handsome one in three stages – square, octagon and spire.

Beyond Seillans the still beautiful D19 winds its way to **Bargemon** – the summer wild flowers varied by delicate blue harebells and the glowing pink of rampant wild peas. Bargemon is on a smaller scale again, but it still has its mediaeval ramparts and its quiet unexpected corners where you can sit under the trees and relax to the cool sound of fountains. There is a true Provençal clock-tower, and the church is built on a sheer rocky outcrop, which means that its east end stands enormously high above the town. Unfortunately the west end and the tower have been spoilt by over-enthusiastic restorers, and the inside has little character. The town and its people are full of it, though, as you will realise if you tune in to café conversation during the lunch hour. Turning south on the D25 you come to **Callas**, a smaller, poorer and more remote version of the hill town, though the situation and the views from it are superb.

The way back to Fayence lies along the D562, which may seem a tame road after the others, but no road in Haut-Var is dull or predictable. This may be a time to consider another base to explore it from, and if you want a quiet spot in romantic surroundings I would warmly recommend the Auberge du Puits Jaubert beside the lake of St-Cassien. Listed in the *Guide Michelin* under Montauroux (simply because there is no other town or village within miles) it is primarily a *restaurant avec chambres*, but the rooms are comfortable and the food has to be good to attract clients from a distance. Riding parties have special attention, and there are horses in the paddock. The lake is not visible from the hotel, but you can walk through the woods to one end of it – a vast expanse of water which must keep half the male population of the neighbourhood happy fishing at weekends.

There are more places within easy reach of either Fayence or St-Cassien which you should keep at the top of your list for visiting while in Haut-Var. Most of them lie on the rim of a wide semicircle north of Fayence, and it seems superfluous to suggest one route or another for getting there. You could however begin by joining the main D562 from Draguignan and following it in the direction of Grasse. Grasse is a major town of the Alpes Maritimes which specialises in scent manufacture, but it would be a pity to break the spell of Haut-Var by getting involved there now. Instead you can turn away to the north a few miles out and have a look at **Cabris**, one of the smaller hill towns and one which has remained proudly individual. If you stand high on the terrace of the ruined château and look south, the view is phenomenal even for this part of the world. The hillsides with their lavender fields fall away steeply below Grasse, and you can follow the course of the river Siagne all the way down to Cannes. Beyond Cannes the Îles de Lérins seem to float on the sea, and if conditions are right you can sometimes make out the mountains of Corsica on its farthest rim. The parish church is not an old one – 1617 is its date – but a good example of the period, and it has two unusual treasures to display. Behind glass to the right of the apse is a vivid marble sculpture of the Last Supper, and over the high altar a genuine Murillo of the Holy Family.

Overlooking the upper Siagne is **St-Cézaire**, a pleasant place like the other hill towns. It has more open spaces and fountains, and three towers and a gateway left of its fourteenth-century fortifications. Earlier than those is the cemetery chapel dedicated to the obscure St Sardaigne, which seems unusually big and solidly built for its purpose and date, but until the eighteenth century it was the parish church. Authentically Romanesque, from its plain west end and simple belfry to its spacious rounded apse, it stands out boldly among the conventional modern tombstones. Inside, it goes one better, for at the west end there is an early stone sarcophagus, identified by the splendidly Roman name of Julia Sempronia.

Nearer again to Fayence is **Callian**, a cheery little town full of nice people, with the well preserved remains of an eleventh-century castle which has been sensibly converted during the last few years to provide dwellings for several local families. They seem not at all overawed by the roll of former owners, displayed with their emblazoned arms on the walls of the entrance archway. They include families who held the title of Prince of Callian for four hundred years (1030 to 1421); branches of the de Villeneuve family were here from 1240 to 1793, when the castle was wrecked by the revolutionaries. Other surviving buildings seem to date from the sixteenth century, and there are the usual fine fountains and leafy squares.

Most intriguing and aptly named of all the hill towns is **Mons**, 2,500 feet up and thirteen kilometres north of Fayence. Mediaeval and outwardly unsophisticated, it has three hundred inhabitants, no hotels, one simple café-restaurant, one *épicerie*, one *boulangerie*, a *poste* and a *mairie*. There is hardly any traffic through its narrow streets, which carry (a bit self-consciously) signs in Provençale with French translations underneath. All is in fact not quite what it seems, for as at Callian the surviving quarters of the mediaeval castle have been adapted as little modern dwellings; the choicest one is built between the walls of the seigneurial chapel with its Romanesque windows still showing. While prowling the silent streets look for the workshop of M. Robert Audibert, an impassioned naval historian who makes wooden ship models of all periods, from galleons to aircraft-carriers, out of millions of matchsticks cut exactly to the right length and fineness.

To see the church, which is a curious mixture of dates and styles, enlist a most knowledgeable lady who lives next door to the *poste*. It began with a single Romanesque nave and apse in the twelfth century, built in the middle of an ancient cemetery, with the usual *porte des morts* in the south wall, now blocked up. In the thirteenth century a Gothic side aisle was added; in the seventeenth the east end seems to have collapsed, and curious alterations made which resulted in the high altar being moved into a false apse at the west end, with a monumental baroque *retable*.

It soon becomes clear that though Mons seems genuinely unsophisticated its inhabitants know what they are about. All traffic entering the town is routed round to a large open promenade, which combines a perfect site for a market with a large car park, and has a view point which matches most we have seen. Beyond and below it there is a purposeful and well designed modern school; to sum up, this is French local organisation at its best.

The next objective should be one of the most romantic of all ruined castles, to be found in the village of **Bargème** – which at exactly 3,589 feet is the highest in Var. From Mons it is reached by driving north up the narrow Vallon du Fil to join the famous 'route Napoléon', at the Col de Valferrière (3,500 feet), turning left there and left again on the D21. You sight the great castle on its hill to your right, about three kilometres after leaving la Bastide. If you should be starting from the neighbourhood of Bargemon or Callas there is a more straightforward route which crosses a big military training area known as the Camp de Canjuers, and reaches the D21 south of Bargème.

From whichever direction you come, you may run out of adjectives to describe the beauty of this countryside and the magnificence of this huge ruined keep; it was the Château des Sabran-Pontevès, mentioned in 1235, and its four round corner towers stand intact after a little discreet renovation to one of them. Its other fortifications spread along the spine of the hill, with an inner bailey ending at a point with another strong square tower. The village is mediaeval, carefully and proudly preserved; its twenty houses all lay within the outer walls of the castle.

Cars can be left on a terrace outside the entrance gateway which overlooks the broad valley of the Artuby, an important river which winds its way down from the northern hills to Comps-sur-Artuby, then passes through a deep canyon into the Gorges du Verdon. You can hear sheep bells sounding along the slopes of the valley below, but on this level you can walk for hours over moors covered in clumps of thyme, with butterflies sampling every wild flower in the book, it seems.

On your way to the castle you pass the **Church of St-Nicolas**, which shares the same grand situation on a spur of the hill above the village. Outwardly unassuming, it was restored in 1898, and in 1904 the bell tower had to be replaced after it was struck by lightning – the weights of the clock fell through the tribune at the west end. The inside is not to be missed, though, and you should have little difficulty in contacting the curator of the village museum who is always glad to show it to visitors. The church was built in the eleventh century – long before the castle – on the site of a wooden Carolingian one burnt down in the ninth century.

A unique object which survived the fire is a wooden panel covered by canvas and painted with scenes from the early life of the Virgin, with delicate gilded strips of material between the pictures. It was rescued from the burning church almost intact, perhaps because the wood is walnut, always slow to catch fire. At the west end the original eleventh-century arch supports the restored tribune, and to the right of that is a font from the Carolingian church – just a plain round basin, as in early Christian times. The present altar is a baroque gilded affair, but on the north wall there is a fine centrepiece from a fifteenth-century triptych, of which the side panels were stolen many years ago.

The road south of Bargème – which will be hard to leave – runs westward into **Comps-sur-Artuby**, a pleasant village with an historic inn where for a modest tariff you can stay and refresh yourself for the next stage in your journey. The Grand Hotel Bain has nothing to do with baths or spas, and though spotlessly kept is is not at all grand. It has been kept by the family of Bain for eight generations and two hundred and fifty years. Three generations are still in evidence, the youngest in his teens and waiting to take over, and nothing could be warmer than your welcome here. Apart from its family history, its was a popular stopping place on one of the regular *transhumance* routes for flocks travelling north to the alpine pastures in spring. It has modern central heating and a lock-up garage.

Though the hotel may be your chief reason for stopping here, if you do, you will see on the hillside above the village an upstanding church surrounded by the ruins of houses. This was the parish church which in the thirteenth century served the village before it moved down beside the road, and it has recently been restored with much care. The apse has been re-roofed with the traditional heavy tiles, or *laves*, and the tower has been given a new topknot hung with coloured tiles after an old Provençal pattern.

Your circuit of Haut-Var is almost complete. From Comps you can travel swiftly to the spectacular canyon of the Gorges du Verdon, and that would be a short cut to the last chapter of this book, but perhaps it would come too quickly on top of the gentler scenes you are leaving. Instead I suggest a quiet descent to the valley of the Artuby by the D955, which crosses again the Camp Militaire before entering the Gorges de Chateaudouble. Not as dramatic as the Gorges du Verdon, this is a deep tree-lined valley from which the road emerges a few miles short of Draguignan, which used to be the capital of the whole department until it was supplanted by Toulon.

Draguignan is not a town to stay in, and you would be better off either at Comps-sur-Artuby or at les Arcs, ten kilometres further on. Nor is it an easy town to drive in, for a great deal of urgent traffic passes through it, and parking is difficult. Your entry from the north will bring you into the Boulevard de la Liberté opposite the Porte de Portaiguière, which is the best way into the old town. *Parking* is needed quickly, for the streets are uncompromisingly narrow, if not reserved as pedestrian precincts. This was one of three gates in the thirteenth-century town walls, which encircled the hill on which now stands the finest of all the clock-towers of Provence. It could be taken for the keep of a castle, with its three strongly built sections divided by drip-courses, and turrets at each of the four upper corners, but the elaborate iron basket-work which supports a bell and a weather vane signals a more peaceful and decorative role.

Known as the **Tour de l'Horloge**, it did replace an earlier keep which was demolished by Louis XIV in 1659 after a period of local unrest. You can make a clock-wise circuit of this remarkable monument, following the line of the earliest fortifications as far as the Porte Romaine – a misleading name for a mediaeval gateway, though it may have earlier foundations. If you pass through it to enter the old town you will find yourself near the east end of the church of St-Michel, a disappointing nineteenth-century building which was not improved by an earthquake soon after it was built.

It does however contain two gilded wooden statues of St Hermentaire, a peculiarly local saint who earned respect and veneration by killing the dragon who is supposed to have given the town its name. From the west end of the church a wider thoroughfare passes the head of a crowded market place, which is the natural centre of the old town, and bigger and more colourful even than the one in Aix. Beyond this point the rue Cisson is conveniently shut off as a pedestrian precinct, and you can walk down it past the Hôtel-de-Ville, which was once a Franciscan convent. Turn back when you reach the Boulevard

Clemenceau, or you will be overwhelmed by the traffic. The rest of Draguignan is a big modern town of no lasting interest.

I mentioned earlier the idea of a base at **les Arcs** as an alternative to Comps-sur-Artuby – a good one, because this little town has a romantic history as well as an original kind of hotel. We hear of it first in 909, when the 'Villa Arcus', or 'House of the Arch', belonged to one Foucher de Valensole, who was a brother of St Mayeul, abbot of Cluny. The town grew up round a castle built in the eleventh century, then known as the 'Castello de Archus'. Over the next hundred years the castle was enlarged as a seat of the counts of Provence, and in 1200 it was given as a feudal possession to the same family of de Villeneuve who for five hundred years held the château of Callian near Fayence, and other properties round about.

The nobility of Provence in those days was closely connected with that of Aragon, and the titles of count of Provence and count of Barcelona were almost interchangeable at times. Raymond de Villeneuve had come over with his overlord Raymond of Barcelona when he inherited the title of Provence, and was enough of a personality to be included by Dante among the dwellers in *Paradiso*. Two generations later the head of the family was Arnaud II de Villeneuve, and January 1263 saw the birth of his eldest child Roseline, round whom were woven many of the most charming legends of mediaeval Provence.

At a time of famine and hardship when she was seven, she insisted on taking food from the castle to feed the hungry people of the town. Though a kindly man, her father eventually ordered her to stop depleting his own stores, and followed her out of the gate one day, suspecting she was disobeying him. He was right, but when he challenged her to show what she was carrying in the folds of her apron she opened them and let fall a bunch of roses. This miracle confirmed what everyone knew, that this lovely girl was a saintly young creature destined for the service of God. To this day one of the postern gates into the 'town of the arches' is called 'la porte du miracle'.

The people of Provence have always loved fairy tales, and to find this delightful story told as a matter of fact in a printed brochure is most endearing. The Catholic church has never discouraged a belief in miracles, even to the point of adding picturesque details to a story, so we have to allow for some licence when we are told that St Bruno, founder of the Carthusian order, came one day from the Chartreuse de Montrieux as a guest of the family and encouraged the fifteen-year-old Roseline to join a religious order. It seems ungracious to object that by then St Bruno had been dead for 150 years. However there is no need to doubt that she did join the Carthusians, and after her novitiate at St-André-de-Ramières near Mont Ventoux, and five years at the mother priory of Bertaud in Haute-Provence, she was delighted to be transferred to the priory of la Celle-Roubaud, within a mile or two of les Arcs. More to the point, her father's sister Jeanne had for some time been installed there as prioress.

It should be remembered that until the end of the thirteenth century women members of the religious orders were not strictly confined to the *clôture* of their convent, and could take part in the ordinary life of their own families, visiting and being visited as they wished. Pope Boniface put an end to that in 1298 by decreeing that the 'brides of Christ' should no longer be exposed to any contact with the world outside, and the walls of the convent became their prison. Roseline was allowed a last emotional visit to her family at les Arcs, where her father had grown old and feeble, and from where her favourite brother Hélion had left for the Crusades under the banner of St John of Jerusalem – the order of which he would later be elected Grand Master. Roseline accepted the new rules without question, and in 1300 at the age of thirty-seven she was chosen to succeed her aunt as prioress of la Celle.

One can easily imagine the gracious life lived by her family in the château de Arcs. Its fortifications were demolished in the Revolution, and the only warlike feature that remains is the tall

Tour de Barras, sometimes known as the Tour Sarassine because watch was kept from it for marauding Saracens approaching from the coast. Below it the *parage* – the open space where the men-at-arms assembled at times of danger – has become a peaceful courtyard with a fountain in the middle. Many quiet corners have been discreetly converted to houses for the well-to-do, with flowers and flowering trees peeping over walls and round the arches which are still a feature of the *ensemble*.

At the far end is the Logis du Guetteur, a *restaurant avec chambres* which takes its name from the watch-tower, and occupies the site of the *donjon* – so much so that the dining room is fitted into a low-vaulted chamber they say was the prison. Advertised as an *étape gastronomique*, it makes a very comfortable and refreshing stopping-place for a night or two. Many of its rooms look out over a drop of several hundred feet, with an eagle's eye view of the town below, and you can take your breakfast *al fresco* (when not too fresh) on the battlements. The town has a comfortable and prosperous look, and the tall houses with their painted shutters are roofed with the true Provençal tiles.

From here it would be natural to make an early visit to the place where Roseline de Villeneuve ended her life after nearly thirty years as prioress of the abbey of la Celle-Roubaud. During this time miracles attributed to her hardly ceased, and the most dramatic story of the time came when her brother Hélion was captured by the Saracens in Rhodes. Her spirit appeared to him in prison, struck off his chains, unlocked the gates, and spreading her nun's veil like a sail she transported him safely back to Provence. To read these fairy tales helps to explain the veneration that Roseline inspired in later generations, and the extraordinary range of offerings to be seen in the chapel where her body lies.

To get there, take the minor D91 out of les Arcs to the east, which crosses the N555 on its way to la Motte. Before the crossing you will see on your left a farm which obviously belongs to a *vigneron*, with its premises entirely given over to the wine trade. This is all that remains of the priory buildings, but to the left of the farm is the chapel you have come to find.

A curious building, basically Romanesque, it has one principal nave which ends in an elaborately carved wooden choir screen – beautiful work, reminiscent of Grinling Gibbons and dated 1635. The carving also embraces choir stalls on both sides, making an enclosure which frames an enormous baroque gilded altar and *retable*. The entrance is by the north door, facing which is a glass case containing the effigy of St Roseline, life-like yet corpse-like, with blackened face and hands showing through her nun's habit. Her arrival here is part of the fairy tale, for in the first place she was buried simply in the Chartreuse cloister after the custom of the order. Then everyone protested because pilgrims were not allowed in the *clôture*, and in 1334 the Avignon Pope John XXII agreed to her body being exhumed and transferred to the chapel. It was found to have suffered no change since it was buried five years earlier, and – most remarkable of all – her eyes appeared to be still alive and conscious of the occasion. Thereupon her brother Elzéar, who as bishop of Digne was in charge of proceedings, decided that the eyes should be removed and placed in a suitable reliquary.

In 1660 Louis XIV arrived at the neighbouring town of Cotignac with his mother, Anne of Austria, and having heard of these miraculous eyes he sent his personal physician to establish the truth of the story. The only way the doctor could think of doing this was to insert a needle into the corner of the left eye, whereupon the eyeball immediately reacted in protest. Against the west wall of the south aisle is a fantastically elaborate reliquary which actually contains the eyes, and you can see that the left one is duller than the right. Unfortunately this dubious work of art, constructed in 1883 by an artist from Lyon, has replaced the original – though no one knows what happened to that.

Now for more surprises. The whole wall-space of a blind arcade to the left of the reliquary is filled by a gorgeous many-coloured mosaic. It depicts a kind of *fête champêtre provençale*, attended by angels. A table is laid in the open air with food, wine and suitable utensils, a bird sings from a tree above, and the rays of the sun light up the scene. The colours are blues, greens and soft reds, and it represents all the best things of life in Provence. It is signed by Chagal and dated 1975. At the east end of this aisle there is a graceful iron lectern made in the form of a tree in bud – by Giocometti. He also did the vivid gilded bas-relief of the miracle of the roses.

The date of the exhumation and translation of Roseline's body was 11 June 1334, the first Sunday after Pentecost, which is also Trinity Sunday. Then and on the first Sunday in August a pilgrimage to the chapel takes place, and Mass is celebrated every year on the anniversary of her death, 17 January 1329. For the faithful this was the day when she entered heaven as a saint, though the church of Rome delayed this final recognition until 1857. Provence has always had a special place for her in its heart.

15

Centre-Var

West of Draguignan the land is flatter, more predictable and not nearly as beautiful. Towns are no longer built on isolated hill-tops; the country between is agricultural, cut into by the many small rivers which feed the Argens before it reaches Fréjus. There are plenty of vineyards, but they produce no wine which deserves a regional *appellation* other than the blanket *Côtes de Provence*, and at first sight all seems rather dull after what we have seen further east. Yet Centre-Var is not only central to the department of Var, but in many ways crucial in the history and development of Provence. There is a lot to see, and communications are a good deal easier than in Haut-Var.

The nearest to the west of les Arcs is **Lorgues**, where you will find fountains and plane trees and an atmosphere more like the hill towns of the Haut-Var, though the town itself stands at no great height. The church of St John the Baptist is a big seventeenth-century building on the lines of a Romanesque basilica. The walls of the apse are covered with wooden panelling right up to clerestory level, and a classical touch at the west end is the organ tribune supported by four Doric columns. On the last pillar to the right of the choir a marble tablet tells how after a disastrous drought, which lasted four months, a procession of three thousand people was formed to intercede with St Roseline at her chapel near les Arcs. Rain fell that very day, 8 May 1817.

The ground rises more steeply to the north of Lorgues, and rock begins to show along the minor road which leads to St-Antonin-du-Var. Do not miss the eccentric little pilgrimage chapel of **Notre-Dame-de-Ben-Va** which appears suddenly on your right above this road soon after it leaves Lorgues. A tiny thing, clamped to the rock and enveloped by low trees and greenery, it probably took the place of a hermit's cell and became much frequented by pilgrims. The porch here actually bestrides the old pilgrims' pathway through the woods to the chapel, whose name can be read as Notre-Dame 'de la Bonne Voie', or even 'de Bon Voyage'. The occasional modern pilgim still arrives on foot, but for most of the day the big goana lizards sun themselves undisturbed on the rock.

Apart from its enchanting situation the chapel is unique for the wall paintings which cover not only the vaulting and arches of the porch, but most of the interior as well. The date of 1511 can be made out on the pillar to the right of the entrance. Only recently have these frescos been freshened up and some unsightly graffiti removed; the result is an exceptionally happy little scene.

North-west of Lorgues by way of the D10 and the D77 – a lovely road – you come to **Tourtour**, a town best known these days for the hotels it has attracted to the neighbourhood. The more wealthy French and Belgians patronise the four-star Bastide de Tourtour south of the town, whose restaurant has a Michelin rosette, while the less pretentious Petite Auberge further out in the same direction is just as quiet and comfortable. To the east is the expensive-looking residential development of St-Pierre, where the Auberge St-Pierre has a swimming pool and fifteen comfortable rooms at prices which are not outrageous.

Why this area should have attracted so much holiday trade is a puzzle, but a certain sophistication has spread into the old town

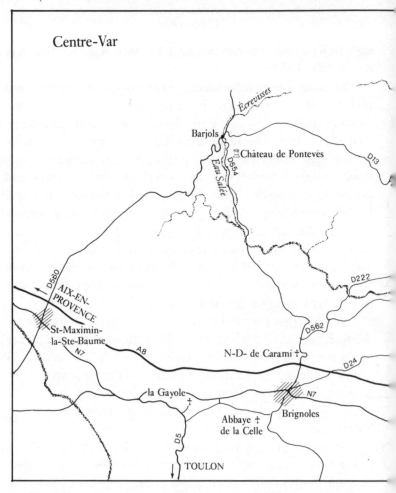

Centre-Var

of Tourtour itself. The remains of the mediaeval château are now occupied by the Mairie, and one of the town's historic features has disappeared. The two great elms, 'les Ormes de Sully', planted in the central *place* by Henri IV's old minister to commemorate a visit by his new mistress, Anne of Austria, have had to be replaced by mundane plane trees. Built into a surviving section of the ramparts is a seventeenth-century oil mill – mark of an essential industry in the land of the olive.

To the east of the town the ground rises steeply to an escarpment occupied by the parish church; the wide terrace

beside it commands a breath-taking view of endlessly interlocking hills to the south and east. The high western façade of the church and the important-looking tower above it disguise a surprisingly small Romanesque interior. Though the walls of the nave have been whitewashed and cut up by chapels with gaudy altars, the apse has been well restored in natural stone.

Between Tourtour and Aups the D77 runs along the limestone ridge of the Montagne des Espiguières, which rises to a peak of nearly 3,000 feet. It passes the *manoir* of la Beaume, to the left in a loop of the road, and a little further on you have a good view of the fortified farmhouse of **Taurenne**, a magnificent group of buildings in a circle of trees down below you on the same side of the road. It is said to contain a collection of tapestries and Provençal furniture, but a locked gate blocks access by the public. It remains one of the sights of the district – the equal of many more written-up châteaux.

A scholarly eighteenth-century *curé* worked out mathematically that **Aups** was the centre of the world (presumably on the flat-earth premise), but it turns out to be a strange mixture of sophistication and decay. You enter in style through a gateway in a Tour Sarassine, and the big *place* is planted with well grown plane trees, lined with cafés, and provided with parking space for a great number of cars and coaches. You may wonder what their occupants have come to see, for the old quarter is very much run down and in need of repairs; the church is late Gothic and unremarkable except for some seventeenth-century panelling. Perhaps they will be hunting for the seven sundials claimed by the Syndicat d'Initiatives, of which one was designed by the mathematical abbé Jean. I spotted an indistinct one high on a wall near the west end of the church, but on my only visit to Aups the other six escaped me.

This is as far north as we need to go for present purposes. To the south is the valley of the Bresque, where the town of **Salernes** is chiefly noted for the manufacture of the hexagonal red clay tiles, or *tomettes*, which you find everywhere on the floors of Provence. Beyond Salernes there are two towns which have strong but different claims for attention, but if you like waterfalls on a grand scale stop at the cross-roads in a small village called **Sillans-la-Cascade**. A footpath here leads to a spot where the flow of the Bresque is interrupted by a cliff some 130 feet high, down which an enormous volume of water pours into a series of deep green pools. Some fair-sized trout are caught here – and eaten locally.

From the crossroads the D22 goes on to **Cotignac**, the most attractive of the smaller towns of Centre-Var, tucked in at the base of a sheer 200-foot cliff from which sprout the remaining towers of a substantial castle. The old streets are narrow but not mean, running between impressive four-storey houses of the seventeenth and eighteenth centuries, and opening out here and there into little *places* with fountains, a bit like Venetian *campielli*. The centre of life is the Cours, which may remind you of the Cours Mirabeau in Aix, though here it is a long wide terrace shaded by three rows of plane trees and raised a few feet above the road, so that it effectively becomes a pedestrian precinct. Café tables are set out under the trees, with a row of genuinely useful shops behind. At the top end is a big fountain, encrusted with moss, and again reminiscent of Aix. They say that the huge cliff above the town is honeycombed with caves and galleries, but the access to them is dangerous and visitors are not encouraged to attempt it.

Entrecasteaux, the other town you must not miss, can be reached either from Salernes or by a cross-country road from Cotignac. Little more than a village, it stands poised above a gorge of the Bresque, and is itself overlooked by a big seventeenth-century domestic château built on eleventh-century foundations. From below you see a high wall with regularly spaced windows on three storeys, with an attic floor above, and you climb to it by a long inclined ramp which lands you on a broad terrace with a Renaissance doorway on the far side of the château.

The mediaeval castle had been burnt down in 1600 and was rebuilt by the Comte de Grignan who married the daughter of Madame de Sévigné – who criticised in her letters the extravagance with which he ran it, though no doubt enjoying her visits. Before his death de Grignan sold it to Raymond de Bruny, Treasurer-General of France and a member of a family which had become very rich through trade and speculation in maritime armaments during the reign of Louis XIV. Another branch of the family acquired the chateau of la-Tour-d'Aigues in the Luberon, and until the end of the eighteenth century the life of

265

both establishments must have been as luxurious as anywhere outside Versailles. The good times ended when Jean-Baptiste de Bruny was convicted of murdering his young wife, and though the property passed to a son-in-law, Gérard de Lubac, and was spared destruction in the Revolution, life at Entrecasteaux was never the same. The de Lubac family did keep it till after the last war, but by 1949 it had fallen into ruin and was taken over by the *commune*.

There were no funds available to restore such a large building, and it must have seemed a miracle when in 1974 a buyer was found for the derelict property – who was one of the most extraordinary characters of the twentieth century. He was a Scotsman, Ian McGarvie-Munn, and his career had already been so remarkable that to summarise it here may give a clue to the way he set about restoring Entrecasteaux.

Born in India in 1919, he went with the first expeditionary force to France in 1939. After Dunkirk he joined the King's African Rifles, serving first in East Africa and then in Burma. After the war he took a course at the Royal Military College of Science at Shrivenham and qualified as a member of the Royal Institute of Naval Architects. He then emigrated to Central America, and became President of the National Association of Colombian painters; four years later he was appointed Commander-in-Chief of the Guatemalan Navy, and President of the *Gran Flota Centroamericana* – not bad going for a former subaltern in the K.A.R. Next he entered the Guatemalan diplomatic service with the rank of Ambassador, but in 1962 he was seriously ill and had to give up both his professional and his diplomatic career. Returning to Europe he bought and restored a *manoir* in the Auvergne – a move which gave him the experience to tackle a much bigger enterprise at Entrecasteaux.

So much for his published *curriculum vitae*. What it does not reveal is that while in Guatemala he married a lady of the country, from whom he was subsequently divorced, nor that he made a lot of money on the Stock Exchange which enabled him

The Tour des Abbés, Abbaye de Montmajour

Aix-en-Provence: cloister of St-Sauveur

The prison fortress of Château d'If, off Marseille

Opposite: Abbaye de Silvacane: Cistercian windows at the east end of the nave

Provençal countryside: belfry of the church of la Pépiole in the background

Draguigan: Tour de l'Horloge

Collobrières: Hôtel-de-Ville and Place de la Libération

Narthex of pilgrimage chapel of Notre-Dame de Ben Va

Pilgrimage chapel of Notre-Dame de Carami, outside Brignoles

Early rock burial passage, Prieuré de Carluc

Notre-Dame de Salagon: decorative detail on west façade

la Pierre Ecrite: a fifth-century Roman inscription near Sisteron

'Tardons' – autumn lambs in the high pastures

The village church of St. Martin-de-Brômes

to begin his restoration without any subsidy or grant. The vast expense involved taxed even his means, and as the work proceeded everything was sacrificed for it. The family worked round the clock and throughout the year, even installing the electricity and central heating themselves. Ian McGarvie-Munn died in 1981, having in six years achieved results which the most experienced domestic architects would have envied. His family is carrying on the work, but so far only two floors have been properly dealt with.

Inside the château the many facets of this man's genius begin to show. Of the two beautifully furnished rooms which are shown on the ground floor, one is decorated with his own paintings, and you realise that he was a considerable artist whose work recalls Matisse and the early Picasso. The walls of the second room are hung with seventeenth-century *chinoiserie* panels painted on silk, and a lovely early Chinese painting of birds and trees hangs over the fireplace. In the same room there are glass-fronted recesses which contain an exquisite service of Venetian glass, made in Murano to his own designs. The remaining rooms on the ground floor are set aside for contemporary exhibitions, with sponsors who contribute to the restoration funds.

Down below are the kitchens and barrel-vaulted cellars, part of the eleventh-century castle, with mediaeval iron implements and a charcoal-fired cooking stove. The *buanderie*, or scullery, was ingeniously supplied with water running into a cistern which could be heated by charcoal underneath, and from there into a trough for the washing-up. From one cellar a shallow flight of steps led down to the level of the moat, with a boat drawn up ready for launching.

On the first floor yet another world is revealed. First you can see some elaborate documentation and illustrations of the work done on the château, but the really fascinating part is taken up with records, written and pictorial, of an expedition undertaken by Admiral Joseph de Bruny to find out what had happened to

267

the explorer la Perouse in his attempt to circumnavigate the world. Both expeditions were inaugurated by Louis XIV, but de Bruny's was brought to a disastrous end by disease and shipwreck in Tasmania, while la Perouse returned safely. One of de Bruny's fleet was rescued by a British squadron and found to contain his log book, which is exhibited along with scale drawings of the ships involved. A charming bedroom is furnished in Louis XIV style, with portraits of Madame de Sévigné and her daughter, so we can imagine this great letter-writer here at her desk.

Lachlan McGarvie-Munn is now in charge of the work his father began, and he lives here with his wife and family. They hope that by opening the château to the public, and by other sponsored activities they can defray some of the cost of the work still to be done, and the upkeep of what has been achieved so far. In 1982 the château was opened to young French musicians for study before getting involved in national and international events. The concerts they gave at the end of their stay have developed into an annual music festival, and the place is alive with all kinds of enterprises.

Though the *commune* of Entrecasteaux has not been called on to help with the restoration of the château, it has made an important contribution to its setting by reconstituting the formal gardens laid out at the foot of the curtain wall by le Nôtre, the fashionable seventeenth-century landscape gardener. What badly needs restoring is the fourteenth-century chapel which once was enclosed in the *enceinte*. It stands forlornly at the top of the approach ramp, on the same level as the château, with badly stained masonry and vegetation growing from its tower, but no doubt it too will eventually be taken in hand.

With so much to see round about you may find it convenient to have a different base for a day or two. **Carcès**, a few kilometres south-west of Entrecasteaux, has no tourist attractions, but a modest family-run hotel called Chez Nous is worth considering. At Cotignac you were very close to **Barjols**, an important town which stands at the confluence of two rivers, the Écrevisses and the Eau Salée – which must surely combine to produce salt-water shrimps – and it has the finest of the large churches in Centre-Var. It was founded in the eleventh century by Archbishop Raimbaud of Arles, but the Romanesque nave was extended in the sixteenth century to include a south aisle, and a row of chapels replaced the cloister in the following century, when a college of canons took over its administration.

The entrance to the nave is down a flight of fourteen steps, and the interior detail repays study. The pillars on each side of the entrance to the apse are crowned by unusual strips of carving. To the left is a hunting scene, with archers confronting a centaur and other strange creatures; to the right the scene is the Annunciation. The vaulting is filled in with a pinkish brick which blends with the stone of the pillars. In the apse and choir there is some good seventeenth-century panelling – a range of *trompe l'oeil* designs of classical arches with fluted pilasters and Corinthian capitals. The choir stalls have fixed *misericorde* seats, each with a different subject carved beneath it: there is a horned devil, a bagpipe player, a monk with ass's ears, a duck, a man using a hand mill, and two strange characters sitting on what looks like a commode, back to back, one with hands over ears, the other with hands over eyes – seeing and hearing no evil? The corner panels to right and left have a Nativity and a Crucifixion, and Adam and Eve faced with the Tree and the Serpent.

The church is unusual, but to find something unique follow an alleyway to the west of it, which opens out to reveal a series of waterfalls which once provided the power to drive a classic Provençal oil-mill. The water gushes from the side of a sheer cliff, above which you can make out the walls of an early castle, and it falls in separate cascades which used to drive different parts of the machinery. Most of this has been reconstructed and set in restored masonry, but they have preserved the original 'undershoot' water-wheel which drove the mechanism for crushing the olives – the first step in a long process which produced one of Provence's main exports. A striking architectural feature is the pair of round-arched recesses on the left, which would probably have contained the vats ready to be filled. With all this water available, Barjols seems to have even more inexhaustible fountains than the other Var towns.

Three kilometres east of Barjols is a village overlooked by the rather sad remnants of the château of **Pontevès**, which belonged to a branch of the Sabran-Pontevès family of Bargème. Only the four round corner towers of the original castle are left, with a Renaissance gateway opening on empty space. In between is a grassy enclosure, much used for exercising the village dogs, and there are views over the valleys which converge on Barjols from all directions.

If you should be staying in or near Carcés, your main objective should be the **Abbey of le Thoronet**, the eldest of the three 'Cistercian sisters' of Provence, and in some ways the most impressive. You should not be put off by the curious landscape which surrounds it, for the hills between it and the Lac de Carcés have been quarried for years to produce bauxite. The brick-red scars in the wooded hillsides are bad enough, but the constant movement of heavy plant to and from the quarries has covered every surface round about with a pervasive red dust, which in wet weather turns to red mud.

Never mind – the jaunty little spire and orange tiles of the abbey show up cheerfully behind the evergreen trees which shelter it from the world. Older and even simpler than Silvacane, the church is supremely beautiful, within and without, in its Cistercian balance and proportions. Its genealogy, as it were, goes like this: Cîteaux in Burgundy begat Bonnevaux in the Dauphiné; Bonnevaux begat Mazan in the Vivarais; in 1136 monks from Mazan founded a community near Tourtour beside a tributary of the Argens called the Florège, at the instigation of Count Raymond Bérenger (the second of Provence and the fourth of Barcelona). The site proved unsuitable for the monastery they planned to build, and after a further grant of land near Lorgues, confirmed in 1196 by King Alfonso II of Aragon, who currently held the title of count of Provence, they began to build the abbey which took its name from the nearby village of le Thoronet.

During the next century lands and possessions were showered on them by noble families of Provence; while this led to a spiritual decline in the community it failed in the long run to avert a material one. There was no regular income except from its lands, and after 1430 all this went to an absentee abbot who benefited from the revenues but rarely visited the abbey. From then on, though the few monks – there were never more than about twenty of them – managed to live fairly comfortably on local produce – they had neither the resources nor the will to maintain the fabric, and even before the Revolution they had been ignominiously taken over by the bishop of Digne when their numbers fell to eight. Le Thoronet was only rescued by the attention of Prosper Merimée, who stirred the Historic Monuments Commission into action in 1873; since then, over a period interrupted by two world wars, the abbey buildings have been gradually restored by the governments to which they have belonged since 1857 – though they have had no religious function since the Revolution.

It is easy to forget the more depressing part of its history now that we can see this wonderful place in something like its original state. The mathematical beauty of simple proportion has rarely been better demonstrated than in the church's western façade – such a contrast to the heady Gothic extravagancies of later centuries and other climates. Its plain surface is broken only by the simplest window openings, beautifully spaced, and by the two symmetrically spaced doors – one for the monks, the other for the lay brothers – which led into the side aisles.

The interior plan of the church follows the Cistercian rule: nave and two side aisles, a broad transept in which two chapels face eastward from each arm, but are still enclosed in the rectangle of the transept. Only the main apse forms a semicircle projecting to the east, following the example of Sénanque rather than Silvacane, where it is left square. Throughout the nave there is not the slightest ornament; the arcading is carried on pillars with plain flat surfaces, and the cross-arches of the vaulting are supported only by rounded pilasters which in Cistercian fashion end several feet above the ground. Most of the light enters through the two big round *oculi* which catch the sun at its rising and setting with striking effect; the round-headed lancets below play a lesser part in the setting than they do at Silvacane.

The cloister and monks' quarters were built to the north of the church, as at both Sénanque and Silvacane, though here there were no difficulties of terrain to contend with. The sturdy arcading of the cloister – deep-set bays, each with one short, fat central column – is set off by the precise geometry of the circles and semicircles which pierce the inner wall surface, or tympanum, of the bay. The east, west and south galleries were all completed before 1175, which makes them considerably older than their equivalents at Silvacane; as a whole this is the oldest surviving Cistercian cloister. Though the north range was added towards the end of the twelfth century, there is no difference of style, and to this period we owe the delightful hexagonal *lavabo* which protrudes from it; the refectory behind has disappeared, all but its southern wall with an entrance aligned to that of the *lavabo*.

The Chapter House is one of the few places where modestly decorated capitals were allowed, and ribs were used to strengthen the vaulting which had to support the dorter above. This huge airy chamber is one of the finest to survive, and even without any glass in the windows the thickness of the walls and their narrowing embrasures must have made the night air just tolerable except in the coldest weather. Other monastic buildings are in various stages of restoration: the undercroft, the lay brothers' quarters, the guest house, and the tithe barn which still contains an oil press and grinding stones.

The impression throughout le Thoronet is one of an almost primitive strength and austerity, relieved by a magical sense of proportion, and of an architecture which delights the eye by the simplest of means. Though no longer an active religious centre, it remains instinct with the spirit which inspired its builders – something which has no need to be reinforced by the playing of Gregorian chants on tape.

As we continue to work westward, the next interest centres on the town of **Brignoles**, long established on an unmistakeably Roman section of the N7, once the *via Aurelia*. You can understand why it was popular in the days when there were few other roads through Provence from west to east, and it was a half-way house for travellers between Aix and Fréjus. In 1660 Louis XIV stayed here with the Queen Mother, Anne of Austria, during a tour of the region which had consequences for at least two of its institutions. You can approach it today by quieter roads coming south from Carcés or Barjols, and so avoid the rather depressing eastern suburbs. The older part of the town is very good value, though you should find a parking space as near as possible to the Place Carami, named after the river which flows through Brignoles and into the southern end of the Lac de Carcès – an artificial lake created in 1936 to supply water to Toulon. From the Carami comes the water to activate the big moss-encrusted fountain in the middle of the *place* – a civilised open space with the usual plane trees for shade in hot weather, the welcoming Café de l'Univers on the north side, the Hôtel-de-Ville to the south.

From the *place* you can climb by way of the rue St-Esprit and the Grand Escalier – three flights of broad steps under a series of low arches – to the centre of the town and the church of St-Sauveur. Of this only the western doorway is Romanesque, and the doors themselves, with their carvings of St Peter and St Paul in high relief, were made as you might expect in the seventeenth century. The fifteenth-century nave is high and handsome, with no side aisles; the transept and choir are a century later, and the apse is disfigured by a monstrous *baldachino*. As at Cotignac the pillars of the nave are decorated with Maltese crosses, and the road to the east of the church is called the rue des Templiers, and it led to their *commanderie*. The little courtyard to the north has a classic Renaissance doorway with a plaque announcing that in this ancient palace 'St Louis' was born in 1274. Do not be misled – this was not King Louis IX, but the archbishop of Toulouse, son of Charles II of Anjou.

The counts of Provence converted the mediaeval castle into a summer residence. Not in itself a notable building, it has been converted again into a museum of local antiquities, among which there is possibly the oldest object connected with Christianity in Roman Gaul. This is the upper part of a second or third-century sarcophagus, with a sculptured frieze of subjects which can be interpreted in different ways. Some have read Christian symbolism into them all – St Peter is catching his fish, the Good Shepherd is carrying his strayed lamb into Paradise, and so on. Unfortunately there is a hole where the central figure was seated with a small girl at his feet, so the most important clue is missing. If you clear your mind of the Christian connection – and there are no specifically Christian symbols – you can see it as a much more pagan scene depicting the country residence either of the missing central figure or of the man so comfortably seated at the far right. The trees are full of birds, there are other small animals as well as sheep, and what looks like the head and shoulders of a sun god appears benignly up in the left-hand corner. The style is really Hellenistic, and derived from the classical *stele*; make of it what you will, it remains a piece of refined, vigorous and inventive sculpture from a period not usually associated with such qualities.

A later inscription shows that it was re-used in the sixth century for the burial of a lady called Syagria, who is said to have founded the chapel of la Gayole, close to the N7 west of

Brignoles. When discovered there it was first brought to the church of St-Sauveur, and only recently transferred for safety to the museum. Also in the museum is an early Christian altar of the fourth or fifth century, which used to be in one of the St-Sauveur chapels.

Close to the southern outskirts of Brignoles are the remains of the **Abbey of la Celle**. As in the case of St Roseline's abbey, la Celle-Roubaud, the word 'celle' comes from the Latin *cella* – originally the inner sanctum of a temple, then the retreat of a hermit, and so applied to any religious establishment which had begun as a hermitage. All that is left now is the substantial abbey church and the chapter house of the monastery. The former has recently been restored, and the interior has emerged as a good plain example of thirteenth-century Provençal architecture, but the western façade is a curious composition which incorporates an older archway, off-centre and set in very rough masonry. Except for the chapter house, which is a typical early Gothic vaulted chamber, and a corner of the cloister, the monastic buildings have either disappeared or been incorporated in a hotel.

In the seventeenth century the Benedictine nuns of la Celle were all members of aristocratic Provençal families, had their own servants and enjoyed a comfortable and care-free life. This seems to have scandalized the royal party who visited Brignoles in 1660, and Mazarin ordered them to move to the Augustinian convent of St-Esprit in Aix, where he hoped the bishop would keep them under better control. When the Revolution came there was no one to resist its confiscation, and the buildings were all *morcelés*, sold off in lots to private buyers for the benefit of the *commune*.

The minor road which passes la Celle runs parallel to the N7 for a short way before it becomes the D5 and joins the main road to Toulon. To find the chapel of **la Gayole** where the sarcophagus in the Brignoles museum was discovered, turn right at the junction and right again up a track which leads to a prosperous-looking farmhouse. You will see no sign of a chapel, because it is round at the back of the farm at the edge of a field, and it would be as well – and is probably essential – to ask at the farm for permission as well as guidance.

The chapel is an extraordinary survival from what are so misguidedly called the 'dark ages'. You will be told that it dates from the fourth century, but though there are signs of re-used Roman material historical evidence suggests it was founded in the early Merovingian period, perhaps when the worthy Gontran, grandson of Clovis the first Christian king of the Franks, was king of Burgundy in the sixth century. This was the time when the lady Syagria is said to have imported two 'second-hand' sarcophagi of the second or third century, of which one was to be the tomb of her cousin, a member of a leading Gallo-Roman family called Ennodius Felix; he had retired from the world and come here to live a hermit's life, and he is known to have corresponded with many of the early bishops of the church.

This sarcophagus was bought by a seventeenth-century *savant* from Aix, who carried it off to his home there. It disappeared when the house was demolished in 1787. The other sarcophagus Syagria reserved for herself, and this is the one whose beautifully decorated top part is now in the museum at Brignoles with her name on it. The chapel became a popular burial place, and several other anonymous sarcophagi can be seen scattered around outside.

The building itself is difficult to date architecturally, and it could be later than the time of Syagria and Ennodius. The three apses which project north, east and south from a central crossing recall the Greek Cross plan of the Byzantine model, but the fourth apse has been replaced by a short nave. The north and south apses were used as separate chapels, and at each entrance, framed by short columns with classical volute decorations, are the bottom parts of the sarcophagi once occupied by the two patrons. Another possibly classical relic is the column to the right of the central apse, which has a Corinthian capital with acanthus leaves. This apse is the deepest of the three, with a single window opening, and there are traces of fresco colouring on its half-dome. The stucco which covers the columns and parts of the walls has also been coloured, though it would be difficult to say when.

All is very dilapidated, but here that adds to the romantic effect – at least in fine weather. One day perhaps la Gayole will be discreetly restored, but you can understand why the owners of the farm and chapel prefer not to have it turned into a tourist attraction. In the meantime they have done well to preserve a unique monument from a very distant past.

The N7 will now carry us swiftly back to Aix. The autoroute would be even swifter, but apart from its horrors it bypasses the important town of **St-Maximin-la-Sainte-Baume** – to give it its full sonorous name. St Maximin was the Roman martyr Maximius, who according to the popular legend landed in the Camargue with the Saintes-Maries in the first century. When the little party dispersed, he and St Mary Magdalene came to preach the Gospel in Aix, from where Mary left to spend the last thirty years of her life in her cave on the mountain of la-Sainte-Baume. When she died her body was brought down and entombed alongside Maximius in what is now the crypt of the great Gothic basilica of St-Maximin.

The crypt belongs to the same world and much the same time as the chapel of la Gayole, for it was once a burial vault belonging to a fifth-century Roman villa; the sarcophagi you see here, though not as old as Syagria's and unlikely to have contained the bones of first-century saints, must be of about the same date as the others around la Gayole. What really happened to the Magdalene's remains is a matter of controversy. To begin with you have to accept the legend of the Saintes-Maries, and that she died in the Sainte-Baume cave. In the tenth century the monks of Vézelay in Burgundy were claiming that her relics had been taken there for safety during the Saracen invasions, and for over two hundred years pilgrims came there in their millions to pray at her shrine. In 1279 however Pope Boniface III was persuaded to declare that the relics had never left the crypt of St-Maximin, and the tide of pilgrims was diverted away from Burgundy into Provence.

Two years later Charles II of Anjou, King of Sicily and Count of Provence – and nephew of St Louis, King of France – commissioned his own architect Jean Bautici to build a new church to honour the 'rediscovered' bones, and though he never completed the project his designs were respected by later architects. It was part of a priory run by the Dominicans, a practical order chosen by Charles d'Anjou to organise the pilgrimages and maintain the buildings. The result is the loveliest Gothic church in Provence, and its beauty is not hard to analyse. Its great height comes as a surprise after even the loftiest Romanesque naves, and we owe the unity and purity of its style to the designs of Jean Bautici, and to his successors who never deviated much from them. The colour of the stonework is telling – a biscuit tone tinged with grey, which combines with the lightness of the structural members to produce a feeling of airy grace. None of the glass in the windows is coloured, so the daylight enters unfiltered, except by a gentle *grisaille*. The height is achieved without any triforium, and the church's beauty and elegance is entirely architectural. There is no sculptural decoration, and it shows that Dominican Gothic at its best could rival Cistercian Romanesque.

The only intrusions of a later date are a Renaissance wooden screen enclosing the choir, the choir stalls themselves, the organ tribune, and some baroque altar *retables*, one of which is in any case exceptional. This one is in the chapel at the head of the north aisle, the work of a sixteenth-century artist called Rouzen in gilded and painted wood. Its centrepiece is a Crucifixion, but the exceptional feature is the series of eighteen panels which enclose it on either side. The outer ones to right and left are vivid scenes of the Passion; the inner ones portray the martyrdom of various saints in the cities of the south. This was an opportunity to include views of Rome and Florence, of the *piazzetta* at Venice and the leaning tower of Pisa, and the earliest known painting of the Palais des Papes at Avignon.

The crypt, whatever its date, is little more than an underground cell, a short simple barrel-vaulted chamber. As well as the tombs of St Mary and St Maximin, there is an elaborate carved marble sarcophagus for St Sidoine, another arrival in the Camargue boatload whom we met as St Restitut in the Tricastin. The reliquary supposed to contain the skull of the Magdalene is obviously of the nineteenth century.

The conventional buildings, known as the 'Ancien Couvent Royal' in deference to its founder, were built alongside the north aisle, and begun at the same time as the church. There is no access to the cloister from the church, which is a basilica with no transept, except through the sacristy. Instead the visitor has to leave by the west door and walk through a passage in the Hôtel-de-Ville to reach the reception office on the far corner of the Place J. Salusse, where you have to buy an entrance ticket.

Big enough to encompass several trees, and so pleasantly shady, the cloister has a plain Gothic elevation on all four sides. A fine vaulted chapter house opens off the east gallery; to the north is the refectory, extended westward into a chapel now equipped for lectures and concerts. The walls of the *chauffoir*, next to the chapter house, are covered with photographs which illustrate the Dominican way of life, taken with the monks acting their parts somewhat self-consciously. The Dominicans follow the rule of St Augustine and their own 'Constitution of Preaching Brothers' founded by St Dominic in 1216. They were thrown out at the Revolution, but the church and convent were saved from destruction by a happy coincidence. Napoleon's younger brother was employed by a provision merchant in the town, and his superior intelligence was acknowledged when he was elected president of the local Jacobin club. He set up a provision store for the army in the church, and the organist learned to play the *Marseillaise* in time for a visit by the army

279

commander, Barras. The Dominicans returned in 1859, and it was here that their great theologian Henri Lacordaire wrote a life of Mary Magdalene. Exactly a hundred years later they withdrew to Toulouse, and the Couvent Royal is administered by a secular body of patrons of the arts, known as the 'Collège d'Échanges Contemporains'.

16

Aix to Sisteron

This is a straightforward journey which should suit travellers who want to see something of the far northern regions of Provence, to which Sisteron is one of the principal gateways. It follows very closely the course of the river Durance, alongside which a major highway has always run, so we can expect to find things of interest on the way. For most of it the N96 follows the right bank of the Durance; so does the A51 autoroute, which will reach Sisteron very much more quickly but will give you little chance of stopping before you get there. From Aix the N96 has only a short distance to go to reach the river crossing at the Pont de Mirabeau, where it also vaults over the autoroute. The village of Mirabeau, to your left after the crossing, was the seat of the family which produced the revolutionary marquis who left his mark on Aix-en-Provence.

The road then joins the main railway line from Avignon, and follows it into **Manosque**, a mediaeval town which has grown into a big commercial one without losing too much of its character. It owes this to a sensible move which has closed the whole area between its two mediaeval gateways to traffic, and so created a *zone pietonné* which winds its way through the centre of the old town. Arriving from Aix you will have to leave your car in the *parking* on your left a little way short of the **Porte Saunerie**.

Approaching it from this side you have the best view of this magnificent battlemented and machicolated fourteenth-century gateway; having passed through it you will find yourself in a relaxed world of traffic-free streets, with every kind of shop needed to support life, and numbers of little *places* at intervals with inviting café or restaurant tables.

Your way passes two big churches, of which **St-Sauveur** – the first you come to on your right – is the more interesting architecturally, though only the apse, choir and transept are genuinely Romanesque. The octagonal cupola is particularly fine, and the fanlight over the apse is an unusual departure. At the west end is a superb baroque organ, which you may hear being played during the midday lunch hour – when the church is surprisingly open. Further on you come to **Notre-Dame**, in the corner of the irregularly shaped Place de l'Hôtel-de-Ville. The architecture here is a bit of a muddle after a good deal of alteration in the seventeenth century, but it contains two outstanding works of religious art. The full name of the church is Notre-Dame-du-Romigier, where the word *romigier* is an old form of *rôncier*, meaning 'bramble bush'. This is an instance of the familiar legend by which a statue of the Virgin was discovered or re-discovered in some unlikely place – in this case (like Brer Rabbit) in a bramble bush; we met it last at Notre-Dame-de-l'Ormeau near Fayence. The curious statue preserved here was carved in a dark wood in the twelfth century, and is known as a 'Black Virgin'. The other object to look for is a very early marble sarcophagus (fourth or fifth-century) now used as an altar in a chapel off the north aisle.

You will eventually come to the **Porte Soubeyran**, which was the main point of entry to the town from the south. Named after a prominent Provençal family, it is of the same date as the Porte Saunerie and looks very much like it, except that it has lost its battlements – they have been replaced by a peaceful Provençal clock-tower with an ironwork belfry. If you have left your car at the other end of the town there is no point in going out through

Aix to Sisteron

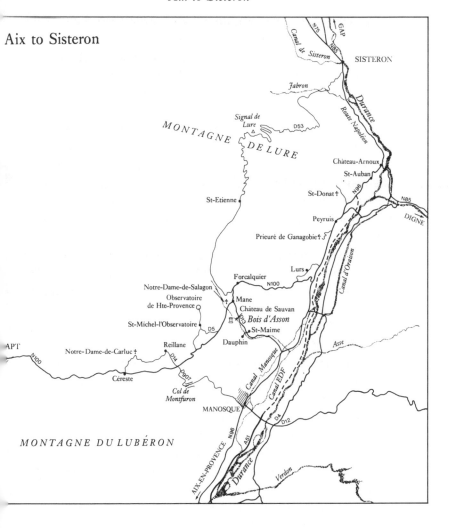

the gateway unless you want to photograph it from the far side. Instead the return journey through the town may find you ready for lunch, or at least a drink, somewhere on the way. Remember as you walk through the streets of Manosque that the novelist Jean Giono was born here, and that in *Jean le Bleu* he describes the life of his father as a shoemaker in the town.

At Manosque you have crossed the border from Var into the Alpes de Haute-Provence, which is a huge territory, not all of it mountainous but with some of the wildest scenery in France. If you carry on along the N96, which sticks strictly to the valley of the Durance, you will miss one of the most important towns in the history of Provence, Forcalquier. It would also mean missing several places on the way there which are surprisingly little known. The alternative is a detour which for maximum interest should leave Manosque by the D907, signposted for Apt. The first objective is the most elusive, and calls for some careful map reading – you will need an up-to-date edition of the Michelin series to have a chance – but it is one of the most intriguing places in Provence.

The priory of **Notre-Dame-de-Carluc** is not mentioned in any regular guidebook, and apart from the problem of finding it it is hard to see why. The D907 climbs steadily to the Col de Montfurin at the north-eastern tip of the Montagne de Luberon, from where a pretty road comes down to meet the N100 highway from Apt to Forcalquier. Turn left here, and just before the village of Cereste take a very minor road to the right. After about two-and-a-half kilometres take a fork to your right which should be signposted to Reillane. Keep a sharp lookout to your left, and you will sight the grey stonework of a church up among the trees and overlooking a small stream – beside which you can leave your car.

The church is practically all that is left of the main buildings of a twelfth-century priory, but by no means all there is to see. Built on an earlier foundation some time before 1150, it was dependent on the great abbey of Montmajour outside Arles.

Hard as it is to believe this now, it controlled in its turn about fifteen other rural priories in the neighbourhood. Its fortunes declined in the sixteenth century, its buildings decayed, and by the time of the Revolution little remained except the principal priory church, where Mass was still said on Sundays and feast days. There were in fact three churches associated with the priory at different times, though traces of the two older ones are minimal. In such a remote situation the surviving church of Notre-Dame has to be kept locked, but there are guided visits every afternoon (except on Fridays in June) from 1430 onwards, or from 1300 at weekends.

There is no great loss if you fail to get inside, for much of it has been restored after several collapses of the fabric. It originally consisted of two square bays of equal sizes, which formed the nave and the choir, with a polygonal apse projecting to the east. There is a good view of the apse from the outside, where into each of the corners to north and south is tucked a short fluted column with a carved capital: to the south a pair of sprightly doves nestle among the acanthus leaves; to the north a man supports the weight of the cornice – it might be the world, judging from his expression – on his sturdy arms.

The real interest and mystery of the place lies in a long sunken gallery extending northwards from that side of the choir, though not until 1960 did anyone investigate it and try to fathom its purpose. For the first twenty metres or so it was covered by a low roof supported on short stumpy pillars with elaborate capitals, of which three were put back in position by the excavators. The further end of the gallery needed no roof, for it continued into the mass of rock on which the priory was built. Along the right-hand side, cut into a raised stone shelf, is a row of open rock graves; at the far end, where the gallery runs into the rock, there are more graves on the left and a little group, including some small enough for children, outside it to the right. At this point the gallery narrows and ends in a square-sectioned shaft with a floor about six metres below the previous level, just where a spring emerges from the rock. The excavators concluded that this was part of an earlier church, or at least a baptistery, recorded in 1074 as dedicated to St John the Baptist. You can just make out part of an arch which would have supported its vaulting.

Further on still to the north you come to what looks like the ground plan of a primitive cell, and the archaeologists maintain that this was the kernel of the whole monastic establishment and grew into the earliest of the three churches of Carluc, recorded in 1011 as dedicated to St Peter. It is tempting to imagine that a subterranean passage containing rock graves goes back to an early Christian period, but a remote site like this can only have been developed as a monastic complex site round about 1100. The two ancient chapels connected with the abbey of Montmajour, also built on a rocky outcrop, are surrounded by similar graves, and so is the little church of St-Pantaléon in the Vaucluse. More and more graves were discovered as the excavations proceeded, and Carluc must have encompassed a much bigger cemetery than either of those sites. It seems to have been a popular place for both baptism and burial.

The long roofed gallery can be looked on as the equivalent of a cloister in more sophisticated establishments, as well as a passage connecting the church with the baptistery. The rock graves along the side would have been occupied by monks rather than the general public. You will look in vain for more than the vaguest trace of other monastic buildings, though masonry can be seen on the hill above Notre-Dame. Once the site was abandoned natural decay was quick, the worked stone was carried off as valuable building material, and the rock itself was quarried for more. The remarkable thing is that from what was left the archaeologists were able to deduce so much of the original plan and its uses.

From Reillane there is an easier way back to the N100. Turn north at the junction, and after four kilometres you come to a road on your left which leads to a monument of the twentieth century which could hardly be more different from Carluc. In 1938 the government decided to build the Observatoire de Haute-Provence at a height of 650 metres on this northern tip of the Luberon. One of the best equipped in Europe, it takes advantage of the pure air of Provence and a site rarely affected by heavy cloud or mist. The road to it passes through the village of St-Michel, now known as **St-Michel-l'Observatoire**. It has a small Romanesque church which was built on much the same plan as Notre-Dame-de-Carluc, and not much later in date.

This is what is known as the 'haute église de St-Michel', and must not be confused with the later church in the village below. High in two senses, you climb to it up a steep path, and its walls tower above you as you reach the top. The inside is more interesting than at Carluc, for the original cupola over the choir section has survived, complete with its fan-shaped squinches, and it makes more telling use of those neat corner pillars, or *colonnettes*, to decorate and soften the angles of the walls. On the other hand the semicircular apse was demolished and the east end extended in the sixteenth century to make a squared-off sanctuary. It has two notable fittings: the high altar is a single plain rectangular block of limestone with a decorated cornice and a stepped base, and at the entrance you are greeted by a gorgeous marble *bénitier*, or holy water stoup, where the basin is carried on the backs of two well nourished lions.

If you should arrive on a Wednesday afternoon you can take advantage of a guided visit to the Observatory; otherwise you can admire its fourteen cupolas from a distance, before rejoining the N100 by a diffrent road. Turning north again you will soon see on your right the entrance gates of the **Château de Sauvan**. As distant from twentieth-century technology as it is from the Romanesque world, this eighteenth-century château is now one of the finest in France, and quite the best example of its period in Provence. I say 'now' because although it was built to designs by the celebrated architect Jean-Baptiste Franque between 1720 and 1725, and hardly damaged by the Revolution, it was neglected by its later owners, wrecked by the German army which occupied it during the last war, and barely habitable by 1980. At that point it was bought by the present owner, who has restored it to a state no less splendid than when it was hailed as the 'Petit Trianon de Provence'.

The man responsible for building Sauvan was Michel-François de Forbin-Janson, a brigadier in the army of Louis XV and a kinsman of the archbishop of Arles; in 1793 a descendant of his was involved in an episode worthy of Dumas. The *châtelaine* of the time had married into a princely family, and the Princess Galléan was not only a close friend of Marie-Antoinette at Versailles, but also resembled her closely. She thought up the bold plan of changing places with the queen, who was by then a prisoner in the *Conciergerie*, and mustered a million francs – the whole of her fortune – to further the plot, by bribery if necessary. All had been privily arranged, but at the last moment the queen smuggled out a message to say that she could not allow her friend to risk her life on her behalf. As it was, the princess came under suspicion, was denounced, and had to escape abroad.

This story, and other highlights of the history of the château, have been put on a tape which is played to visitors while they assemble on the back terrace for a guided tour. The visit is extremely well organised, and the usual guide is pleasant and expertly informative. The whole exterior, especially the main western front, is a perfect example of eighteenth-century French architecture at its best; you will not see its like in Provence, nor probably outside the Île de France. The new owner has assembled a remarkable collection of period furniture, ceramics and other works of art to adorn a series of beautiful rooms on two floors. A Provençal peculiarity in the furniture is a number of pieces with feet in the shape of 'sabots de biche', or deer's feet, but most of it is in the classic Louis XV or Louis XVI style, with a few additions from the Directoire and later periods.

A fine stone staircase leads to the first floor landing, which also gives access to a long gallery *à l'anglais*. The staircase, we are told, suffered badly from the habit the last young *châtelaine* of the Forbin-Janson line had of riding her horse up to her bedroom. The animal was quartered in the music room, which did the room no good, and had to be coaxed down backwards next morning. A small chapel containing a painting of St Bruno, founder of the Carthusian order, seems an uneasy neighbour for a Charles X billiards room and a side staircase *à la dérobé*, by which lovers and mistresses could traditionally depart unseen. The music room, now beautifully restored, has an auditorium with a tiny gallery just big enough for a harpsichord.

Your guide will explain that there is still a lot to be done, but the only obvious need is to clear the overgrown garden levels below the rear terrace. In a *château de plaisance* there was never any need for a moat, unless it was decorative, but opposite the north front, and reflecting it, there is a beautiful rectangular *bassin*, or ornamental lake, on which swans (white and black) float serenely; it took four years to clear it of the rubbish which the Germans had tipped into it. A number of the original windows were blocked up to avoid the tax imposed by the Directoire, but their blankness was concealed by *trompe l'oeil* decoration; the new owner is gradually opening them up again, one by one.

At the end of my visit I was intrigued enough to ask our guide who the proprietor with such impeccable taste might be. The answer was a conspiratorial whisper: 'C'est moi!'

The road in to Forcalquier crosses the river Laye just before the village of Mane, and very soon after the crossing you will see on your left an indeterminate group of buildings which turns out to be an important mediaeval site – the priory of **Notre-Dame-de-Salagon**. We are back now in the early twelfth century, for this offshoot of the Benedictine abbey of St-André in Ville-neuve-lès-Avignon is recognised in a papal bull of 1118 as its chief dependency in the neighbourhood of Forcalquier. Yet it seems never to have been a full monastic establishment, which explains why the only building alongside the church was the Prior's Lodging – he being in sole charge of its affairs and the only resident cleric. Little is known of its early history, and though it was prominent in the records of Forcalquier under Raymond Bérenger IV it is only occasionally mentioned thereafter.

The interest of the church is more architectural than historical, though it is intriguing to find that in 1723 the nominal holder of the benefice was Jacques de Forbin-Janson, archbishop of Arles, whose kinsman was building the château of Sauvan just across the road. It has suffered so much natural and malign damage in its time – *dégâts* is the more succinct French word – that its details are easier to assess than its overall character, especially as so much of it was rebuilt in the sixteenth and even the nineteenth century.

The outer walls are entirely plain except for the western front. This appears lop-sided because the north aisle is not matched by one to the south of the nave, and the entrance doorway is not centred under the deeply sunk quatrefoil *oculus* in the gable, but the doorway itself is worthy of a cathedral. The shafts of the pillars which support the archivolts, three a side, are all fluted in different ways, and the acanthus-leaved capitals are simpler and more elegant than some you will see inside. The most original touch is in the treatment of the outer arch, which with its 'billet' moulding is continued to right and left of the doorway, where it projects rather like a drip-stone. Above the centre of the arch and below its extensions runs a deliciously carved frieze of linked leaf and flower patterns.

The arrangements inside are more confused, after a good deal of reconstruction at different times. As you would expect, the oldest part is the apse, and excavations have found beneath it a primitive square cell, or *cabanon*. The nave is pure twelfth-century Romanesque, a very wide one with massive pillars supporting a barrel vault. The north aisle was built at the same time, and may have had a third bay with a second apse projecting to the east. If so it was altered in the fourteenth century to make a Gothic chapel, while the main part of the north wall had to be completely rebuilt in the sixteenth century, either after an earthquake or because of damage caused in the wars of religion. Most of the capitals in the nave and side aisle are conventional, but look for the one on the inner side of the north aisle which has a lively if archaic carving of the baptism of Jesus. I especially like the possessive and watchful dove representing the Holy Spirit, and the shy-looking angel holding a shawl for Jesus to put on when he emerges. The most unusual decorations are the inset panels which occur in odd places, usually high up on the walls, carved with a strange variety of animal and human figures. We have seen them before in the Tricastin churches of St-Paul-Trois-Châteaux and St-Restitut, and they are thought to have been unsolicited *jeux d'esprit* by enterprising masons to enliven a dull expanse of wall.

The building attached to the south side of the church is the *Prior's Lodging*, though not the original one. In the fifteenth century the humbler Romanesque quarters were replaced by a more substantial 'modern' building on two floors, serviced by an impressive newel stairway. Its architectural details, especially the mullioned windows, are of what we should call the 'Tudor' period, and it looks like a home for a man who felt his own importance and liked his comforts.

As usual, the Revolution resulted in the whole property being sold into private hands, and the church was abandoned until 1857. After more than a century of vicissitudes, during which the church was used for storing grain, and the priory as quarters for Italian troops during the last war, the real work of restoration began only in 1981. Then the last private owners sold it to the *commune* of Mane, who bought it with the help of a state grant on the understanding that the cultural organisation called *Les Alpes de Lumière* would sponsor a comprehensive programme of repair and rehabilitation. They began by making it the base of the formidable-sounding *Conservatoire du patrimoine ethnologique de la Haute-Provence*, which is the body now responsible for everything that goes on here. This explains some otherwise puzzling activities, in particular a publicity display (including an excellent documentary film) which illustrates the history and practice of *transhumance*, the spring and autumn migration of huge flocks of sheep from the drying pastures of southern Provence to the fresh grazing of the alps after the snows have melted. The valley of the Durance has always been one of the main routes in either direction. As another diversion they have planted an area north of the church as a mediaeval herb garden, and they have concerts and even theatrical performances during the summer. As for the structural repairs, a lot has been done in a very short time, and the history of Salagon is still being rewritten almost daily as the works proceed. It will be some time before the whole of the Prior's Lodging is open to visits, but the rest is open all day and every day.

From the terraces of the château of Sauvan you will have had comprehensive views of a countryside which has been compared with Tuscany, a rolling mixture of valley, plain and wooded hills. To the north the citadel of Forcalquier stands out against the background of the Montagne de Lure; to the east you look down on the many channels of the Durance and its attendant Canal de Manosque. You can also follow the line of the Roman *via Domitia* as it crosses the plain below; this is the trunk road which Strabo says was used even more heavily as a route from the Rhône valley into Italy than the *via Aurelia* to the south. It ran from Arles north to Cavaillon, and from there it followed roughly the line of the N100 to join the valley of the Durance east of Forcalquier. It ran on north through Sisteron and eventually entered northern Italy by the Mont Genèvre pass. This section is easy to follow, as it runs very straight from Reillane to Lurs on the Durance, bypassing both Forcalquier and Salagon.

In the foreground of the view will be **Mane**, with some solidly built sixteenth and seventeenth century *hôtels*, and a ring of narrow streets below the ramparts of the twelfth-century citadel. Mane has become more of a dormitory suburb of Forcalquier than a village, but a few kilometres further south a pair of unspoilt *villages perchés* face each other across the D13 and the river Laye. The more substantial one is **Dauphin**, where you will find quiet little paved and cobbled streets, archways and flights of steps, old ladies popping in and out of doorways, and lizards disappearing into cracks in the walls. The streets have names like Rue Torse, Rue du Figuier, La Grande Rue; narrowest of all (two feet wide at the most) is the Ruelle de l'Église. Parking is on the Terrasse du Château beside the church, but the only sign of a château is a gateway at either end of the terrace. The fifteenth-century church has a Renaissance front but is kept locked. If you cross the main road and drive up to **St-Maime** (a contraction of St Maxime) you will find a smaller and less interesting village, but right on the top of its hill there is an odd-looking polygonal tower which is all that remains of a castle once belonging to the Raymond Berenger family. There is an enjoyable walk up there by a path which ends in a grassy scramble among wild flowers – difficult to follow until the grass is cut, but populated by some rare butterflies. Before you reach the tower you will pass what is called the *chapelle castrale* of Ste-Agathe, just a tiny rough stone nave with a lean-to south aisle and single lancet window, reputed to be of Carolingian date, but not in use for many years.

What you will not expect to be told about these two villages is that in the nearby Bois d'Asson are mines which in this century have produced large quantities of lignites, gysum and rock salt, and that the resulting cavities are now used for storing the national strategic reserves of petroleum.

Forcalquier today give no hint of its importance in mediaeval Provence. The castle where the counts of Provence held court for two centuries was demolished in 1601 on the orders of Henri IV; the 'cathedral', though it once claimed equality with

Sisteron, never had a bishop, and the Franciscan Couvent des Cordeliers was ravaged during the wars of religion, sold for agricultural use after the Revolution, and only came to life again after being almost completely rebuilt in the 1960s. All the same you will find it a sensible and well organised town, and there is a small mediaeval nucleus to the south of the cathedral.

To understand the all-but royal status of the court of Forcalquier a brief genealogy may help. The first count of Forcalquier, William Bertrand (who died in 1065), belonged to a junior branch of the family which had ruled all Provence as sovereign counts since the tenth century, and was descended from William 'the Liberator', who had thrown the Saracens out of la Garde-Freinet in 973. As for the Provençal dynasty, in 1112 the charmingly named countess Douce married Raymond Bérenger, count of Barcelona, who thus by marriage became Raymond Bérenger I of Provence. In 1151 their son Raymond Bérenger II married the heiress to the Catalan throne, thereby becoming King of Aragon, and was succeeded by their son Alfonso II who inherited the two titles of King of Aragon and count of Provence. On his death the kingdom of Aragon passed to his elder son Pedro, the *comté* of Provence to his second son Alfonso, while his daughter Constance married the emperor Frederick II.

In 1195 Alfonso reunited the families by marrying Garsinde, the last Forcalquier heiress. It was their son Raymond Bérenger IV (his elder cousin Raymond Bérenger III having died without issue) who ruled Provence from his castle in Forcalquier for nearly thirty years, and though he had no sons he has never been rivalled as a matchmaker for daughters. Marguerite the eldest married Louis IX of France (St Louis), Eleanor married Henry III of England, Sancia married Richard duke of Cornwall (Henry III's brother who became King of the Romans), while Beatrice married Louis XI's younger brother Charles, duke of Anjou. It was the youngest daughter's marriage which affected Provence most, for her husband also held the titles of King of Naples and Sicily (sometimes called 'the two Sicilies'). Several generations later 'le bon roi René' could still call himself King of Sicily as well as count of Provence. You will sometimes find the father of the 'four queens' called Raymond Bérenger V; this is because his great-uncle of the same name held a brief regency which does not strictly entitle him to be called count.

Armed with all this information there is no excuse for not taking the winding path from the south of the *vieille ville* which leads up to where the castle of the dynasty once stood. Of all its fortifications only one tower and a few bits of wall survived the attentions of Henry IV, and in its place rises a surreal confection called the **Chapel of Notre-Dame de Provence**, built in the 'Romanesque' style of the nineteenth century. To be fair, it looks more original than the new cathedral of Marseille, and it could almost get away with its octagonal base but for its mechanical frieze and the crowded and badly proportioned cupola. The view in all directions from the terrace is worth the climb.

Another disappointment is the church of **Notre-Dame**, known as the 'cathedral without a bishop'. The transept, choir and apse have an early Gothic elegance, but the nave has been harshly restored in Romanesque style, and a good deal of baroque detail was added in the seventeenth century; I found the interior surprisingly neglected and dilapidated for a big city church. The **Couvent des Cordeliers**, which you reach by way of the Boulevard des Martyrs to the east of the church, was established by Raymond Berenger IV in 1236 – the 'cordeliers' being the popular name given to Franciscan monks because of the 'cord' with which they traditionally gird up their habit. Its buildings suffered many indignities after the Revolution, on top of severe damage in the wars of religion, but they have been restored to something like their original state, and parts of them are used for concerts and exhibitions during the summer. Guided visits are possible every day in July, August and the first half of September, but in the other summer months they are limited to Sunday and public holiday afternoons. One of the few relics of the town's mediaeval fortifications is the **Porte des Cordeliers**, which was not the entrance to the *couvent* but straddles the street parallel to the Boulevard des Martyrs.

If you have found Forcalquier in some ways disappointing, there are better things to come. If you rejoin the N96 near Lurs and turn left for Sisteron, look carefully for a sign about three kilometres further on which points the way left to the **Prieuré de Ganagobie**. The road rises through the trees in a long series of startlingly abrupt *virages*, and ends on a wide grassy plateau. Here you must leave your car and walk forward until you see a long stone wall on your right which partly conceals the west front of a monastery unlike any we have so far seen in Provence.

The formation of this plateau recalls in an odd way Conan Doyle's *The Lost World*. A flat-topped island site, about 1300 metres long and on average 400 across, it was part of the prehistoric cliff along the right bank of the Durance. The drop of nearly 350 metres to the river bed is almost sheer. However the black-winged figures fluttering about the monastery walls will be Benedictine monks, not pterodactyls from the Lost World. The site had indeed been occupied in prehistoric times, but records began in the Carolingian period, when the bishop of Sisteron – whose family owned the land – built two churches up here and in about 960 presented them to the Benedictine abbey of Cluny as the nucleus of a monastery. It was a natural connection, because at the time the abbot of Cluny was St Mayeul, a Provençal by birth and possibly related to Jean III of Sisteron. Gifts of land and property followed, and in the early twelfth century the Benedictines began to build a new monastery with an abbey church dedicated to Our Lady. At the same time a small town grew up at the narrow northern tip of the plateau, protected by fortifications which ran right across from east to west.

Though the only access to the whole plateau was by a steep

mule track, all went well until the end of the fourteenth century, when both financial and spiritual resources seem to have failed. By 1404 the complement of monks had fallen from twelve to four or five, the buildings were in ruins, and by 1471 the 'vieille ville' to the north was uninhabited. There were brief attempts to revive the monastery in the early sixteenth century, but it was sacked during the wars of religion and its archives were burnt. In 1579 a visitor from Cluny found nobody living on the plateau but a few shepherds. Another partial revival in the following century was eclipsed by the Revolution.

At the turn of the last century the owner of the land gave it back to the Benedictine abbey of Ste Madeleine in Marseille, but the real revival of Ganagobie did not begin until 1957, when the *Service des Monuments historiques* took it in hand, and fifty Benedictines from the abbey of Hautecombe in Savoy, who had found their privacy too much threatened by tourists, moved in to worship and work in peace.

The first sight of the west end of the abbey church will show that this is not a Cistercian but a Benedictine foundation. Whereas the doorways of Silvacane, Sénanque and le Thoronet are deliberately inconspicuous, the one at Ganagobie explodes in a riot of sculpture. The tympanum of the deep-set archway could have been designed in Burgundy, though it seems that Provençal masons come nowhere near the standards set at Vézelay and Autun. We have the familiar Burgundian design of Christ in his oval *mandorla* surrounded by the symbols of the four evangelists, with two winged angels to fill in the corners. We have a lintel where a row of apostles gaze fixedly out from between the pillars of a Romanesque arcade. Although there are twelve figures, notice that the one on the far left has a halo, and so must represent Christ – which means that Judas has been left out. Peter is identified as usual by his outsize key. The three detached *colonnettes* which support the arches on each side look more typical of Provence, especially the one on the left with zig-zag fluting, but the unique feature of the whole doorway is the

297

pattern of cut-out blocks of stone – almost like fretwork – which frame both the entrance itself and the two main archivolts. The architectural term is *festonné* (from *festons*, or 'festoons') but we are assured they will not be found anywhere else in France.

The single nave inside is more Cistercian in feeling, rising serenely without a triforium and without any ornament; there is a double transept with only two side apses. The east end was wrecked by a deliberate explosion in the Revolution, and though the central apse has been beautifully restored the cupola and vaulting of the transept have been replaced by wooden rafters. Tucked into the corner between the north transept and the nave is a rectangular chamber, entered only from the outside and not usually shown, which was probably the chapter house and only remaining part of the earlier eleventh-century monastery.

The revolutionary explosion in 1794 was the beginning of an extraordinary story. When the vaulting of the east end collapsed it covered and concealed a mosaic pavement which filled all the space before and behind the high altar, and extended in front of both the side chapels – a work commissioned by the thirteenth-century prior Bertrand which took fifteen years to complete. For over 150 years no one knew it was there, until one day in 1950 Père Lorézi, then the only resident Benedictine, discovered what lay under the rubble. He called in the local and eventually the State authorities, and the *Commission des Beaux Arts* decided to have the whole pavement restored. Small sections of it were removed in turn and sent off to a firm of experts in western France; treated and restored, they were returned and gradually replaced until the whole surface could be revealed as it was first laid down.

The pavement is unique. Unlike Byzantine mosaics, these are full of life and movement, composed in a spirit of elegant fantasy, with some deliberate fun in their treatment of animals. The only colours are red and creamy white against a black ground, and the motifs are said to be Celtic. I have seen other thirteenth-century mosaics in a similar position in Burgundian churches, but nothing like these. They would take half an hour to examine properly and just as long to describe, but specially memorable are the scene of a knight on horseback spearing a dragon, a graceful antelope, and some good attempts at elephants.

The cloister galleries are divided into two main sections each side, where an arch curves low to enclose a row of four inner arches supported by pairs of columns. There is plenty of solid wall space compared with the open archways, an arrangement which gives more shelter in the extremes of climate up here. The restoration of the cloister, refectory and other monastic quarters has been undertaken by the monks themselves, and is still going on. They have also prepared fifteen guest rooms to receive those who wish to spend a few days in rest and retreat from the world below, and they are always glad to welcome groups of young people. One hopes that the dream of a peaceful refuge for prayer, meditation and work will not be spoilt by coachloads of insensitive tourists. As things are, visits are well organized and discreetly handled by a body of highly intelligent and articulate men – and are never allowed to interfere with the daily offices of the church.

To get a last feeling of the place, first go round outside to the east end and look at the simple but satisfying build-up of the *chevet*. Then walk further east down the avenue to a point where a crucifix has been set up on a spur of the cliff overlooking the Durance. No view, except from the air, could take in so much of a river at one time, but then most things about Ganagobie are unique.

Between May and October one visit is allowed every morning at 1100, three in the afternoon at 1500, 1600 and 1700. In the winter you can visit only on Sundays, in the morning again at 1100, in the afternoon at 1500 and 1600.

Returning to earth, and resuming the journey towards Sisteron, you will find the N96 increasingly busy and its surroundings less attractive. At St-Auban there is an airfield beside the

river, and at Château-Arnoux the road joins the Route Napoléon, which is the only way from Nice to Sisteron. To avoid all
this and enjoy one more discovery, follow the main road out of
Peyruis but very soon turn left at a junction where the right-
hand turn crosses the river to Les Mées. Soon you will have left
all traffic behind you as you climb into the woods of the Val-St-
Donat. Watch the skyline ahead of you, and after about a mile
you will see the outline of a building standing high and clear of
the trees. This is the **Church of St-Donat**, the only substantial
survivor of a little group of primitive shrines connected with this
saint. Thanks to a rare twelfth-century *Vita Sancti Donati* we
know a good deal about him.

First heard of as a Christian priest at Orleans at the end of the
fifth century, he retired to the *pays de Sisteron* at the foot of the
Montagne de Lure to live a hermit's life. Hermits were expected
to live in rough and desolate places, but at the same time to be
reasonably accessible to those who wished to pay their respects
to a holy man. The Val-St-Donat is still a rough territory, but it
must have been very beautiful then; it was certainly accessible,
because through it ran the *via Domitia*, bypassing Château-
Arnoux on its way to Sisteron. There are no records of building
here until the eleventh century, but in 1018 we read that
William II of Provence presented the whole site (which he
described as a 'monastère') to the abbey of St-André at
Villeneuve-lès-Avignon. Exactly a hundred years later the text
of a papal bull includes among the properties of St-André two
churches dedicated to St Donat, an upper and a lower one;
other sources indicate there were two small chapels as well.

Deep in the scrub of the neighbouring hills are the vestigial
ruins of the church of St-Donat-le-Haut, and the chapel, or
'église mineure' of St-Donat-le-Bas, but they would take some
finding. What we see now is the 'église majeure' of St-Donat-
le-Bas, and it ranks among the earliest of early Romanesque
churches in Provence. It was probably built by the abbey of
St-André in the middle of the eleventh century, and it seems

certain that the site had been a religious centre since the beginning of the sixth. In the fourteenth it emerges as a priory under the wing of Ganagobie, and until the Revolution it was a popular goal for pilgrims. It was sold then as public property, but such a substantial building in this situation was too useful to destroy, and for the whole of the nineteenth century the nave was used as a barn and the choir as living quarters. Since then this magnificent church has remained empty and untended, but such is its appeal in its present state that one would almost prefer it never to be 'restored'. In fact some fitful work has now begun through local enterprise, and you can see that a couple of window embrasures have been carefully rebuilt.

You can leave your car in a kind of layby among farm implements on the corner of the road, from where there is a short scramble to a rough clearing among pine trees and scrubby vegetation. You arrive at the foot of the cathedral-like east end – or perhaps a better simile would be the bows of a great ship riding a green sea. Walk round to the west and look through the iron grille which cuts off the entrance there – there is no formal doorway. What you see is Romanesque church architecture in the raw, in its earliest, purest and simplest form. The plan is that of a basilica, with a high wide nave flanked by side aisles so narrow as to be little more than passages leading into the transept, but well lit by high lancet windows on the south side. There is no ornament, no capitals; just pillars, arches and walls, and a still perfect cupola over the crossing. The central apse is unusually wide and high (though only half as high as the whole eastern wall) whereas the two side apses are tiny. This is what makes them look from outside like a hen with two chickens. The stone floor is all broken up, and there are graffiti on the pillars, but the grandeur of this church is irresistible. If the western entrance is barred, you may be able to get in by the doorway of the south transept, where there is a removable grille.

My visit here was made even more memorable by an encounter with Pan. From down below we heard the sound of a

301

flute coming from inside the church, and when we arrived there we found a young man with curly black hair standing in front of the apse and playing plaintive music on a reed pipe. His audience was the girl who came with him, but when we spoke he said he came there often by himself to play because the acoustic was so responsive. He showed us his pipe, and from his pocket he produced a set of real Pan-pipes – short stems cut to difficult lengths and bound tightly together, each producing a different note. He had made them himself from reeds which grow by the stream below, and

> 'The music in my heart I bore
> Long after it was heard no more'.

All this time the background to the north has been the Montagne de Lure, which is really an extension of the Mont Ventoux range, just as high and rather wilder. I have not yet in this chapter made any suggestions about hotels to stay at, but if you are looking for a base near Forcalquier to explore the area I have described, and perhaps to probe the fastnesses of the Montagne, you will do no better than the St Clair, just south of St-Etienne. It stands in its own peaceful grounds beside the D13 to Forcalquier, has twenty-seven moderately priced rooms, an enterprising chef, a sunny terrace and a swimming pool.

From St-Etienne there is a spectacular drive right over the top of the mountain, past the Signal de Lure at 1800 metres, and down into the valley of the Jabron a little way west of Sisteron. Much the same route is taken by the Grande Randon-née GR6, but walkers should remember that this is a wild and uncompromising mountain in bad weather. In fine weather the scenery is magnificent, the trees include beeches and oaks as well as pines, and there are rarities among the flora and fauna.

17

Sisteron and Haute-Provence

Sisteron is easily the most dramatic town in Provence –
dramatic in its history, dramatic in its situation. It stands at the
junction of two great rivers, the Durance and the Buëch, after
which the Durance is joined by the Bléone from Digne, and
forces its way south and west to join the Rhône. Sisteron (the
Romans called it *Segustero*) was on the *via Domitia*, so it was the
northern gateway to the Roman *provincia*. Unlike Forcalquier it
was a genuine bishopric from the fifth century up to the
Revolution, and its bishop Jean III virtually founded the
monastery at Ganagobie.

The Saracens occupied it during their campaigns of conquest
in the ninth century, as a key northern outpost; the otherwise
unknown St Bevons is still venerated as the leader who got rid of
them in 974. The counts of Forcalquier and Provence relied on
it to protect their northern borders against any intrusion from
Savoy or the Dauphiné, but in 1481 it passed with the rest of the
comté into the hands of the French kings. François I stayed here
three times during his Italian campaigns, and in 1815 Napoleon
arrived after his escape from Elba. The road he took, now the
N85, has ever since been called the Route Napoléon.

Nothing is left of its eleventh-century fortress, and the later
history of Sisteron is inseparable from the rock citadel which

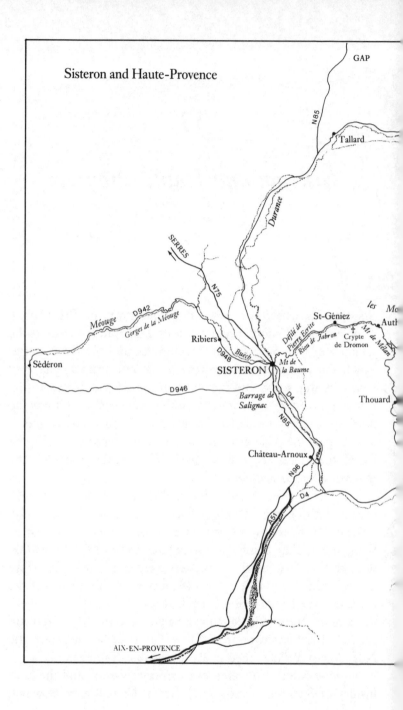

Sisteron and Haute-Provence

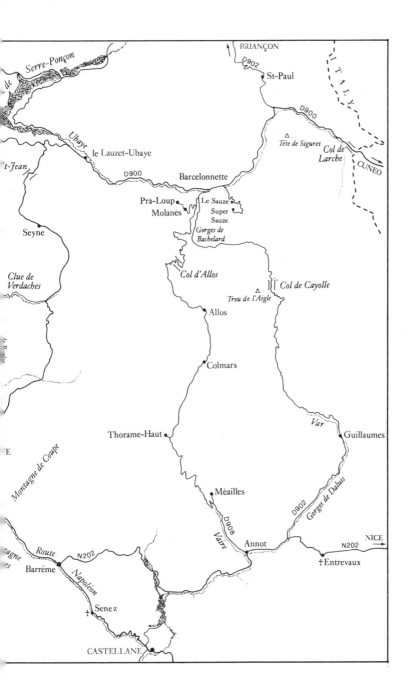

Henri IV built to guard his eastern frontier. He employed the military engineer Jean Érard, and though Louis XIV's Marshal Vauban drew up plans to extend it, they were never carried out. It remains an extraordinary and imaginative feat of engineering, and to walk round its battlements at any time is an unforgettable experience. Its watch-towers are built over sheer drops, and one – the 'Devil's Lookout' – has a vertiginous view across the Durance to the Rocher de la Baume. This fantastic formation, where the strata of a 1,500-foot limestone crag run vertically, is reflected in the deep still waters of the river. The most alarming part to walk along is a narrow projection of the *chemin de ronde*, built on a knife-edge of rock to reach the westernmost watch-tower. I shall never forget looking west from here just before sunset, as a fiery red sun went down behind the jagged Montagne de l'Ubac.

The fortifications have many ramifications and levels, and there is a sensible system of directive signs to help you find your way around them. Before you reach the highest levels you pass the *donjon*, where Richelieu managed to imprison Duke Jean Casimir of Poland, and the fourteenth-century chapel of the counts of Provence – or rather its handsome modern incarnation, which brings us to the most recent drama involving Sisteron and its citadel.

On the night of 15 August 1944, the day when the Allies landed on the Riviera coast, a squadron of United States bombers was detailed to destroy the bridge over the Buëch above the town. Their aim was not good, and they dropped all their bombs either on the citadel or on the old town beneath, killing three hundred French civilians. They made little impression on the citadel, clamped so firmly to the rock, but they wrecked the lovely little Gothic chapel.

This story had a more cheerful preface. The Germans were using the *donjon* and other quarters to house a party of civilian prisoners awaiting deportation to concentration camps. Apparently knowing nothing of the planned bombing raid, the local

Resistance had fortuitously decided to rescue the prisoners the night before. A small party dressed in German uniforms marched smartly up to tell the guards they had come to escort the prisoners to the railway station. It worked, and the whole lot were marched down to the town and disappeared into the *maquis*, leaving only the German guards up there to endure the American bombardment. I had a vivid account of this story from the *gardienne* at the ticket office; as a girl of fifteen she had seen the party go by, and had survived the next night's bombardment.

Naturally there is little left of the old town, except where the narrow stepped alleys go down to the river bank. Yet it seemed like another miracle that no bombs directly hit the cathedral church of **Notre-Dame-des-Pommiers**. Its title is a misnomer, for Our Lady here had nothing to do with apple trees, and the word *pommiers* is a wilful corruption of the Latin *ponemurum*, meaning the open space 'behind the wall' of a fortified town – which is exactly where the cathedral was built. It is however a noble building, strong rather than beautiful, and a true example of Provençal Romanesque. The nave is high, the side aisles narrow; there is a fully rounded barrel vault, and an octagonal cupola complete with squinches. The arcades are high enough to carry the vaulting without any triforium or clerestory, and there is no sculptural ornament. The outside is less satisfactory, in spite of the fine octagonal tower over the cupola, mostly because its proportions are spoilt by a line of chapels protruding to the south. The three rounded towers in the open space to the south of the cathedral are the only remains of the fourteenth-century walls of the town, and they too are lucky to have escaped the bombardment of 1944. The town plays down that traumatic event, and its publicity even equates it with the sad day in 1924 when Sisteron was deprived of its title of Sous-Préfecture.

The reason why the Durance runs so calm and deep below the Rocher de la Baume is that it has been turned into a lake here by the Barrage de Salignac, some way down stream, as part of a huge hydro-electric industry involving an underground power station to the north of the town, which produces 650 million kilowatts a year, and a conventional one below the barrage producing 220 million – and at no cost to the environment.

If you would prefer to stay in Sisteron – and it is a lively and friendly town – the best choice in my opinion is the Tivoli, which is quiet and has the advantage of an open space with parking in front of the hotel. In any case there are at least two worthwhile expeditions to east and west which you could fit in if there is time. The shorter one involves crossing the Durance by the big new bridge under the Rocher, and taking not the D4 back down the left bank but the D3 which strikes out into the hills towards St-Géniez. You will soon see you have arrived in a different kind of Provence – a sub-alpine landscape of narrow valleys where the hills press closer and closer as you climb among them. There are few roads, and the routes they follow take the line of ancient mule tracks.

The D3 climbs quickly to close on 3,000 feet, then embarks on a slow winding course through the Défilé de Pierre Écrite. A *défilé* is a narrow passage between encroaching cliffs, or between cliffs and river, but the **Pierre Écrite** requires more explanation. Some time in the fifth century, presumably before barbarian invasions entirely disrupted the life of the Roman province, the *praefectus* Claudius Postumus Dardanus (by then a Christian) established a walled community which he called *Théopolis* ('city of God') somewhere on the route we are following.

To enable the inhabitants of Segustero to reach it he must have carved a way through the rocks and made a road; such is the message of a long and beautifully chiselled inscription in Latin carved on a rock to the left of the road at the end of the *défilé*, and two-thirds of the way to St-Géniez. There is a sign pointing to it, but low down on the verge and easy to miss. It is as though the Minister of Transport had unveiled a plaque to record his contribution to a local amenity; it is socially interesting that his name is linked in the inscription with his wife, who was called Nevia Galla and could have been a Gallic woman of property in the neighbourhood. What happened to Théopolis, or where it was, is a mystery, though it seems that Dardanus at the time of his conversion had corresponded with St Augustine, author of the treatise *de Civitate Dei*, and the name could have symbolised something less than a classical walled city.

After the *défilé* we enter the more open valley of the Riou de Jabron, and the road emerges into pleasant fertile farming country, mainly pasture – though still with a background of jagged peaks and volcanic-looking slopes. The village of St-Géniez is poor and a bit tatty, and when I asked a passer-by if he could direct us to the chapel of Dromon we were treated to a stream of hostile invective, directed not against ourselves, we realised, but against the church in general, the Pope and all his works, and the local *curé* in particular. The solution as usual is to be found at the Mairie, on the left towards the end of the village, where you will be given not only directions but a key to get in with.

Follow the road for just over a kilometre till you see a track on your right marked by a sign saying **'Crypte de Dromon'**. It ends beside a small farm, where you can leave your car, and from there you walk for perhaps ten minutes across an open grassy slope below the steep face of the Rocher de Dromon. The scene is exhilarating, buzzards wheel overhead prospecting for their next meal, and there, surrounded by tufts of wild lavender and thyme, is an odd-looking little chapel.

It turns out to be the remains of the eleventh-century church of Notre-Dame-de-Géniez, of which only the nave and south aisle, with their apses, are left. Some poor restoration has destroyed much of its character, but from the right-hand side of the main apse a flight of steps leads down into the tiniest of crypts, which was literally hewn out of the rock in the only shape possible – though it did achieve two separate aisles, each with a minute apse facing east. A passage connects the two, so that pilgrims to the site could cross from one to the other, and return to ground level by more steps to the north. The north aisle has collapsed and its stairway has vanished, but enough light comes in by an opening on that side to see the remaining apse and the two little columns on the right of the south aisle. The capitals are carved, somewhat roughly, with familiar Christian symbols like the peacock and the horned ram, and were probably twelfth-century replacements for earlier ones.

However tempting the idea that the crypt goes back to the time of Dardanus and Théopolis, or at least to Merovingian times, the experts tell us that it is no older than the eleventh century. One theory is that it was built to contain the relics of St Genès of Arles, as we read of a priory of St-Géniez-au-Dromon being established in 1030 by the Benedictines of St-Victor in Marseille; another is that it replaced a hermit's cell related to a Gallo-Roman *oppidum* on the top of the Rocher de Dromon. All we can say now is that this oasis among the wild hills of Haute-Provence would be a wonderful place for Dardanus's City of God.

The valley remains open and pleasant as far as Authon, an attractive village from where the Grande Randonnée GR6 climbs almost to the summit of les Monges at well over 6,000 feet. The adventurous driver can now follow the D3 on its tortuous way over the Col de Fontbelle, across the flank of the Montagne de Melan, and past the village of Thouard to join eventually the Route Napoléon between Digne and Château-Arnoux. Alternatively, and perhaps more wisely, you can go back the way you came, and so repeat a lovely drive.

A longer journey, which will take you through more cultivated but still beautiful country, is a round trip which sets off up the valley of the Jabron itself to the west of Sisteron. You can reach the valley by a short cut from the southern suburbs, and follow it all the way up to Séderon, which you may remember was the end of a similar round trip I suggested to the east of the Baronnies in an earlier Chapter. The return journey follows the

D542, a road which gets more and more beautiful as it runs east down the valley of the Méouge.

The most spectacular part of the drive comes when the road enters the **Gorges de la Méouge** before the river joins the Buëch. The rocks on either side of the road are stratified in the most bizarre formations I have ever seen – sometimes horizontal, looking like walls of regular masonry, then diagonal, then curving over like Romanesque arches, even sometimes falling in vertical channels. To reach Sisteron you can avoid the town of Laragne-Montéglin and the N75 highway by taking the minor road through Ribieu down the right bank of the Buëch.

From Sisteron the N85 heads north for Gap, from where Napoleon's cavalcade progressed through Grenoble and Lyon to his eventual defeat at Waterloo. This section of the Route Napoléon is a new and very busy road, but the floor of the valley is covered with fruit trees of all kinds, a marvellous sight in spring, with high wooded mountains filling the horizon to the east. After 34 kilometres the main road parts company with the Durance, while we take a right fork and follow the river into **Tallard**. This is a strange town, partly old and dilapidated, partly modern and cheerful. The run-down church of St-Grégoire was mostly reconstructed in the seventeenth-century, but the best feature here – and well worth a stop to look at it – is a remarkable castle built in the fourteenth century on a rock spur overlooking the Durance.

Its centrepiece is a huge square *donjon* with round towers at each corner which was later adapted to make it more of a *château de plaisance*. At the same time the north wing was extended to join up with a 'flamboyant' chapel. In the last few years a big programme of restoration has been going on, thanks to an unusual initiative by the Knights of Malta, and it will be interesting to see what they make of it. As it is, you get a good idea of the conditions of life for a noble family in the peaceful days before the wars of religion spoiled everything. If you feel like stretching your legs for half an hour after looking over the castle, there is a pleasant walk through oak woods to the south-west, where you are likely to meet red squirrels.

The road now runs east, still following the Durance, until it reaches the outlet of the **Lac de Serre-Ponçon**. This huge lake was formed in 1960 by building a barrage to hold back the waters of the Durance and the Ubaye at the point where they converged. The barrage itself has a core of impermeable clay dug from the bed of the Durance, and it provides power for an underground hydro-electric station with the enormous output of six thousand million kilowatts a year. Nothing of this is visible, as it goes on underground, deep in the rocks to the south of the lake. In any case your attention will be distracted by the scenery, which here becomes incomparably grand. To your left are the still blue waters of the lake, to the right are great cliffs of volcanic rock, and ahead is what looks like an impenetrable wall of immense mountains. The road crosses the river below the barrage, then leaves the south bank of the lake to climb through these volcanic rock formations, keeping its distance from the lake till it reaches the col and a spectacular *belvedere*. Now it plunges down to join the Ubaye where it enters the lake at its south-east corner, and soon arrives at the roadside village of **le Lauzet-Ubaye**. Here the road signs begin to point ahead to Cunéo, only 120 kilometres further east, and you realise that the wall of mountains which closes the horizon is the frontier of Italy.

If you have sensibly stopped for refreshment at the Auberge du Lac, afterwards you can walk down a path to the left beyond the village to a point where a deep narrow gorge is crossed by a little humped bridge, alleged to be Roman. This is a pretty spot, but the bridge with its slightly pointed arch is more likely to be mediaeval.

Another twenty kilometres bring you to **Barcelonnette**, an interesting town in its own right, apart from the glorious scenery which surrounds it. First of all its name, as you may have suspected, marks its foundation in 1231 by Raymond Bérenger

IV, who as a grandson of Alfonso I of Aragon was count of Barcelona as well as Provence. From 1388 it belonged to the princely house of Savoy, but in 1713 it was given back to France under the terms of the Treaty of Utrecht, in exchange for a slice of the Dauphiné. The military commander of the district who arranged this for Louis XIV was Marshal Berwick, an illegitimate son of James II and Arabella Churchill.

The older parts of the town have cobbled streets, but the social centre of Barcelonnette is the Place Manuel, a big sunny open space surrounded by quite smart cafés and restaurants, and overlooked by a tower which was the *clocher* of a Dominican priory in the fifteenth century. Its Spanish-sounding name is explained not by its connections with Barcelona, but by a curious sequence of events in the nineteenth century. In 1821 the brothers Arnaud, whose textile business in Barcelonnette was failing, decided to emigrate to Mexico. There they set up a shop for woven goods and other specialities, which was so successful that other families went out to join them; by the end of the century there was a whole colony of 'Barcelonnettes' engaged in this kind of trade. They never forgot they were French, and when war broke out in 1914 a number of them returned to fight – and some to die – for their country, as a memorial in the town for 'Mexicains morts pour la patrie' shows. The movement back to Provence continued, as life grew more difficult in south America, and these double expatriates have built themselves villas in and around Barcelonnette. There is even a shop in the Place Manuel which sells goods which are obviously of Mexican origin.

An interesting diversion from the main road after Barcelonnette is by way of the D902, which follows the Ubaye up to **St-Paul**, at over 4,000 feet and less than twenty kilometres from the Italian border. The mountain scenery is terrific, but the valley stays green and quite wide for most of the way. This is now unmistakeably the land of winter snows, and you get used to the galvanised roofs which look so incongruous in summer but

313

are covered with snow for months at a time in the winter. This is what makes St-Paul at first sight a shabby town, but it has some character and it contains an excellent example of the *montagnard* style of Romanesque church architecture. The church has a particularly fine tower, with arcaded openings in both upper storeys, and an octagonal spire with the ornaments – 'bobbles and ears' I call them – typical of the district. The key can be had from the Mairie, though that opens only between 0900 and 1200 on Mondays, Wednesdays and Saturdays, presumably because the Mayor's staff do duty elsewhere, which limits your chance of seeing inside – as it did mine.

This is the furthest point north of any of our journeys. To continue that way will bring you to Briançon and the frontier pass of Mont Genèvre; if you carry on eastwards, the frontier post at Larches is only seventeen kilometres away; to the south the 9,000-foot peak of the Tête de Siguret blocks the way. You are still only among the alps (with a small 'a') of Haute-Provence, but though you may not associate Provence with skiing, that is now the main industry in these parts. The facilities and the snow slopes are not up to the international standards of Switzerland and Austria, but they provide a correspondingly cheaper holiday and attract thousands of French enthusiasts, mostly on their own package or group terms.

In the last decade what used to be remote mountain villages have been transformed into hideous conglomerations of 'egg-box' hotels, served by the kind of shopping precinct you would expect to find in a London suburb. Another distressing result is that many of the best mountain pastures have been bought up or rented to build ski runs, hotel complexes and access roads, so that the sheep farmer of the south, who for centuries has brought his flocks up here in the annual *transhumance*, is finding less summer grazing available and the rents much higher.

In summer of course one sees the developments at their worst, without a romantic blanket of snow over everything, but another problem for the summer visitor is where to stay. A hotel built and operated for one kind of client is unlikely to be congenial for all, and a survey of those available up here between June and October is not inspiring. The two main centres south of Barcelonnette (there are no recommended hotels in the town) are at le Sauze and the inelegantly named Super-Sauze, and at Pra-Loup. Of all the hotels listed in either group I would unhesitatingly recommend Le Prieuré at **Molanès**, which is a delightful little backwater village half way up to Pra-Loup from the main road. This cosy inn – though it has a small swimming-pool it hardly ranks as more than an *auberge* – was adapted from farm buildings attached to the mediaeval priory next door, of which the chapel (restored in the last century) is still in use. Run by a young family who know the business, it would make an excellent base for the extended excursion I am suggesting to round off the chapter.

In the whole of Provence you will find no more exciting day's drive. Essentially a round trip, you can take it in either direction from Molanès, or from wherever your base is. It involves a drive of 185 kilometres on mountain roads at altitudes which reach almost 7,000 feet at the two main cols, so you need to be fairly confident about the weather, and to give yourself plenty of time by making an early start.

I would suggest making a clockwise circuit, joining the D902 on its way south from Barcelonnette, which will be signposted for the **Col de Cayolle** – the sign will also tell you whether the route is open or not. The first stage is along the bottom of the valley of the Bachelard, a deep leafy gorge with towering cliffs of rock on either side, where the road dodges from one bank of the river to the other across bridges with flimsy-looking iron railings. Later the views open out as the road climbs steadily towards the col, wide moorland slopes replacing the rock cliffs.

Up here you may spot a number of fat furry creatures about the size of a small badger scurrying about and feeding among the scattered rocks. They are marmots, and they get very active in the late summer and early autumn building up their calories for winter hibernation in burrows under the rocks. Another animal you are less likely to see, though there are plenty of them, is the mountain hare, a much shyer creature and an expert at camouflage. In winter its fur turns to white, which is its chief defence against the eagles which glide majestically out of their eyries to quarter the moors in search of a good meal. The nearest peak to the right of the col is called the Trou de l'Aigle.

So far we have been climbing the north-facing slopes, but at the col the world opens out to the sunnier south, and it comes as a surprise to find cattle rather than marmots feeding on much greener pastures. Below the col is the source of the Var – quite a thought when you realise that the journey it begins here will end at Nice. The descent is more gradual, and the road runs through some pleasantly domestic villages to **Guillaumes,** a little market town where you may like to stop for a rest from driving. Founded by William II of Provence in 1100, it has a baroque church and a ruined castle – neither important enough to spend valuable time in inspecting it any closer. The next stage is one of the most extraordinary of the whole journey, when the rocks turn to a brick red and the road needs about twenty short tunnels to force its way through what are called the **Gorges de Daluis**.

Soon the D902 joins the main N202, which accompanies the quickly growing Var all the way to Nice. Now is the chance for a longer break in the journey, perhaps for lunch, at **Entrevaux,** six kilometres east of the junction. This unusual town owes much of its character to the war which broke out in 1690 between France and Savoy, when Louis XIV instructed his great engineer Vauban to turn it into a strong point on the line of the Var. The key to the fortifications was a citadel on a pinnacle of rock, to which Vauban built a steep zig-zag approach which passes through a fortified gate every hundred yards or so. He also built ramparts to protect the town itself, into which he incorporated the earlier seventeenth-century cathedral – the bishopric of Glendèves goes back to the twelfth century – and gave it a fortified tower.

The older part of the town is on the north bank of the river, which you cross by a drawbridge leading to the Porte Royale, a picturesque sight with two round flanking towers. The two other gates are the Porte de France and the Porte d'Italie, facing as you would expect west and east respectively. Through the Porte Royale you come to the welcoming Place Martin, shaded by chestnut and plane trees, with a marvellous shop which specialises in the local *charcuterie*. If you have time to wander round you will come across other pleasant surprises. Though most of the bigger houses date from the time of Louis XIV, Entrevaux was a flourishing town in the reign of François I, a century earlier, and had successfully defended itself against the invading imperial army of Charles V. The street names are eloquent: the *rue du chapitre*, the *rue des hermitages*, the *rue basse*, the *rue de l'horloge*. This last might well be called the *rue des chats*, for the steps which lead up to the clock-tower have strategic doorsteps for cats in the sun. One corner is described on a plaque as the Bastion de la Portette, built in 1707 under the direction of Vauban to replace an ancient bridge carried away by floods from the Var in 1651.

The cathedral is an eighteenth-century extravaganza grafted on to an early seventeenth-century original. The west end has a pair of fine wooden doors, carved with episcopal emblems and decorative swags in the best contemporary manner. Beyond it to the east is the Porte d'Italie, approached from the outside by two drawbridges – and here you can appreciate Vauban's skill in fortification. Whenever he could he built his corners at a very acute angle, giving maximum fire power and minimum target area; the tall narrow slits for musket fire are another Vauban speciality. He spent two periods here, in January 1693 and November 1700, which seems to have been long enough to get the work started and later approved.

In spite of all this it would be wise not to start too late on the return journey – though of course you could equally well carry on down to Nice, or turn westward to Castellane on the Route Napoléon. Otherwise the northern leg begins at Annot, a not very interesting town, and follows the valley of the Vaire as far as the village of Méailles, which overlooks the road from a rocky vantage. This is the line of the Nice-Digne railway, which soon disappears into a tunnel to reach Thorame-Haute-Gare – a station which actually has a ticket office and people waiting on the platform for the next train for Nice. You are now on the D908, which sticks to the valley of the Verdon all the way up to the **Col d'Allos**. As far as the town of Allos the going is easy and the gradients gentle. On the way you bypass another important piece of fortification by Vauban, the town of **Colmars**, which also has its Porte de France and a Porte de Savoie, each with a fort to protect it. It seems appropriate that the name Colmars comes from the Latin *collis Martis*, or 'hill of Mars'. Allos is now an unattractive modern ski resort, surrounded by 7,000-foot mountains.

From Allos the driving is more demanding – corniche work all the way to the col, itself nearly 7,000 feet up – and the mountains look bleaker than they did at la Cayolle. The descent is if anything trickier, especially if there are *travaux* in progress, which is not unusual on this road after the winter. One autumn however I was rewarded by seeing an early stage of the modern *transhumance* in reverse, when thousands of sheep are rounded up from the mountain pastures and brought down to a point on the road where they can be loaded on to *camions* for the long journey back to the south – as far even as the Crau and the Camargue. At 6,500 feet it was quite an encounter, with two trucks already loaded, a big flock still grazing round about attended by several dogs, and even a donkey which had come down with one of the shepherds.

He had a gun slung over one shoulder, and had brought with him a brace of hares which he handed over to the driver of a truck. These mountain folk are a type apart – tall and fair-skinned, not at all like the little dark men from the north Italian mountains – and as you pass or stop by the way they look through you as being less than nothing in the lives they and their ancestors have lived for centuries.

Eventually the road spirals its way down to the junction with the Pra-Loup approach, and if you are staying in Molanès you will be very grateful to relax in the comfort of le Prieuré, and to enjoy its good food – which always includes 'specialités de la région'.

18

The Return to Aix-en-Provence

For my last chapter I have chosen to describe a journey from the far north-east of Provence to the town deep in the south which for five hundred years and more has been its natural centre. It should, I believe, recapitulate all the traits which make up the character of this most individual region of France. We start among the highest mountains close to the Italian border, and the first leg of the journey begins at the eastern end of the Lac de Serre-Ponçon. This is where the river Ubaye comes in, having started in a little lake on the shoulder of the 10,000-foot Bric de Rubren – which is exactly on the frontier between France and Italy.

As you approach from le Lauzet-Ubaye, the turning south comes soon after the *belvedere*, and is a continuation of the D900 you are already on. After a quick climb to the Col St-Jean the road runs easily down into **Seyne**, another mountain town one feels would be happier under snow. Vauban was at work here too, as part of the programme he began at Entrevaux in 1690. To his designs the local engineer-architects Viquet and Creuzet de Richerand built a fortress to enclose the existing twelfth-century watch-tower. Now after long neglect there is some extensive restoration going on, but most of it is open for visits in July and August. From the outside you can see the typical

Vauban trade-marks – the massive walls sloping outward towards the base, the sharply angled corners of the lower bailey, and plenty of narrow slits for musket fire at just the right angle.

The church of Notre-Dame de Nazareth is another example of *montagnard* Romanesque, which will remind you of St-Paul; the tower is very similar, if not quite as fine. The inside is impressive but dark, both because of the dark stone used and because the big rose window over the west doorway is the only source of light.

The forty-two kilometres between Seyne and Digne make another marvellously scenic drive, especially if you take the right-hand fork after fifteen kilometres on to the D900A, which involves an even more spectacular encounter with nature than the road up to the Col de Cayolle. The word *clue* which often appears on the map in these parts means 'cleft', and on this route you pass through two of them, the Clue de Verdaches and the Clue de Barles, where the road narrows to a single track between perpendicular or overhanging cliffs of rock. The Clue de Barles is the more startling of the two, where there seems hardly any room to pass, and the rock faces on either side are more like mountain precipices than cliffs. The trees in this uninhabited valley are all deciduous, turning to glorious colours in autumn, and a little burbling stream called the Bès runs down it to join the much wider bed of the Bléone just before Digne.

Digne was the most important staging post on the Route Napoléon before Sisteron. Its more modern part has a long tree-lined central boulevard and several distinguished *places*, while the older quarter is grouped round the ugly nineteenth-century cathedral of St-Jerome, built on a prominent hill. Digne was the diocese whose bishop Miollis was taken by Victor Hugo as the model for Mgr Myrillin, who figures in the story of the bishop's candlesticks in *Les Misérables*. The building not to miss is the former cathedral of **Notre-Dame-du-Bourg**, but you need to work out carefully how to get there. Le Bourg is now a residential suburb at the northern end of the Boulevard

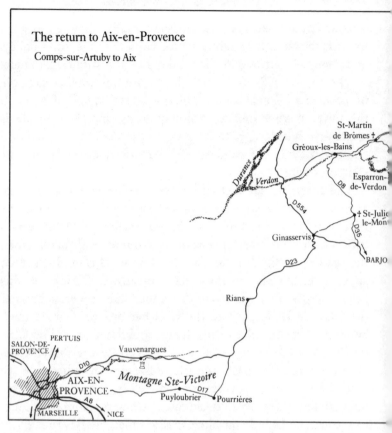

The return to Aix-en-Provence

Comps-sur-Artuby to Aix

St-Martin
de Brômes †

Gréoux-les-Bains

Durance

Verdon

Esparron-
de-Verdon

D8

D554

† St-Julie
le-Mon

D35

Ginasservis

D23

BARJO

Rians

SALON-DE-
PROVENCE

PERTUIS

Vauvenargues

D10

AIX-EN-
PROVENCE

Montagne Ste-Victoire

D17

A8

Puyloubrier

Pourrières

MARSEILLE

NICE

Gassendi (named after a seventeenth-century astronomer) though it was the nucleus of the Carolingian town and bishopric.

Notre-Dame is easy enough to find if you are coming in by the main D900 road from the north, as it stands close to the right-hand side soon after you enter the town. Unfortunately if you have chosen the D900A approach you will have to drive on to the central roundabout and turn left from there up the Boulevard Gassendi. Avoid leaving your car in the town centre, as it will seem a very long walk up to Notre-Dame at the far end of the Boulevard. Just before you reach it, look out on the right for the classic columns and entablature of the Grande Fontaine of 1829.

322

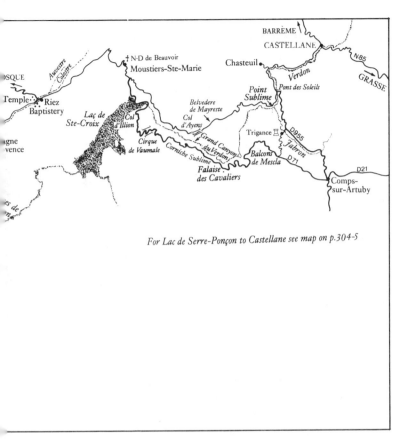

For Lac de Serre-Ponçon to Castellane see map on p.304-5

The church is special for several things. From the outside you register a Lombardic façade, guarded by a pair of amiable lions; the tower is on the south side, and has a Carolingian base, though its upper storey was added in the twelfth century. The inside has been undergoing extensive and overdue restoration, during which bones galore have been disinterred from under the nave, where archaeologists were looking for Carolingian foundations. You should by now be able to see the famous fourteenth-century frescos in a better state, as well as some later fragments from the fifteenth and sixteenth centuries; these include a sequence of the Last Judgment, with Heaven and Hell populated by appropriate mediaeval virtues and vices. The

323

single nave has the blind arcading on either side which is typical of Provençal Romanesque, and the white marble altar in an alcove on the north side is said to be Merovingian. There have been very few structural alterations since the sixteenth century, which is unusual in Provence.

South of Digne the Route Napoléon takes the only route possible between the Montagne de Coupe and the Montagne de Beynes, juggling with the railway line along the valley of the Asse. At **Barrème** there is a house with a plaque saying that Napoleon spent the night of 3 March 1815 there, and you can imagine the excitement in the little town when first his outriders arrived, then the cavalcade with the man who still called himself emperor at its head. It was a day not yet two hundred years ago – perhaps somebody's great-grandfather saw it all. Only a year later Nicéphore Niepce of Châlon-sur-Saône made the first photographic negative, but sadly there were no photographers in Barrème that day.

The next stop is at **Senez**, which surprisingly has a twelfth-century cathedral – and the surprise is even greater when you look inside it. The bishopric dates from the fourth or fifth century – its first recorded bishop was called Ursus, or 'the Bear' – but it was never a rich diocese and it vanished in 1801 after the Revolution. Another typical example of Provençal Romanesque, with signs of the Lombardic influence we saw at Digne, it has the usual single nave, with a central and two side apses opening off the crossing. As at Notre-Dame-du-Bourg the tower is offset to the south of the nave.

Its greatest treasure is a set of sixteenth and eighteenth-century tapestries hung behind the choir stalls on either side. You will find framed descriptions of them all beside the door in the north transept – now the usual entrance.

The earlier set comprises five Old Testament scenes worked in *toile de Flandre* which are mainly concerned with the prophet Elias and his set-to with the priests of Baal, with vivid scenes of preparations for the sacrifice. They were bought for the church by a seventeenth-century bishop of Senez, and the colours are a striking mixture of deep blues and browns. The rest are early Aubusson tapestries with a more varied selection of scenes from the Old Testament and Apocrypha, of which I find especially delightful the *Return of Tobias*, accompanied by his dog and carrying his fish. These tapestries are extremely valuable, and the church naturally stays locked for most of the time. The key is kept at a little café close by, but you may have to wait till the proprietress is free to let you in – sometimes not till the afternoon.

Castellane is still a mountain town, or at least a town surrounded by mountains, for you will find it more sophisticated than others further north. It was important in history through being at a crossroads in a region where main roads are scarce because of the terrain. Besides being on the Route Napoléon it has an easy connection with several routes to the north, and a branch road follows the line of the Verdon westward down to the Grand Canyon and the Lac de Ste-Croix.

Today its position makes it a good centre for tourists, though there is not a great deal of choice of accommodation. A sensible choice would be the Grand Hotel de Levant – agreeably old-fashioned and not at all as grand as it sounds – if only because it commands the central square and has a big garage alongside. It also has a good view of the most distinctive attraction of the town, the chapel of Notre-Dame-du-Roc on its pinnacle of rock away to the east. Otherwise there is nothing much to Castellane except for the colourful market which springs up overnight in the Place Marcel Sauvaire. The church of St-Victor was first built in the twelfth century, but after years of neglect it has fallen out of use and is being restored as a venue for exhibitions.

At Castellane – where Napoleon had his *déjeuner* before arriving at Barrème – we leave the Route and take that branch road down towards the Grand Canyon du Verdon. Not too quickly, though, or we shall miss a little turning on the right, signposted to **Chasteuil**. This is the strangest and most evocative of all the high villages of Provence, no more than a hamlet hidden in a fold of the mountains west of Castellane, and in a world which has little to do with modern life. A self-contained farming community lives here as it would have lived a hundred years ago – a rough life, but in surroundings of great beauty and peace. This is what has attracted a few young people to do up one or two of the enchanting but dilapidated little houses, and even to open a tiny *buverie-cum-crêperie* with an eye on adding a couple of *chambres d'hôte*. There is no shop, no *mairie*, and the little belfried church has no *curé* to celebrate Mass even once a month. This happy village occupies a sunny shelf between the mountains to the west and the deep valley of a tributary to the Verdon; it is overlooked by a crag with the jagged ruins of a castle on it – ruins which you can hardly distinguish from the rock itself.

The road you are now on splits at the Pont de Soleils, where the left-hand fork goes on to Comps-sur-Artuby, while the D952 keeps right for the Canyon. Six kilometres down the road to Comps a sign points to right to **Trigance**. Though this is another little mountain community, it could hardly be more different from Chasteuil, for its life depends mainly on the château which crowns the spur above it. Mediaeval in origin, altered in the sixteenth century, it has now been converted to a three-star hotel, where you can obviously stay in great style in a superlative situation. It has eight rooms in separate 'lodgings', the road up to it is private, and cars have to be parked on a terrace below the battlements, leaving all luggage to be hoisted by an external lift to the hotel entrance. The choice between a room here and a *chambre d'hôte* in Chasteuil would be an interesting test of character.

The **Grand Canyon du Verdon** is the best known of the Provençal gorges, and certainly the most spectacular. Approaching it from the east you have the problem that there are two roads commanding it from north and south, but no way of crossing from one to the other so as to make a round trip. You just have to decide which route to take, though if you are staying in the neighbourhood you can eventually follow both. The northerly route is the shorter, and though it takes longer to reach the most dramatic parts it passes a place called **Point Sublime**, where there is a little inn which would make a simple base for exploring the area in more detail by car – or indeed on foot. The Grande Randonnée GR4 connects the Auberge du Point Sublime directly with the more modern hotel-restaurant called the Grand Canyon Cavaliers on the far side of the gorge, though this is a very strenuous walk (including the passage of a tunnel) which needs caution and careful homework.

The scenery in the Canyon is beyond description. The French guide-books use adjectives like 'sauvage', 'grandiose', 'mysterieux', 'étonnant', but none equal the reality, and perhaps the popular names given to certain spots match it better. The *Couloir de Samson* is a place quite easily reached from Point Sublime, where the arrival of a side stream called the Baou brings even more confusion to the river bed, littered as it is with enormous blocks of stone such as the strong man of the Old Testament might have torn from the cliffs; the drop from the viewpoint to the bottom of the gorge here is more than seven hundred feet. The *Chaos de Trescaire* is another name more expressive than any adjective.

To continue along the northern route, which is also the shortest way to Moustiers-Ste-Marie, you stay clear of the gorge until you reach the Col d'Ayens at about 3,000 feet. Here you have the first view of the Verdon in full flow, but a more striking one comes at the *Belvedere de Mayreste*, where you are clear of the trees and can look back up the gorge to take in the superb cliff wall on the far side. For a while the road runs close to the river, then it takes one more climb through the woods to the Col d'Olivier, followed by a slower descent to Moustiers.

The southern route, known as the Corniche Sublime, is more spectacular, but to follow it you have to approach from Comps-sur-Artuby on the D71. The two great view-points on this side are the *Balçons de Mescla*, a rocky terrace overlooking the point where the Artuby merges with the Verdon, and the *Falaise des Cavaliers*, a sheer limestone cliff face rising a thousand feet above the gorge. The tree cover is thicker, with oaks at first predominating, then some fine beeches. The road as a rule runs higher, and the river far below looks like a pale blue ribbon. The *Cirque du Vaumale* allows a final view of this indescribably grand scenery, where a million years ago some vast flow of water cut its way through the rocks from the plateau above – rather as the famous Samaria gorge in Crete was created.

At last the road turns inland at the Col d'Illion and makes a steep descent with many *virages* to the shores of the **Lac de Ste-Croix**, which has another hydro-electric barrage at its southern end. It is also a splendid sheet of water, with sandy beaches and all sorts of facilities for aquatic sports.

One serious warning: try to avoid the weekend when taking either of these routes through the Canyon. Such a popular venue attracts hundreds of cars all day on Saturday and Sunday outings; worse still, the sharp turns and steep gradients are a challenge to motorcyclists in aggressive mood. In these conditions driving the narrow corniche roads can be a nightmare when it should be exhilarating.

Either way leads eventually to **Moustiers-Ste-Marie**, and here too you would do well to avoid crowded times and seasons. The site is exceptional, for the town is built just at the point where the Ravin de Notre-Dame splits the limestone cliff above it to let in the *torrent* of Rioul, which feeds the river Maire on its way to the Lac de Ste-Croix. On the north side of the ravine above the town is the chapel of **Notre-Dame-de-Beauvoir**, built probably about 1100, though there is a legend that it was founded by Charlemagne. A more likely one is that grottos in the rock were first used in the fifth century as a hermitage by St Maximin and his followers from the Îles de Lérins. The name of the town does indicate that there was once a monastery here dedicated to the Virgin Mary, and a connection with the

Crusades suggests that it was here by at least 1250.

The great iron chain which spans the ravine is said to have been fixed there to fulfil a vow made by a knight taken prisoner in St Louis's seventh Crusade, a vow which involved hanging from it a five-pointed star in honour of Our Lady. Chain and star still hang there, but are unlikely to be the originals, for a nineteenth-century illustration shows no sign of them. The chapel was a good deal altered in the fourteenth and sixteenth centuries; the east end is Gothic and the Romanesque porch was extended in 1782 by a lean-to porch with multi-coloured tiles. The panelled wooden door is obviously Renaissance. Access to the chapel is by a true pilgrimage route, a long climb by pebbled steps which takes nearly an hour from the town, allowing for stops on the way to look at the view. A pilgrimage is still staged during the first week in September, though it seems odd that the occasion is connected with the Roman goddesses Diana and Aurora – which makes one wonder about the chain and star.

The church in the town, like the chapel above, was altered in the fourteenth and sixteenth centuries, and again by a not altogether felicitous restoration in 1928, but it has a genuine Romanesque nave with the blind Provençal arcades on the south side walls. Its great architectural triumph is the tower, a magnificent structure with the tall window arcades and the shallow four-sided spire we associate with the Lombardic tradition in southern France – compare the tower of Notre-Dame-d'Aubune in Vaucluse, as well as some we have recently seen in Haute-Provence.

I have left to the last the best known aspect of Moustiers, its reputation for the glazed and painted pottery known as *faïence*. It probably sells more than it manufactures, for not all of what spills out from the shop fronts all over the town was made here, the trade having died out at the end of the last century. It was revived by a writer called Marcel Provence in 1925, but even what is made locally today is poor stuff, with little sense of form or design. You can see the real *faïence* in the Musée de Vieil Aix and other reputable museums. The trouble is that during the summer Moustiers is crammed with tourists looking for souvenirs, and if you add to them the motorists converging from both sides of the Gorges du Verdon and coming up from the Lac de Ste-Croix, the town with its narrow streets becomes a bottleneck for traffic, with ten-minute waits not unusual at the lights in the centre.

Though still in the department of Alpes de Haute-Provence, we shall soon be leaving the mountains behind us and heading for the valley of the lower Durance. Having extracted ourselves from Moustiers we can stop next at **Riez**, where there are two of the oldest monuments in Provence. There is little to be seen in the town itself, but that is because the original colony of *Julia Augusta Apollinaris Reiorum* (a title sensibly shortened by the Romans themselves to *Reia Apollinaris*, and then by the usual scramble to Riez) was established more to the west, at the confluence of the rivers Colostre and Auvestre.

The only recognisable Roman legacy still standing is a row of four granite columns of the Corinthian order, complete with marble bases, limestone capitals and a marble architrave, which was the southern arcade of the *pronaos* of a temple built on the lines of the Maison Carrée at Nîmes. This temple stood beside the main road from Digne to Aix, on the north bank of the Colostre. To find it, ignore a misleading sign immediately north of the bridge, and continue round to the left of the road leading to Manosque. To the south of the bridge, and to the right of the D952 to Gréoux-les-Bains, is a **Baptistery** of the fifth century, one of the best preserved early Christian buildings in France. It comprises a high octagonal chamber enclosed in a square of which the outer walls were rebuilt in 1818. In the chamber there is an ambulatory formed by eight Roman columns similar to those of the temple, and in the centre an octagonal baptismal font sunk in the floor. Over all is a cupola, not I think the original one, but probably rebuilt in the twelfth century. At each corner of the octagon there is a semicircular niche, as in the baptistery at Fréjus. This one is also used as a *musée lapidaire*, but the fragments of sculpture displayed are not very revealing.

You can see most of this through an iron grille on the east side, though a guided visit can be arranged if you apply to the secretariat of the Mairie in Riez. The notice-board outside supplies some fairly accurate historical information, but you may find some of its descriptions puzzling on the ground. The baptistery is clearly related to the scanty remains of a three-aisled basilica church on the far side of the road. Indeed they were probably part of the same building (on the foundations of a Roman civic basilica) and it looks as if the whole area by the river was an important Roman centre. You can see that Roman materials were re-used in the church, notably the same kind of columns as in the temple. If you look back from the east end of the excavations towards the baptistery you will see that it stands at the south-west corner of the whole complex, in the same context as the one in the cathedral of Aix. The bishopric of Riez was founded in the fifth century, and this could have been the original cathedral of Notre-Dame-du-Siège; it was still in use – though by then much altered – up to the sixteenth century, when it was pulled down and replaced by a new cathedral in the town.

Eight kilometres down the road to Gréoux is the much smaller town of **Allemagne-en-Provence**. You may well ask what Germany is doing in Provence, and there is some talk of a settlement of Germanic tribesmen in the dark ages; even given the Provençal penchant for fairy stories it seems no more likely that the name is derived from a fertility goddess called Alemona, or from the Latin *area magna*, so the mystery remains. Anyhow the interest here is in a large square building which was begun as a *château-fort* by the Castellane family in the fourteenth century and extended two hundred years later to make a *château de plaisance*, with huge mullioned windows and stone lions on the roof-line. Its inhabitants had a rough time during the wars of religion, when it came under siege by Catholic troops. Its *seigneur*, the baron d'Oraison, was just celebrating a victorious defence when he was killed by a sniper's bullet from an arquebus. In revenge his widow put to death twelve Catholic gentlemen who had been held as hostages in the cellars. The French religious wars had something in common with events in Northern Ireland today.

The grounds are attractive, though run down, and there are guided visits in the afternoon during the summer (except on Mondays and Tuesdays). The Renaissance *décor* inside is a bit overpowering, especially after 'improvements' in the last century, so you may be content with an outside view of a pleasantly eccentric building in an otherwise dull town.

There is a different feeling about **St-Martin-de-Brômes**, a delightfully informal hill village, well kept and with attractive corners. Up at the top is a very plain early Romanesque church, reached by a flight of cobbled steps from the village. Its tower has a lot of personality – four-square and chunky, with a jaunty pyramidal stone spire; the body of the church looks almost domestic, with tiled roofs sloping different ways at different levels. Inside all is Romanesque except the south aisle, which ends in a Gothic window, but it opens only for Mass on Saturdays and for weddings and funerals – the cemetery is fifty yards away on a lower level.

The plateau where the church of St-Martin stands is now empty but for it and a tall clock-tower with a machicolated top, which was built as a watch-tower for a Templars' *commanderie* and looks much like the one at les Arcs. Its stonework has been well restored, and the ground floor is used as a museum of Gallo-Roman antiquities – opened only for educational groups on request. In the village below there is a tiny *place* with a moss-covered fountain and two hotels. The one called La Fontaine is a Logis de France and has comfortable rooms at a very reasonable price.

A short détour at this point will take in the formidable château of **Esparron-de-Verdon,** of which the huge square *donjon* is said to date in part from the tenth century. It was another seat of the Castellane family in the thirteenth century, and they developed and lived in it till the eighteenth. The château has recently been bought again privately and is being restored – possibly for visits later. The old French word *éparron* meant 'spur', and the château is built on a spur which overlooks the Basses Gorges du Verdon – almost the last we shall see of that river, now turned into a lake by the Barrage de Gréoux at its northern end.

Gréoux-les-Bains would be easy to dismiss as a modern French holiday spa, which it is, but its warm sulphurous waters were known in Roman times and discovered and exploited in the fourteenth century by the Templars. It was they who built the big square château at the top of the town, which after long neglect is – like its neighbour at Esparron – being extensively restored. The town itself, though very crowded in summer, preserves its dignity and even a certain chic. It was a favourite resort of Jean Giono, who found its waters did his rheumatism good.

A fitting end to the last of our journeys through Provence is at **St-Julien-le-Montagnier,** which I maintain is the most perfect of all its villages. Though not particularly remote – nothing like Chasteuil – it is sufficiently far from a main road to be able to preserve its special atmosphere of peace and happiness. You reach it from Gréoux by the minor road D8, which turns into the D35 before landing you in a not very encouraging patch of houses and shops known as St-Pierre. If you look up from there to your right you will see what looks like a typical *village perché*, but fortunately there is no access to it from St-Pierre. Instead, continue south until you reach a crossroads with a right-hand turn to St-Julien. After quite a long climb you find a small parking area on your right, where it is best – though not essential – to leave your car. From there on you walk into a world of simple enchantment. There is one 'main' street, where the old

333

houses on each side have creepers on the walls and enclosed gardens full of flowering shrubs. The sequence is interrupted on one side by a little café – the only one in the village – and opposite it by an *allée de boules*, with young trees to shade its spectators. If anything the houses further on, and also round the corner to the left, are more attractive still, and all beautifully kept. You will guess rightly that the people who live in the village know its value, and will guard it jealously.

Before you reach the café, a path on the right leads up to the **Church of St-Julien**, which turns out to be a superb Romanesque basilica, an astonishing find in such a tiny village. Seen from the outside the body of the church is not immediately impressive – a long stoutly buttressed nave, whose true height is disguised by comparison with a noble tower which rises straight from ground level, and looks twice as high. The main entrance is on the south side, but before you go in have a look at the smaller Romanesque doorway to the left, where the original tympanum has been replaced by a rectangular marble slab (which is an obvious misfit) incised with a pattern of Greek crosses linked together by *entrelacs*. Another piece of the same slab is let into the lancet window of the central apse, though it can be seen only from the outside; inside there is a marble step in the middle of a short flight leading from nave to sanctuary. These are all remains of a Merovingian church which stood here in the seventh century; the present one is first named in 1182 as being dependent on St-Victor in Marseille.

The nave and south aisle are simple and majestic, and together with all three apses they clearly belong to the twelfth century; the north aisle, with its Gothic arches and vaulting, must be a century later. The lantern over the crossing is an unusual development, with a semicircular barrel vault running north and south but squared off to east and west to make room for windows to light the sanctuary – the true function of a 'lantern'. A cabinet in the south aisle contains a collection of *santons*, one of the best in Provence, with the crib at its centre and the figures all dressed as usual according to their *métier*. An ingenious switch lights it up when you step on a rug in front of it. New glass was put in the windows in 1970 and the roof was renewed in 1988 – you can see that the church is supported with pride by the whole village.

Beside the church a big round tower has been built for a table of orientation, beautifully set out and painted in enamel by local artists. It encompasses a full 360 degree view of the surrounding countryside, and some fascinating statistics are supplied: from here to Rome is a distance of 570 kilometres, to Athens it is 1600, and to Dublin 1460. No mention of London. To the west the ground falls away slightly to reveal the remains of some mediaeval fortifications – a gateway and a pair of barbican towers. This end of the village is a cul-de-sac, and if you have driven up you need to follow carefully the signs indicating the way out to Gréoux-les-Bains – if you can bring yourself to leave a village of such penetrating charm. Personally I should like to buy a retirement cottage and learn to play *boules*.

There are several ways back to Aix from here, but to avoid the obvious main roads you can take the D36 south-west to Ginasservis (where there is a nice country hotel which specialises in *gibier* at the right season), then on to Rians, and from there join the road which runs through Vauvenargues along the north side of the Ste-Victoire. When you get to Aix, remember to keep left along the inner ring road until you reach the Place General de Gaulle at the western end of the Cours Mirabeau – otherwise you will be in trouble. In writing about Provence I have chosen Aix as its focal point because it remains a truly Provençal as well as an international city – and one to which like many other people I am terminally addicted.

Food and Wine in Provence

The problem of writing about regional food these days is that the traveller sees very little of it. More and more of the kitchens of provincial hotels and restaurants are run by chefs who have been trained in some general and central school of cookery, where they learn to present the standard national dishes, as well as any number of dubious tricks of the trade. In the higher gastronomy skills may be passed on from master to pupil, but whatever its subtleties or refinements the food produced will be international in character, designed to make the German, British or American client feel at home, while giving the ubiquitous food journalist something a little *recherché* to enthuse about.

Throughout France there are, thank goodness, inns and restaurants where the experience and wisdom of an earlier generation – perhaps of a *grandmère* – persist, and what a joy it is to find them. In Provence they are easier to find than elsewhere – only perhaps in Normandy and Gascony are there as many – and in a land which extends geographically from the Mediterranean coast to the Alps on the Italian border you can expect plenty of variety in basic produce, which is what counts most. The secret of good cooking, which is not the same as *gastronomie*, lies in a tradition which knows exactly what to buy locally and when, and how to make the best use of it in traditional ways. Anyone discussing Provençal food must take account of the basic ingredients which come from the land itself, and lend a particular character to most of its dishes. The whole way of life in Provence matches and grows out of the land, or springs from the sea, and that is even more true of its cooking.

Fishermen off the Mediterranean coast bring in a bewildering variety of fish, many of which have no English names to identify them. They range from the familiar red mullet (*rouget*), the John Dory (oddly sanctified as *St-Pierre*), and the sea bream (*daurade*) to the more outlandish swordfish (*espadon*), the hog-fish, or *rascasse*, and the gurnard, or *rouget-grondin*. All these, and many more, may go into the traditional *bouillabaisse* so inadequately translated as 'fish soup'. Supposed to have originated in Marseille, it will be found anywhere along the coast, and it was interesting to find it being served on the quayside at Bonifacio in Corsica.

Inland the gamier meats are favoured – rabbit, hare, and the 'wild boar', or *sanglier*, though he and his young offspring the *marcassin* are now bred for the table in farms rather than hunted in the forests. Beef is not common, though a good beef stew, or *daube*, is popular; when steak in any form appears on the menu you can be pretty sure it comes from a different part of France and has spent a good deal of time refrigerated, if not frozen. Lamb on the other hand is plentiful – sheep-farming is one of the oldest industries in Provence – and given the Provençal treatment it can even match our own from the Welsh mountains or the Sussex downs. Pork is an ingredient both for stews and for many excellent varieties of *charcuterie* – again as it is in Corsica.

The Provençal treatment is based on herbs and the more strongly flavoured market produce. Few authentic dishes will omit some combination of onions, garlic and olives, while tomatoes, aubergines and fennel put in a regular appearance. In the autumn the big wild mushrooms, or *cèpes*, will be found in the markets, or very often picked specially that day for the table. Nowhere in Europe, except perhaps in Corsica, is there such a wealth of aromatic herbs – you smell them on the air and savour them with your meals.

These are only generalizations. Among individual dishes look out for the *bourride*, a *soupe de poissons* which many prefer to the more haphazard *bouillabaisse* and should be accompanied by a hot pimento sauce and garlic toast; the *pissaladière*, a kind of pizza or quiche with a filling of onions and olives; the *brandade de morue*, which is a concoction of pounded-up cod with garlic, olive oil and truffles; and with almost any fish or cold meat the distinctive Provençal mayonnaise called *aïoli*, which again relies on a lot of garlic as well as lemon and olive oil. They say the Provençal garlic is not as strong as you find it in other regions, but that I believe to be a faint-hearted view.

Near Seyne in Haute-Provence I have recorded and enjoyed eating a *civet de porcelet*, a rich dark stew of a young porker cooked with onions and carrots; in Comps-sur-Artuby both a gutsy *civet de lièvre* and delicately grilled lamb cutlets brushed with olive oil and dusted with herbs; in Gigondas the old favourite '*pieds et paquets*', a stew of pig's trotters and savoury forcemeat in sausage membranes; at Sisteron a choice of first courses between *quiche au fromage de chèvre* and an *anchoïade* (*crudités* served with a paste of anchovy and garlic on toast); at Molanès near Pra-Loup a *charbonnade de boeuf* (lightly panned thin slices of beef served with an assortment of spicy sauces on the side); near the Camargue a *daube poivré gardian*, which explains itself; at Castellane a *sauté d'agneau printanier*, accompanied by a rousing *ratatouille*. From the Ferme St-Michel in the Tricastin came at different times a *daube à l'ancienne*, a *salade de museau* (slices of pig's cheek on a bed of frizzy lettuce), a *brioche tricastin* (the brioche stuffed with a game *paté*), and *panaquets à la reine*, which are *crêpes* filled with a variety of savoury meats; these are traditional recipes.

The common factors in all these dishes are the freshness of

the ingredients and the simplicity of their presentation. Not one was served in a hotel or restaurant which rated more than two stars, let alone a rosette. Most of them were included not in the *à la carte* category, but in one of the fixed-price menus. Often it was the *plat du jour*, made from that day's market produce and chosen for the family meal by the *patron* or *patronne*.

How far do the wines of Provence match its food? As we know from the more famous wine-producing areas of Burgundy and Bordeaux, you cannot produce really good wines from unsuitable terrain, and whereas the resources of the table are pretty widespread throughout Provence, it has only a few areas where a grape of sufficient quality can grow to make a fine wine. We are not talking about quantity, for the comparatively recent *appellation controlée* of Côtes de Provence covers a vast tract of land from Aix-en-Provence (which has its own 'Côteaux' *appellation*) to Nice, most of which lies in the region of Centre-Var. It supplies the table wines and *vins de maison* for countless hotels and restaurants, and nowadays for many of our own high street wine merchants and supermarkets.

A high proportion of the wines from the Côtes de Provence are *rosé*, which is fine for drinking with *bouillabaisse* or the more recherché dishes of the *midi*, but is a pale accompaniment to the gutsy food of Vaucluse and northern Var. The grapes most commonly grown are the Grenache and the Syrah, but even the latter fails to produce a red wine here to challenge or even resemble the great vintages of the Côtes du Rhône. One can always find the odd exception to rules of this kind, and it is a pleasure to find the red wines of Bandol and the whites of Cassis still of a standard well above their neighbours'. Bandol indeed qualifies as a *vin de garde*, needing as much as six years for a good vintage to mature.

There is a noticeable difference when you come to the Côtes du Luberon, where the red wines have an aroma and a body which makes them far more suitable for the countryside and its provender. Further north again, the Côtes du Ventoux seem by comparison surprisingly anaemic, considering how close they are to the left bank of the Rhône.

More wine is probably produced under a Côtes du Rhône label than anywhere else in the world, though two of its most famous vineyard areas lie outside Provence. We cannot invoke Côte Rôtie or Hermitage to accompany our *civet de lièvre*, but we do have a wine of ancient renown to call upon, the Château-neuf-du-Pape from north of Avignon – and no red wine is more suitable or comforting to drink when the mistral is howling down the valley. As many as thirteen varieties of grape can be used here, though the Grenache is the most reliable, and the grapes ripen quickly in the hot sun reflected from the big stones deposited on the prehistoric riverbed.

Lirac and Tavel lie outside our limits to the west, so for further joy we have to keep to the left bank between Bollène and Avignon, and look at the lands between Orange and Mont Ventoux. The Côteaux du Tricastin produce a light and refreshing red from grapes such as the Grenache, the Mour-vèdre and the Cinsault varieties, as does the little 'Enclave des Papes', which has recently taken to wine-growing under the general appellation of Côtes du Rhone.

To my mind and palate the prize for reds in this part of the world goes to the district south of Vaison-la-Romaine, and in particular to the slopes below the Dentelles de Montmirail – which in any case score heavily for scenery. Between Gigondas and Vacqueras there must be something in the soil and *climat* specially suited to the Grenache grape. The vineyards extend not only along the left bank of the Ouvèze valley, but climb higher into the foothills of the Dentelles than I have seen others do in any part of France. At their best the wines of Gigondas and Vacqueyras, with a long tradition behind them, match those of Châteauneuf, yet you rarely see them on a wine list outside the region, let alone in this country.

In the same area the little village of Beaumes-de-Venise has won fame in recent years by producing a fashionable sweet dessert wine with which expansive British hosts will regale their guests on social or business occasions. It costs a great deal less than Château Yquem, and goes down quite well with a ripe peach.

That really completes this brief – and, I stress it, amateur – survey of Provençal wines. In Bouches du Rhône you can rely on the wide resources of the Côtes, but far away in the alps of Haute-Provence you would – dare I say it? – do better to drink an Italian white from Savoy, or even an Alsatian if available, with your mountain trout. This is not vineyard country.

TABLE OF EVENTS

416	Abbey of St-Victor founded in Marseille
471	Arles captured by Visigoths
507	Frankish king Clovis defeats combined Goths at Poitiers
536	Ostrogoths cede territory east of Rhône (Provence) to the Franks
726	Saracen raids begin
730–50	Saracens sack Arles, Tarascon, Avignon, Apt and Cavaillon
759	King Pepin the Short clears Provence of Saracens
800	Pepin's son Charlemagne is crowned Emperor of the West by the Pope in Rome
843	Treaty of Verdun: Charlemagne's grandsons divide the Empire between them. Lothaire is king of the Netherlands, Burgundy, Provence and Savoy
c.850	The kingdom of Provence becomes independent, based on Arles
910	Abbey of Cluny founded in Burgundy
	Provence invaded by Saracens, Normans and Hungarian Magyars
924	Hugues of Provence defeats the Saracens
973	William the Liberator captures the last Saracen stronghold in Provence
1032	Kingdom of Arles annexed by the Emperor Conrad II; Provence thereafter ruled by counts subject to the Holy Roman Empire
1049	St Hugues abbot of Cluny
1084	St Bruno founds the Carthusian order
1098	St Robert founds the Cistercian order
1112	Count Raymond Berenger III of Barcelona becomes Raymond Berenger I of Provence
1114	St Bernard arrives at Cîteaux in Burgundy
1136	Abbey of le Thoronet founded

1137	Abbey of Aiguebelle founded
1147	Abbey of Silvacane founded
1148	Abbey of Sénanque founded
1178	Coronation of the Emperor Frederick Barbarossa at Arles
1209	Raymond Berenger IV count of Provence
1226	Avignon falls to Louis VIII in the Albigensian 'crusade'; Count Raymond of Toulouse pledges the Comtat Venaissin to the Pope.
1234	Margaret of Provence marries Louis IX of France
1236	Eleanor of Provence marries Henry III of England
1243	Sancia of Provence marries Richard, duke of Cornwall
1245	Beatrice of Provence marries Charles, duke of Anjou, King of Naples and Sicily
1248–54	Seventh Crusade under Louis IX (St Louis)
1274	Comtat Venaissin formally ceded to Pope (Avignon excluded)
1279	Bones of St Mary Magdalene 'rediscovered' at St-Maximine
1305	Clement V elected Pope
1309	Papacy moved to Avignon
1335	Benedict XII Pope; builds Palais Vieux
1342	Clement VI Pope; builds Palais Nouveau
1348	Queen Jeanne of Naples sells Avignon to Clement VI for 80,000 florins
1376	Pope Gregory XI returns to Rome
1378–1403	Anti-Popes in Avignon
1434	René of Anjou succeeds as king of Naples and Sicily and count of Provence
1480	Death of René; his nephew Charles leaves Provence to Louis XI of France
1524–36	Emperor Charles V invades Provence;

repulsed by François I

'Wars of Religion' between Catholics and Protestants

1545   Vaudois 'heresy' in Luberon crushed

1713   Principality of Orange annexed by France

1720   50,000 die of the plague in Marseille

1789   French Revolution: storming of the Bastille

1791   Avignon and the Comtat annexed by the revolutionary government

1793   Napoleon captures Toulon from the Austrians and British

1815   Napoleon escapes from Elba and lands at Nice

1854   'Félibrige' founded by Mistral and friends to revive the Provençal language

1888   Van Gogh arrives in Arles

1904   Mistral awarded Nobel Prize for literature

1942   Germans occupy Provence

1944   Allies land on Riviera coast; liberation of Provençal cities

The Counts of Provence

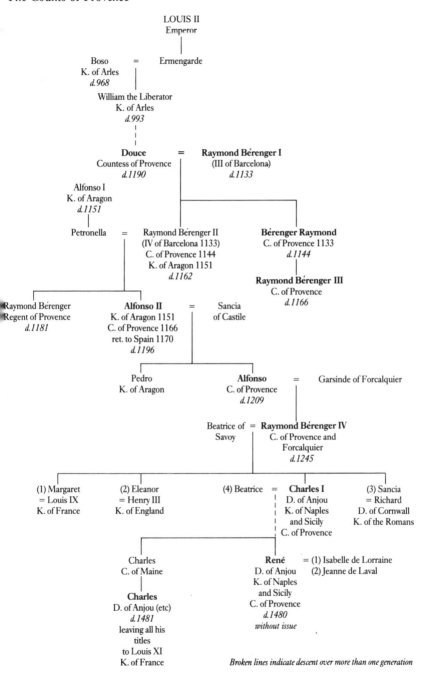

SELECT BIBLIOGRAPHY

Donald Attwater, *A Dictionary of Saints*, 1938
Robert Bailly, *Chapelles de Provence*, 1988
François Cali, *Provence: Land of Enchantment*, 1965
Theodore Cook, *Old Provence*, 1905
J. E. Drinkwater, *Roman Gaul*, 1983
Michel Droit, *Camargue*, 1963
H. A. L. Fisher, *History of Europe*, 1936
Alexis Lichine, *Guide to the Wines and Vineyards of France*, 1979
Archibald Lyall (revised A. N. Brangham), *Companion Guide to the South of France*, 1963
Violet Markham, *Romanesque France*, 1929
Georges Pillement, *La France Inconnue*, 1963
James Pope-Hennessy, *Aspects of Provence*, 1952
Zodiaque Press, *La Nuit des Temps: l'Art Cistercien*, 1962
La Nuit des Temps: Provence Romane, 1977

INDEX

Index

355

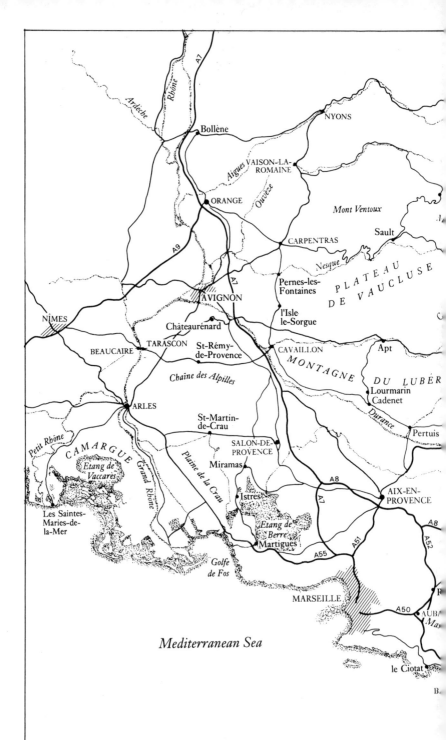